ALSO BY R. EMMETT TYRRELL, JR.

Public Nuisances

The Future That Doesn't Work, ed.

Report on Network News' Treatment of the 1972 Democratic Presidential Candidates, ed.

THE LIBERAL CRACK-UP

R. Emmett Tyrrell, Jr.

Simon and Schuster

New York

Published by Simon and Schuster
A Division of Simon & Schuster, Inc.
Simon & Schuster Building
Rockefeller Center
1230 Avenue of the Americas
New York, New York 10020
SIMON AND SCHUSTER and colophon are registered trademarks
of Simon & Schuster, Inc.
Designed by PAT DUNBAR
Manufactured in the United States of America
1 3 5 7 9 10 8 6 4 2
Library of Congress Cataloging in Publication Data
Tyrrell, R. Emmett.
The liberal crack-up.
Includes bibliographies and index.
1. United States—Politics and government—1977–1981.
2. Liberalism—United States. I. Title.
JK271.T97 1984   973.926   84-13843
ISBN 0-671-52735-5

For Luigi Barzini

". . . Of harmony, and the deep power of joy,
We see into the life of things."

Contents

Contents

Author's Preface

Some years ago, spurred by youth and idealism, I assessed various of the eminent figures of our time in a modest little book, *Public Nuisances*, which, I am sorry to report, some critics considered impolite. Frankly, the accusation jarred me, for I have been a Christian and a gentleman all my adult life, lapsing only once when a rowdy in a Chicago café made sport of my white gloves and bowler. Why would anyone call me impolite—and besides, how would anyone know? American manners have grown very lax. We can blow our noses on the American flag and on some foreign flags too without fear of obloquy or of legal action of any kind. At universities idealists can hoot and howl at visiting speakers. Near-naked joggers sweat and wheeze up Fifth Avenue at high noon unmolested; they pass Saks and Bergdorf Goodman, but no lady shopper would dream of bashing one with her parasol. In fact, few ladies even carry parasols nowadays. My mother carries one, but she is an exception. Most carry whistles and small cans of mugger repellent. So frayed is our system of common courtesies that I have observed young ladies breast-feeding their babes on the Washington–New York shuttle. Moreover, they sit up in the nonsmoking section. Nobody objects. How they have acquired these creatures I do not know. Those breast-feeders that I have observed look quite hostile and are markedly anaphrodisiac. Possibly they were artificially inseminated, which is in itself rather rude.

At any rate, when the critics brought down on me the aforementioned accusation I was very dubious. Something else had caused their indignation. In recent decades the gabble of intelligentsia, so-called, has become increasingly evasive. What they say is rarely what they mean. When they say that they are for equality it is apparent from their actions that they are for inequality. When they are for nonviolent behavior it is clear that there is going to be violence. When some pouted that I had been impolite I knew they were indignant about something else. After all, none of them had ever shown high regard for manners, and some were opposed to standards of any kind whatsoever. What had irked them, I believe, is that they suspected that I had actually had fun writing *Public Nuisances*. It was not one of those labors of *Angst* that they so often confuse with "serious" thought.

Well, I did have fun writing *Public Nuisances*, and apparently my editor, Midge Decter, had fun with it too, for no sooner had I gotten the thing off my hands than she was after me to have at it again. I resisted, not wanting to give further offense to the critics. Yet Midge Decter is as relentless as she is charming and wise.

"You wrote about the public nuisances. Now write about their ideas," she urged one evening as we started in on some very fine *saumon fumé* at a renowned Midtown Manhattan slow-food joint. It was to be a long and fruitful meal; and, come to think of it, it was just as we got to the fruit that my resistance vanished. I believe the fruit was Calvados.

The primary reason that I did not mind the long evening was that Midge's very intelligent husband, Norman Podhoretz, was picking up the check. Another was that they had raised an absorbing subject, that being the palpable absurdity of the major ideas of our time. Practically all of them had entered the public forum more than a decade before when they were boomed as very intellectual and innovative. Alas, by the late 1970s most had shown themselves to be profoundly anti-intellectual; and they had hardened into a cheap orthodoxy, so obvious and vulgar that almost anyone could master it and mouth its dunderheaded pieties. That is precisely what Jimmy Carter did in 1976, but he was not alone. Throughout the 1970s hundreds, perhaps thousands, of impostors latched on to one or more of the orthodoxy's noble causes and gained prominence and riches simply by agitating more ardently than others. By the time the Calvados was warming my esophagus, Madame Decter had prevailed. I would now assess some of the leading ideas of our time, the ideas of post-Kennedy Liberalism, the Liberalism of the New Age, the Liberalism that promised blissful lives all led in suspended and idiotic animation. Madame Decter had her book; and she promptly quit the publishing world.

After reading a vast array of source material and making hundreds of expeditions to historic sites, I have developed the thesis that New Age Liberalism is no longer the sensible, tolerant, highly principled body of thought that Liberalism was in decades past. Sometime in the late 1960s or early 1970s it cracked up into a riot of enthusiasms, usually contradictory, always extremist, often *non compos mentis*. This Liberalism is, then, a misnomer, and it has given birth to dozens of other misnomers, as we shall see. Where it dominates it often ushers in the precise opposite of its stated goals. It is a great flummoxer and somewhat of a Typhoid Mary. Thus what follows is not only a criticism of ideas but also a chronicle of those enthusiasms that have accompanied Liberalism's crack-up.

I am grateful to the indefatigable Miss Myrna Larfnik, who directed my research on this book, and to Mr. William McGurn, Mr. John Steichen and Mr. Paul Vivian, who worked so capably under her. I am also grateful to Mrs. Genevieve Meadows, who never swore, but always returned my patchwork of scribbles and type transformed into a proper manuscript. I should also like to thank my colleagues at *The American Spectator* for their many acts of kindness and also those friends who read the manuscript at various stages in its development. Doubtless they would prefer to remain anonymous, for several teach at the country's finest universities, and therefore have exposed their persons to quite enough danger. Finally, I wish to thank Lois Wallace.

The manuscript was prepared on an Epson QX-10 using

PeachText. Thus, I am not completely opposed to the modern habit of mind. With science and technology I have no quarrel. Even in politics and culture, I have little quarrel with those who acknowledge the facts and do not theorize them away; but are such people in the ascendancy or in retreat? The question has attended me throughout this work.

New York, New York
March, 1984

THE LIBERAL
CRACK-UP

"Whoever hath an Ambition to be heard in a Crowd,
must press, and squeeze, and thrust, and climb
with indefatigable Pains, till he has exalted himself
to a certain Degree of Altitude above them."
—Jonathan Swift
A Tale of a Tub, etc.

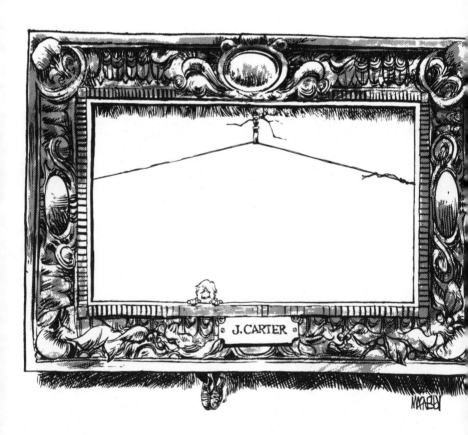

1

Jimmy at the End of the Revels

The Last Yahoo

You hold in your hands the ultimate souvenir of the Carter administration: the official presidential portrait of James Earl Carter, Jr., commissioned by *The American Spectator*, executed by Jeff MacNelly, and offered by the magazine to the government of the United States, the sole proviso being that the government accord it homage and visibility commensurate with that which the French government has given the *Mona Lisa*. As with Leonardo's great work, this too is a masterpiece, if only in its capacity to convey the singular grandeur of our thirty-ninth president and his times.

The American Spectator has never had a response to this generous offer. I like to think that this is because the officers of the National Gallery of Art are even now casting and recasting plans for the exhibition of this jewel. The lighting must be just so, for our portrait's hues are necessarily insipid. There will be large crowds, so security will have to be tight. However, let it not be oppressive. Let it serve what in the 1970s were called human needs. I would suggest having a psychiatrist and a man of the cloth stationed nearby, and for those of us who laughed through the whole buffoonish administration, how about a bartender? Many of those who come to gape will be in need of comfort, but those who were not so credulous will want to have a little fun. Admittedly, it was unprecedented to commission a cartoonist, albeit a Pulitzer Prize winner, to execute a presidential portrait; but then, the Carter presidency was also without precedent.

When the Wonderboy arrived in Washington in 1977, full of solemn oaths and sagacious recommendations for establishing the New Jerusalem right there on the ruins of Gomorrah, one of his first acts of genius was to end the government's voluptuous policy of commissioning cabinet members' portraits. He had promised to get a grip on the budget; thus with one populist swoop, his administration came thousands of dollars closer to controlling what was then a $402.7 billion budget. There was grumbling, but the great helmsman of cornpone populism stuck courageously to his guns: no portraits. Also no White House limousines, fewer White House television sets, no more lavishing of public funds on the presidential palace. When the Reagans moved in, four years later, the newspapers were reporting mice in the Oval Office, and the well-fed cockroaches in the Old Executive Office Building had grown so self-assured that they were almost condescending toward the new tenants.

Think of it: while a lush array of entitlement programs was fattening the budget to the point of elephantiasis, Jimmy was wowing the gulls with such goofball measures as eliminating official portraits. How successful were the Wonderboy's much-publicized economies to be? His budget for fiscal 1982 had swollen to almost twice the budget he had inherited from Gerald Ford.

After the first month of Jimmy's reign the pundits should have been ready for all the loony episodes that lay ahead. Let history record, however, that the giants of the press corps sensed nothing amiss. They called him "brilliant." He was the "political genius" of 1976, certified and sanctified by no less a journalistic colossus than Norman Mailer, weirdly laying out his estimate in the third person singular: "In answer to the people who would ask, 'What do you think of him?' Mailer would be quick to reply, 'I suspect he's a political genius.' It was all he knew about Carter, but he knew that much."[1] In time, with the plaster falling from the walls, the chickens refusing to lay, and the cow gone plumb dry, Jimmy the genius turned to his Rafshoon. His assistant presidents leaped into action, and soon the genius appeared at a press conference, with his hair parted on the left. Now the journalists called him "enigmatic." As late as 1980 they were still calling him enigmatic! By then the enigma had chosen a conscientious objector to head the CIA.[2] He has used a canoe paddle to fight off a seagoing rabbit.[3] He had dangled Baptist salvation before an aghast Park Chung Hee, South Korea's Buddhist dictator.[4] At the crack of dawn he had jogged lap after lap around the deck of the Mississippi riverboat *Delta Queen* while fellow passengers lay sleepless in their beds.[5] In Poland he had startled the morally upright by informing them upon his arrival at Warsaw's airport that "I desire you carnally."[6] At the Venice summit he took leave of the assembled leaders, visited Benedictine monks, and returned full of wonder to notify Pierre Trudeau and Margaret Thatcher of the adventure: the monks ate wholesome cheeses and spoke!* These

---

* The visit was unannounced and became known only when the president returned to the Hotel Cipriani and, in the presence of reporters, told Trudeau all about it just before a private meeting between the two men.

Trudeau's reaction, and later that of Thatcher when told of the early-morning excursion, appeared to be mild bewilderment.

"I had breakfast at the monastery," Carter said.

"Did you have a nice breakfast?" Trudeau inquired.

"Yes, we had milk and bread and cheese," the president said.

At this, Trudeau's lip curled as Carter explained how each of the monks had described his job at the monastery during the breakfast.

"I didn't know they could talk," Trudeau said in a reference to the vow of silence taken by members of some orders of Roman Catholic monks.

"At the meal they let them talk and at special occasions," Carter said.

"They ordinarily talk?" Trudeau inquired.

"Ordinarily they do," the president said. "They have prayers before breakfast and they had a special prayer for me. I told them I needed it."

After the Trudeau meeting, it was Thatcher's turn as she arrived at the Cipriani for her private meeting with Carter. The British prime minister seemed uncertain how to reply as reporters listened to this dialogue:

"Had breakfast with the monks," Carter said.

"Oh, did you?" Thatcher replied.

"They're really wonderful . . .," Carter added.

"Yes," Thatcher said.

"There are some who do special work on Gregorian chants . . .," Carter said.

Thatcher replied again with "Yes."

Not for nothing is the president's Secret Service code name "Deacon."[7]

whole four years had been a wonderful time for Jimmy. In the argot of the time he "went through changes." He grew. He experienced. In fact, in the first three years of his presidency, Jimmy personally experienced things that Grant, deep in the sauce, had only dreamed of.

American foreign policy became a ribald joke before the world. American domestic policy wheezed and groaned as more and more flapdoodle was piled onto it. Galoots and wretches manned our government. Our culture flaunted the worst of fourth-rate vulgar. The Great Republic seemed to be taking on the appearances of a banana republic. Europeans long given to patronizing us suddenly fell silent and began to worry. Was that the sound of Soviet tanks revving up off to the east or was it just a growl from the Politburo? By 1980 things had grown serious. Jimmy Carter was the worst president of the twentieth century. Harding has been redeemed.

There will be those who will find that appraisal harsh. Some are simply ignorant of our history. Others are deceiving themselves, and if they are persons of influence they are probably accessories to the offense, people who, through most of the Wonderboy's reign, sought refuge in sophistry and euphemism while Jimmy grinned and tumbled headlong into the White House china. The same critical standards they had so recently applied to the Ford administration became mysteriously defunct during the Carter administration until it was too late in the farce to matter.

What was afoot? The economy was in ruins. The government was malfunctioning in practically all departments, and in place of foreign policy we had only sonorities. Yet through the corridors of public commentary, no one ever said out loud: "The President is an ignoramus." This was an opinion voiced only by the few. Even when the Wonderboy was back in the bush country, far from power, the pundits remained silent. How does one account for it? Well, there are many truths about American public life that we dare not utter. One is that American public life is thoroughly dominated by the personae and ideology of Liberalism. Another is that today's Liberalism has become radicalized. Still another is that Jimmy tried most

Jimmy at the End of the Revels

of the Liberal panaceas and practically blew up the country.

There have always been whistle-brained pontificators at large in the Republic, all promising a New Age full of wonder and kookery. Generally they are kept far from center stage. However, in the 1960s these New Age visionaries multiplied. Together they conjured up a wild and absurd vision of the good life, and to the astonishment of many, they gained influence. During the 1970s their analyses, ideals, and juvenile shouts overwhelmed the sensible Liberalism of yore. The result was a Liberalism that was profoundly utopian, embracing a view of man that transformed him into a perpetual child, degrading him almost to the level of an animal caged in a zoo. It was a Liberalism that steadily became illiberal in its policies, inane in its oratory, and irretrievably corrupted by ambivalent purpose and an all-consuming baseness. The historic failure of the Carter administration revealed the crack-up of American Liberalism for all to see.

To assess the Carter glory is to indict the adepts of the New Age. In 1976, lost in their unctuous reveries, they proclaimed Jimmy plausible, and during the following farce most continued to view him as plausible. By election time 1980 they believed that the voters shared their delusion, though by practically every measure Jimmy was a sure loser. Still the New Age Liberals insisted that he would pull it off. They even insisted that Jimmy had come out of his televised debate with Ronald Reagan unscathed. Now, this speaks volumes about the extent of their delusion. Remember, for twenty years the Liberals had explained to us how a cool, handsome JFK had whipped a hot, thrashing Richard Nixon and won the debate of 1960. Reagan had achieved practically an identical victory over the labored, hissing Jimmy. Yet the Liberals called it a draw. Practically every poll of ordinary Americans called it a Reagan victory. Still the Liberals called it a draw. Some of them even argued that Jimmy had won. When he was thumped so mercilessly in the subsequent election the Liberals were stunned. Events have continued to wobble the New Age Liberal not because we inhabit a New Age requiring new wisdoms but because *he* inhabits a New Age, a personal hallucination that has lost touch with *all* wisdoms, even the wisdom of yesteryear's Liberalism.

By the end of the 1970s New Age Liberalism had become not only illiberal, but also irrational and inhumane. It had become a series of poses assumed by the precious and the opportunistic frantically attempting to maintain cultural and political dominance. An important key to understanding the vagaries that swept through the 1970s is the realization that during that decade celebrity and preferment generally went to those who could accurately calculate the drifts of the *Zeitgeist* and then intone the requisite bromides with neither a blush nor a snicker. Remember the curious exculpation of the lout John Dean? Would he so readily have been accepted as a "writer" and "commentator" had he remained unrepentant and refused to affect the self-guilt, self-improvement, I-am-better-for-having-been-a-creep soap opera that accompanied his conscience-raising? Remember the great leaps into *Jugendkultur* made by such eminentos as Galbraith and Schlesinger? Would they have retained their eminence had they maintained intellectual standards and scorned the idiot enthusiasms of the hour? Self-respect, integrity, dignity, and intelligence had very little to do with making it in the 1970s. All was dependent on cunning and a prevenient nose for the fashionable. A shapeless dynamic like this gave enormous social and cultural leverage to the arrantly gaga; and the gaga joined the rogues in shaping the interests of the time.

It was to be Jimmy's hour. He was a scamp mountebank from jerkwater America whose knowledge of government and of history was somewhere between that of the washroom attendant at "21" and a modestly educated welfare queen. Yet so superficial and juvenile had the bromides of New Age Liberalism become that the scamp could intone them fluently. So degenerate had the New Age Liberals become that the mere sounds of these bromides pacified them. A peanut farmer from a crossroads village, who had made his way to the governorship of Georgia playing the Kluxian toot one minute and Negro blues the next,[8] now had confected a song and dance incorporating Reinhold Niebuhr, Karl Barth, Bob Dylan,

Martin Luther King, Jr., the Allman Brothers, and a dozen or so Liberal aphrodisiacs.* He wore dungarees, pole-climbing boots, and work shirts. He carried his own suitcase (most likely empty). He smiled with a grim assiduity that sent small children leaping for cover. Yet the intelligentsia of Liberalism warmed to him.

There were, of course, holdouts. The fashionable Georgetown set was particularly uneasy about developments, and with good reason. Soon Jimmy's yokels would be crowding into their salons, ordering Moon Pies, complaining about the cold vichyssoise, dipping their soup spoons into finger bowls, and staring in awe at the chocolate mousse. Yet the majority of Liberals were very agreeable to this new genius. Said Norman Mailer upon returning from Plains: "There was such happiness in the smile that followed, and such good humor; it was such an astonishingly nice smile that Mailer to his horror understood how people became Carter converts on the spot. . . . If the smile was not genuine, then Carter was not only a political genius but an artist of the first Satanic rank. . . . Norman Mailer came to the conclusion that Jimmy Carter was somewhere within range of the very good and very decent man he presented himself to be, and he thought he would find himself on Election Day happy to vote for him."[10]† It was a gamble. The Liberals were betting that a Snopes could be a successful president at least as long as he exuded their wisdom.

This was to be the New Age Liberals' most reckless gamble since Watergate. Then they had wagered that a little *coup d'état* could be indulged in with impunity. Now, as the Wonderboy sashayed down Pennsylvania Avenue on Inauguration Day, noble visions flickered in their minds. Soon

---

* "I am a Southerner and an American. I am a farmer, an engineer, a father and a husband, a Christian, a politician and a former governor, a planner, a businessman, a nuclear physicist, a naval officer, a canoist, and, among other things, a lover of Bob Dylan's songs and Dylan Thomas' poetry."[9]

† Said James David Barber in the second edition of his nonsensical tome *Presidential Character*, "I believe he will also turn out to be a pleasured [sic] President, finding, as did FDR and HST and JFK, that life in the Oval Office can be fun. . . ."[11]

Jimmy held inspirational telephone call-ins, fireside chats, town meetings. He was, as they say in Washington, making all the right moves.

Of course Jimmy too was gambling. An essentially vacuous, mean-spirited Snopes, he had listened intently to the political debates of the 1960s and early 1970s. He had watched the protest demonstrations. He wagered that the New Politics, as it was called, was most likely to keep him loved, respected, and living in a house full of clean sheets. He would not be a traditional Southern pol. He would be a populist versed in New Age bosh. Yet in the end, as he directed the ship of state off the reef and into the next maelstrom, the Liberals turned queasy, held their sides, and prayed for Dramamine. Finally they leaped from the sinking ship, abandoning Jimmy much as the veterans among them had abandoned LBJ more than a decade before. Jimmy, in truth, never was a true-blue Liberal of the New Age, but he was a gifted poseur. He had packed his government with the champions of every New Age cause. The Liberals should have been grateful. There were the famous, like Dr. Peter Bourne, Andy Young, and Midge Costanza. There were the deeply committed, like Joan Claybrook, and in foreign policy every McGovernite not then employed by a rock band. Yet soon the Liberals' role in the administration was being revised.

After the voters had had their say on November 4, 1980, the Liberals' disavowals were categorical. Ingrates like Jack Newfield asseverated, "We must understand that the main reason Carter was defeated was because he was an incompetent conservative president."[12] Alas, once again the facts pinned the donkey's tail on the unhappy Newfield. "It was a novel idea Jimmy Carter had four years ago," the Associated Press reported as Jimmy headed his mule back to Plains, Georgia. "Instead of staffing the government with the usual appointees, he brought in critics of government, the reformers, the discontented. He hired outside agitators and made them inside agitators."[13] More than fifty public-interest pests from the Nader camorra were given powerful posts in the Carter administration. "He trained a whole generation, which will be back," averred Sam Brown, whom the Wonderboy had made director of ACTION.[14] When the world was young, and the answers to our problems blossomed like bright crocuses after the wintry snows, Brown had organized the Vietnam Moratorium. He had also organized Eugene McCarthy's 1968 presidential campaign. During the Carter administration he attended cocktail parties for the victorious North Vietnamese. Doubtless, he too would be put down as another of Newfield's "incompetent conservatives."

Arthur Schlesinger, Jr., even went beyond Newfield: "What the voters repudiated in 1980 was not liberalism but the miserable result of the conservative economic policies of the last half-dozen years."[15] Arthur had apparently forgotten the huge growth in economic regulation, in transfer payments, in infringements upon every aspect of personal liberty. This was Liberal progress! He had also forgotten the glorious birth of the Department of Education and the Department of Energy, the violent struggles to create a Consumer Protection Nanny and a Department of Natural Resources. There were the threats against the corporations. There were CETA grants, food stamps, school lunches for the middle class, and more. Arthur was unfair.

Perhaps the venerable theoretician of humbug was angered that Jimmy had not gone far enough. After all, he had never tried wage and price controls, and he had never gotten comprehensive national health care. Then too, possibly Arthur had been discomfited by being associated with such an obvious mountebank. Arthur should be more resilient; *all* New Age Liberals who are not utter morons are to some extent mountebanks. The most credible explanation for Arthur's pathetic thrashings is that he had already grasped the great historic fact of the Carter administration, to wit: under the Wonderboy practically every New Age prescription—certainly every foreign-policy prescription—simply came a cropper.

In foreign policy the New Age Liberals' insistence on accommodation, negotiations, legalisms, "openness," disarmament, and so forth was greeted by the Soviet invasion of Afghanistan, the Iranian barbarism, the proxy wars in Africa, at least one Marxist government in Central America, and the fissures in NATO. The Iranian barbarism put the lie to the

New Age Liberals' pious dogmas of restraint, mutual under-standing, and Third World innocence. The Soviet paranoiacs' massive arms buildup revealed the hollowness of the SALT process. The ghastly holocaust in Southeast Asia showed what perverse guff the New Age's foreign-policy alternatives had always been.

In domestic policy the gigantic costs of the New Age's pro-grams for perfect justice, perfect safety, perfect dreaminess grew and impoverished the citizenry. The tax burden rose. So did unemployment. So did inflation. Hockey fans might call this Jimmy's presidential hat trick. No other president had accomplished it in this century. Not even Herbert Hoover.

Here was the age of the little scamp and the great denial. The scamp clawed his way to the White House mouthing pishposh he never understood. His New Age co-conspirators first denied that anything was amiss and then denied any responsibility for the crash. It was one of the greatest acts of denial in the twentieth century. Southeast Asia was not their fault. Our economy was not their fault. Iran was not their fault. Soviet aggression was not their fault. Our diminished place in a dangerous world was not their fault. It was all of a piece with the whole thrust of their thought, which in its maundering about a sunny egalitarian utopia was a colossal escape from human experience, a denial of reality, and an accommodation with nihilism.

The Wonderboy, of course, did not believe in reality either. With pluck and bathos he talked his way into Lincoln's House. He talked his way into Christian saintliness. He talked his way into greatness. In time he was a patron of the arts, fluent in Spanish, a jogger and skier. One wonders. When he collapsed during that footrace or when he fell from his skis did he learn anything about the difficulty of things? I doubt it. During his whole bizarre regime, as the dollar sank and the Russians marched, there emanated from him the sense that nothing really mattered. Nothing beyond himself was real. There was no Iran, no Southeast Asia, no Russian military buildup. At the fag end of his four-year farce, in the hospital at Wiesbaden just before he met the hostages held for 444 days in our Teheran embassy, he was actually incredulous when

informed that their Iranian captors had badly abused them.*
Here was another of his educational experiences, none of
which ever taught him anything. As the Wonderboy's
shrunken and anile figure departed 1600 Pennsylvania Avenue, it is my judgment that he left much the same insufferable
ass as he had been when he arrived. Scamps like Jimmy never
learn.

* The story, unvarnished by Ham's loyal cover-up in *Crisis: The Last Year
of the Carter Presidency*, bespeaks not only Jimmy's naiveté but also his
weirdness. Conveyed to me by a firsthand observer, it is this: an American
doctor told Jimmy in graphic terms of the brutal treatment the hostages
had suffered. Jimmy responded, "Didn't they know that this was wrong?"
  "What do you mean?" responded the doctor.
  "Didn't the Iranians know that this was wrong to do?"
  The doctor replied that he was just an American doctor unfamiliar with
Iranian ways, whereupon Jimmy chirped, "I think they knew it was
wrong," and presidentially exited the room, leaving any further questions
about the hostages' condition or about how they might respond to meeting him moments later all unasked. Make of it what you will.

2

What Ever Happened to Liberalism?

A Trinity of Botches

How are we to plot the catastrophe's course? How does one chronicle the Liberal saga from the mountaintop to the padded cells: the mountaintop on which the first Liberals received the numinous word, took noble vows, and heard a faint ringing in the ear; the padded cells into which decades later the last Liberals committed themselves voluntarily, their placards bobbing above them, their luggage plastered with hortatory bumper stickers. Now the ringing had become a blare. For more than a generation they had tyrannized our culture and bullied our society, but Mammon persisted, and the status quo was always at their elbows, jeering. In fevered depravity the last Liberals ran riot through the 1970s gibbering: consciousness-raising! self-realization! group therapy! sexuality! human rights! animal rights! water beds! wheat grass enemas! sanitary napkins shaped from genuine sea sponges! and on and on, and so forth and so on, and let's get the hell out of here. This is light-years removed from the New Deal.

"The only thing we have to fear is fear itself," Franklin Delano Roosevelt had declared on Liberalism's glad and glorious morn. It was wise counsel for the 1930s, and equally sagacious for capable men and women forty years later. Yet now American commonality had fissured. So many Liberals had become fatalists, solemnly anticipating the end of an era and proclaiming yet another New Dawn, even as they lived in quotidian dread of practically all earthly phenomena. The New Age Liberal became the most intense hypochondriac ever seen in the Republic.

The old philosophical positivist, who had led the Republic through the Depression, against fascism, and into our post-war glories, had declined. He believed in conspiracies; suffered endless visions of doom; fretted about his person: his safety, his health, his psyche. Four decades after FDR's stouthearted declamation, the typical Liberal had curled up into a fetal position, rejected the American eagle, and exalted the ostrich. The popularity of *The Greening of America* had been no accident. Millions of heirs to the Age of Roosevelt had entered the New Age, and it was not as heroic as they had anticipated.

During Liberalism's salad days the infantilism manifest in the 1970s made only infrequent appearances. Liberals of the 1930s were sometimes sentimental, to be sure, and they could dance with the champagne of optimism and the slop of idealism when the topic for discussion was mankind. They saw the heavy club of government as a magic wand, and they were almost totally fooled by the smile on Uncle Joe Stalin's smirker. But then, it must be remembered that these Liberals were innocents in foreign affairs. Power's place in human relations was a difficult proposition for them. They saw the world through the eyes of the apple-cheeked schoolboy capering across the playing fields of Choate. The America they envisaged was a tidy nation of robust workingmen and of wholesome wives whose days were spent packing lunch pails and instructing the children in right conduct. It was, admittedly, a somewhat silly vision, but placed next to the infantile idiocies that came later it shone with dignity. Moreover, in the 1930s few conservatives offered a sounder vision. Had they been in charge of our foreign policy, we would today be either speaking German or negotiating arms reductions with the old men in the Reichstag.

The early Liberals believed in human dignity, freedom, and reason. So fervently did they believe in these things that they were given to universalizing them. Hence it took them a while to get the hang of foreign policy, but in time they came to understand the late Lorenzo de' Medici's advice to his son Pope Leo X: "You should understand that those who speak ill of us do not love us."[1] In the late 1940s these Liberals drew the line with our heroic Soviet allies. They got tough with our domestic Stalinists. Americans for Democratic Action (ADA) was actually founded by Liberals endeavoring to insulate Liberalism from domestic Communism's busy tentacles. As the years passed, ADA began to act as though Communism had simply vanished, but in the early days its members were frisky with anti-Communist hellfire.

When Henry Wallace, professional martyr that he was, stepped forward to lead idiot idealism in a lunge toward the White House, these Liberals had at him with the utmost ferocity. All the anti-Americanism, the dreamy utopianism, and the lust for appeasement that came to characterize the New Age Liberals enlivened the daydreams of the Hayseed Howler too, but back in 1948 ADA had no sympathy for such moonshine. Wallace was judged an ornament of democracy only by the Communists and by fellow travelers.

The Liberals who opposed Wallace were to be known as the Liberals of the Vital Center. Reading their writings today remains an edifying experience. Even Arthur Schlesinger, Jr., was sensible and straightforward—at least, relatively straightforward. In *The Power of Freedom* Max Ascoli, soon to found *The Reporter* magazine, set out a very reasonable assessment of man in society. Acknowledging that mankind's nature was part ambrosia, part arsenic, Ascoli scoffed at utopian schemes. He even doubted the extravagant claims made by some Liberals for natural rights, noting that rights vary among cultures and that they develop differently in different cultures.

In *The Vital Center* a somewhat virginal Schlesinger, uncompromised by purple causes, rejected all totalitarianisms. Issuing caveats about mankind's goodness, he expressed surprisingly modest political expectations, putting one in mind of Irving Kristol, circa 1978. Arthur and his anti-Communist Liberals were, to be sure, propounding a mixed economy, expansion of government ownership, and antitrust legislation. Yet the outright hallucinations of the 1970s were not observable in *The Vital Center*. In the late 1940s these Liberals led a civil war in the Liberal camp and booted Wallace, his Stalinists, and his dreamers back into the shadows. There they remained, nursing the gripes and the phobias that composed their *Weltanschauung*. Then, in the 1960s, the Wallacites returned to fight again.

Now the Liberals of ADA had lost their flintiness. Some, as sociologist Robert Nisbet has observed, had become bored with the bourgeois grind. Others, now widely esteemed and crapulent, were loath to endanger their place at the trough. Consequently, the new radicalism overwhelmed the Liberal community. Neo-Wallacism triumphed in the House of the Vital Center. Bell-bottomed pants, pork-chop sideburns, and crackpot enthusiasms materialized in those hallowed halls of Liberalism where once the New Deal was extolled in a cloud of pipe smoke. Professor Timothy Leary, Professor Charles Reich, Fathers Philip and Daniel Berrigan, and thousands of other *exaltés* of privileged society forsook *The New York Times* and began to swell and to display bizarreries theretofore found only in the classified ads of *The Village Voice*.

It was all rather startling, but to close students of the Liberal saga it was not unimaginable. The New Deal had had its embarrassing moments: nudists among the policy planners, believers in the occult, dietary utopians, and the amazing unending drama of Alger Hiss. Forget not that Henry Wallace was the only presidential candidate in 1948 who came complete with guru, that being the Rev. N. Constantinovich, a theosoph whose memory time has interred but whose lofty place in Wallace's pantheon of minds caused eyes to pop in the late 1940s. Nor were the New Frontier and the Great Society free of embarrassments, the most outlandish of which were often manifested by the chief executives themselves: JFK and his strenuous amours; LBJ conducting the Republic's business from the presidential thunder mug.

Yet in the beginning there was the noble calling. The prophets of Liberalism had gone thither into the land of the Babbitts, bearing tablets proclaiming the rights of man. Now it was the end of an era, and their successors had grown too skittish for lapidary principles. All tenets and good causes went into ceaseless flux. At first the good Liberal was for sexual freedom; then he was alarmed by charges of "sexual harass-ment"; then he was rendered practically celibate by the rise of feminist prudery. There was integration, then black sep-aratism. There was love and compassion; then, endlessly re-peated, there was "rage." The last Liberals had descended into bibble-babble, becoming a mob of scribes and pharisees and nincompoops all convinced that the Law ordained cease-less conflict: the citizens against the government, women against men, the fuliginous against the paleface, youths against adults; even the handicapped were urged to whimper and to harangue and to grasp a U.S. Treasury teat. Liberalism, the party of *fraternité*, had decayed into the party whose doctrine of rights soured every human relationship.

The old dichotomy pitting bosses against workers bored the Liberals of the New Age. They called for a multitude of struggles, all monitored by government bureaucrats following the Liberals' blueprint for social turmoil. Greater community was the Liberals' goal. Using the cement of social justice they would create the greatest community in recorded history. Pursuant to this great goal they went about their crusade of dividing American society into warring factions. Their actions seemed to be based on the philosophical assumption that the means must obliterate the end. In the realm of ethics, this was a breakthrough.

Liberalism had become radicalized—but was this, as adver-tised in the late 1970s, an attempt to get at the roots of issues; or was it an attempt to stomp on those roots? In practice, the movement became a wild and lascivious scramble for what Kenneth Minogue in his splendid book *The Liberal Mind* has called "suffering situations": blacks, students, Hispanics, Indians, women, homosexuals, animals, trees, the balding, the fat.[2] In psychology, however, the movement revealed a grimmer side: that absorption with death that Igor Shafarevich, that brave Soviet mathematician, perceived in socialism in *The Socialist Phenomenon*. New Age Liberalism, having lost its nerve, now sat in anxious anticipation of an end to the heave and roll of history; but an end, of course, that would leave the New Age Liberal on top.

In the 1970s these unhappy people brought about a huge

eruption of uplift, reaching into every area of human endeavor, with practically every reform prefiguring an end to life as lived under liberal bourgeois democracy. Consumerism and conservation became assaults on innovation, enterprise, and labor. "Science" was used to malign science. Traditional conceptions of progress were rendered suspect. The new economic order urged an end to the economics of growth, for growth had meant "future shock," as one of the gimcrack seers of the 1970s had put it. The foreign policy of the New Age became a policy of paralysis, timorousness, and chaos. The feminist movement evolved into a lunatic jihad against femininity and manliness, a neurotic flight from biology, reproduction, and history itself. Indeed, the evolution of the feminist shout was the clearest display of New Age Liberalism's dizzy course. No sooner had the Liberals brought America through the sexual revolution and into carnal bliss than their feminist storm troopers rebelled against the heterosexual paradise. They thundered against both motherhood and the ideals of the late Giovanni Giacomo Casanova. They made coitus and procreation anathema as their precursors in the Women's Christian Temperance Union had made the cocktail of a half-century earlier. By the middle 1970s no Romeo in his right mind would slip between the sheets with a "liberated" Juliet without bringing along a lawyer or, better yet, a grand jury.

New Age Liberalism was in essence nothing more complicated or noble than a running argument with life as it was led by normal Americans. The fact that Liberalism was in the main responsible for modern American life only made the Liberals of the New Age all the more ferocious and perverse. They were out to bust up the joint, to make the bourgeoisie squeal. Led by an array of eminences extending from Herbert Marcuse in the upper atmosphere to Fritz Mondale on terra firma, they would bring America toward a new historical synthesis, the dictatorship of the idiot smile. They would be the dictators. The common folk would smile. And the *Angst* of modern life would be ended forever as all Americans were reduced to a state of piffling infantilism. If New Age Liberalism's furious contradictions would cohere into anything other than a sempiternal pout it was this.

It took nearly twenty years for American Liberalism to metamorphose from a concern for society and progress into an obsession with petty personal indulgences. Liberals began the 1960s with two great and admirable causes, civil rights and welfare. As the decade wore on and the Liberal foreign policy came a cropper in Southeast Asia they acquired a third great cause, immediate withdrawal from Southeast Asia concomitant with the discovery of a proper scapegoat on which to pin their idiotic war, its body counts, its graduated escalation, and all the rest of its technocratic claptrap. Through extravagance, stupidity, and poltroonishness, Liberalism botched each of these great causes so spectacularly that, as a dazed Jimmy headed his mule back to the all-night gas stations of home, the American people welcomed into the White House the Liberals' purest antithesis, Ronald Reagan, a conservative more committed to a body of principles than any American president in fifty years. Moreover, those principles were about the same as those that had been repudiated in the Goldwater debacle. No other about-face in American history could match it. But what the hell, by the end of the 1970s it was apparent for all to see that Liberalism had ripened into imbecility. How long could it maintain its hold even on the yokels of the cow campuses and the foundations? It had betrayed practically all its original values; and during the gaudy reign of the Wonderboy it made an assault on traditional American freedoms analogous only to Prohibition, whose effect was much the same: restricted freedom simultaneous with frayed state authority. Now, however, the assault on freedom was led by not one but a dozen different Anti-Saloon Leagues, espousing a dozen different high-minded infringements on liberty. There were infringements on commerce, on free association, and on the right to organize schools or social groups according to free choice. Social regimentation and social engineering based on the shakiest premises were undertaken; and the American majority knuckled under much as they had knuckled under to Prohibition, "willingly" as Frederick Lewis Allen observed it, "almost absent-mindedly."[3]

Yet by 1980 the Liberals had drunk themselves into a stupor. After years of ceaseless solemnizing and legislating, all they had accomplished was an exchange of absurdities and injustices, those of the past having been heaved aside only to be replaced by new, more impregnable ones: quotas; consciousness-raising; legalized prejudice against men, mothers, and achievers of every variety. Moreover, the government was now empowered to force such abominations into the most intimate spheres of private life. Diminished freedoms and expanded absurdities were not the only consequences of the New Age Liberal orgies. By the late 1970s the economy was suffering an acute case of *encephalitis lethargica*; and abroad the Great Liberal Republic—its foreign aid still flowing munificently—was scorned more widely than the Soviet Union, despite the latter's periodic neighborhood assaults. As France's Jean-François Revel observed the change: "by a sort of tacit, and all the more overwhelming, consensus, [America has] been put outside the law, banished from the international community by its own allies."[4] Ambassadors were assassinated, embassies pillaged, and our diplomats held for ransom. The Liberal order in international relations was now so flummoxed that even America's foreign correspondents, diligently practicing their craft from barstools in the Hiltons of foreign lands, began to perceive a change.

Which of the Liberals' great botches brought the most damage to the Republic? Their domestic botches, I should think, particularly their botch of civil rights, which established the mold for all the domestic stupidities that were to follow. Modern nations with any semblance of representational government must have domestic stability before they can have a successful foreign policy—one thinks of Gladstone presiding over a serene Britain while a host of French statesmen were brought low by interminable domestic conflict. The Liberals' botch of civil rights and welfare kept America in turmoil for more than a decade. These two stupendous blunders loosed a mob of mountebanks into every realm of American life. Along with the mountebanks came witch-hunts for alleged bigots and cathartic melodrama of a particularly ignoble variety. American institutions were filled with idiocy and left in decrepitude. American government became a hectored, driven nanny, ministering to a host of louts, all of whom were ingrates and some of whom were obvious morons.

The chloroform of egalitarianism was spread everywhere in the 1970s. Prior American values of self-reliance, personal liberty, and competence were heaved overboard. Whining and alibiing became the new Fourth of July oratory, and the born loser was crowned as the new American folk hero. Along with this abandonment of older American values came a new class of busybodies to elucidate the new hokum and to harass the productive elements of the Republic. The welfare state had turned many theretofore toiling Americanos into parasites, and this new class of busybodies lived as superparasites, deriving nourishment from the dependence of the welfare clients. The busybodies scudded out of the universities, the institutes, and the foundations, pious in their higher wisdom and ceaselessly counseling more dependence to the dependent, and resignation to the taxpayer. As conditions worsened at home and abroad, these superparasites blandly prescribed submission, or, as they were wont to say, "restraint." There was, as Carter's rubes put it, "nothing that can be done about it."

1

Civil rights was, then, the Liberals' first and seminal botch. This is ironic. For decades the Liberals had opposed the injustices visited upon blacks, injustices that compromised the Constitution itself. Theirs was an invaluable contribution to American life, and it was not composed of cheap gestures, for it was made during dangerous times when one actually suffered for espousing equal rights and equal liberties. Yet as the Liberals moved into the New Age their evolving programs were composed almost solely of cheap gestures, and usually at the expense of established rights and liberties. The excesses of the civil rights movement cost them nothing. They were not denied jobs by hiring quotas. Their children were not bused. They were rarely defamed by phony charges of racism. Civil rights law went berserk in the 1970s, leaving almost no region of middle-class life unpoliced, but the middle-aged Liberals in their tenured faculty positions or their affluent neighborhoods merely struck heroic poses, attended soirees with the fuliginous, and murmured portentously about the forces of bigotry arrayed against them.

Those forces, of course, were, with the exception of an occasional Kluxian stonehead, invisible to the naked eye. There simply were no plausible opponents to equal rights in the 1970s. All pollsters agreed that white tolerance had steadily increased. Yet the New Age Liberals were convinced that bigotry lurked in every dark passage. The religious legacy of Dr. Freud had flattened them, and they believed in the invisible rumble-bumble of the subconscious as piously as ever a one-toothed peasant on a Bulgar slope believed in the spirits and principalities of the air. The forces of bigotry in the 1970s were subconscious, according to the New Age Liberals, which made them all the more formidable.

Southern racism had been courageously and successfully challenged by black activists and intelligent whites in the 1960s. During that decade the Liberals and blacks finally destroyed most of the odious institutions of Jim Crow. Yet it was precisely at this moment of triumph that the Liberals were overcome by their worst impulses: their romanticism, self-righteousness, intolerance, and vindictiveness besotted them. They became flunkies for left-wing zealots. In time practically every extravagant leap into social engineering had their approval. The goal of racial harmony fell away, replaced by the august and far gaudier goal of equality. It is a repellent idea. Nietzsche took its measure well when he observed, "there is no more poisonous poison anywhere."[5]

As the leveling gained steam behind social experiments of prodigious variety and venom, America became one of the century's most heavily propagandized societies. Was it more heavily propagandized than the USSR? I wonder. Everywhere government agencies energetically advertised their good works and good causes. The witch doctors of each egalitarian reform reviewed the language and expurgated it for their progressive purposes: delete Negro, delete Miss and Mrs., neologize with gay, exalt person, castrate history—a total censorship was undertaken. Publishers promulgated thoroughly ideological language guidelines for books published under their imprint. On TV talk shows the citizenry was hectored about nonsexist toys for Christmas; children's books were rewritten to conform with progressive pieties. The very same New Age Liberals who were ever vigilant for the influence of church or big business in the classroom grimly transformed every public institution into a tool of indoctrination.

By the end of the 1960s the Liberals had blown the struggle against Southern racism, and they had blown it so egregiously that not only were new barriers raised up between the races, but strife was incited between the sexes and between lesser groups whose potential for antagonism had theretofore merely fizzed and smoked. In fact, social antagonisms were now grafted onto our political system, where they could provide our litigiously minded Liberals with endless occasions for dithering and incommoding their bourgeois neighbors. More distressing still, bureaucrats, legislators, and judges used the cause of civil rights to frustrate and evade democratic process. Edicts from on high replaced democratic decision-making. Civil rights politics and civil rights law established noxious precedents, encouraging a host of cranks to spring to life wailing and claiming to have suffered the same privations as blacks. Naturally they expected the same remedies.

All the misnamed liberation movements that have disfigured and enfeebled the American polity since the middle 1960s had their roots in the immediate aftermath of the 1965 Voting Rights Act. With it the struggle for the civil rights of Southern blacks was won, but suddenly a grab for special status began. Equality before the law was now assured, but an extraordinary dynamic went into motion. Veteran black leaders like Roy Wilkins and Whitney Young were superseded by newer, brassier operators: men with bloodshot eyes, and fists thrust high in the air. In the style of the late Mussolini and well within the tradition of proven American mountebankery these new black leaders began demanding something altogether different from mere equality. They began demanding reparations; soon they insisted that special areas of American life be reserved for them.

Their first ploy was to reformulate the definition of racism, transforming it from a set of racially biased laws and customs into a kind of American mystery. According to the new definition, racism was a state of mind, somewhat like spring fever only less amusing and more enduring. Were there hem-hems from the Liberals over this idiotic neologizing? Not at all, and so the new black leaders moved on to the next plateau. They announced that racism was as prevalent in the North as in the Old South, possibly more so. Southern racists agreed, glad to divert the Feds' attention northward so that they might hang on to a few of the sacred ornaments of the older order—say, the white-only commodes or the literacy tests querying blacks on the precise number of bubbles in a bar of soap. Sensing huge opportunities for soap opera, the Liberals lined up with the racists: of course racism was as rampant in Dubuque as in Selma! On with the show!

Thus, the new black leaders presented themselves as the world's foremost experts on racism, and from here on the civil rights movement increasingly became a con. Racism was its racket, and by the late 1970s such fantastic spellbinders as the Hon. Andy Young were traversing the whole world lecturing the paleface on the nascent racism that lurked within. Andy found racism everywhere, even in Sweden, even in Abraham Lincoln. "There's a sense in which every American, black or white, is affected by racism," Andy notified a *Playboy* magazine interviewer. "You cannot grow up in the United States of America in the 20th Century and not be tainted by it."[6]

Yet Andy found no hint of racism in Arab lands. Nor did Jesse Jackson, nor the members of the Black Caucus. This was surprising. John Laffin, in a human-rights study published by the Foundation for the Study of Plural Societies in The Hague, summed up the assessment of most historians when he wrote: "Arabs have played the major role in the world slave trade and one of the major parts in the use and exploitation of slaves."[7] Yet the new black leaders remained in the dark. They recognized the Arabs as true brothers engaged in one of the great liberation movements of modern times—namely: the liberation of dollars from Western banks.

It was in pursuit of this noble cause that they created a brand-new racial mythology. In place of all the anti-black myths of yore they confected pro-black myths. The new black emerged as artistically somewhat superior to the honky. He was freer, more natural, and given to pensive moments of profound merit. Morally he was a colossus.

Much as the white racists at the turn of the century used Social Darwinism to control the debate over race, rising black con artists used Freudian and Marxist pishposh to control the contemporary debate—though few opponents showed up to debate. The emerging mythology about American racism grew lurid and terrible, suggesting that throughout American history the honky had devoted all his energies to but one sacrosanct goal, keeping the black man down.

Thus from myth and mountebankery there evolved an entirely new American status: victim status. A weird sociology formed around it, making it the foremost honorific in our welfare state. The courts too labored to make victim status attractive. Acquisition of victim status put one in line for preferments more august and satisfying than any that were ever attached to the One Hundred Percent Americanism of the 1920s or to roots assignable to the old barge *Mayflower*.

An amazing variety of bizarre groups began hustling to dramatize wounds inflicted on them by life in America. The women of the fevered brow confected heinous tales, transforming the nuptial bed into a torture board and chill kitchens into womankind's sole escape. Anon came the horror stories from the student body, the Hispanics, the homosexuals, the herpes sufferers, and the drunks. Soon Ph.D. theses were in the works, and American democracy was being established as a sham and a tyranny. By the end of the 1970s millions of seemingly fortunate Americans took leave of their conspicuous consumption to blubber about how they had suffered rough treatment in the Land of the Free, and to suggest how restitution might be made. To oppose their artifice was to hazard opprobrium of horrible fury. By the end of the 1970s group liberation assumed a place in the American political museum's oratorical wing just down the aisle from red-baiting, bloody-shirt waving, and race-baiting. George Gilder writes that by 1980 some 70 percent of the American people, possessing more than three-fourths of the Republic's wealth, were classifiable as victims of American history.[8] Twenty federal agencies were empowered to pursue the complaints of these newly discovered victims, and if the victims won their cases they stood to profit handsomely. If they lost, the taxpayers picked up the bill. A golden age for the persecution complex had dawned.

Now, of course the victimization of Southern blacks had been very real, and one would have expected black leaders to object to this exploitation of their painful past. After all, they had rarely been reluctant to grouse. In point of fact, they had an enormous gusto for it. Some of the objects of their anger were the now defunct Sambo restaurant chain,* lawn statues of black saddle boys, unauthorized use of black characters by white novelists over the past few hundred years, the singing of "Dixie," rising for the National Anthem. If a white was unaware of their concerns they would grumble, and they would grumble more if he was too knowledgeable. As Norman Podhoretz, the editor of *Commentary*, has observed, their touchiness was of a piece with the black leaders' Southern heritage, redolent of the "Hell no, we ain't fergettin'" mentality of the Civil War diehard. My guess is that the black leaders amused themselves hugely simply by scowling and making the honky shiver. Yet when the feminists, the fat, the bald, and all the other organized bellyachers laid claim to the Southern black's condition—that is to say, a condition wherein they were denied such elemental rights as the voting right—the black leaders entered no complaint. Why?

Thomas Sowell, a black economist of unscotchable independence and resourcefulness, answered the question definitively: "In many cases, their very 'leadership' consists not of their having been selected by blacks but of being regarded by the white news media, white philanthropy, and white politicians as 'spokesmen' for the black masses. Much of the black leadership is not in the business of leading blacks but of extracting what they can from whites, and their strategies and rhetoric reflect that orientation."[9]

Nonetheless, playing to the Liberals' phobias proved to be arduous work, and many of the bogus black leaders of the late 1960s and 1970s staggered into oblivion after tawdry careers,

* Though its name derived from the names of the chain's founders, some black leaders thought it referred to the black boy in the children's story, and it made them mad.

hectic and brief. A book on their eventual whereabouts would make as useful a contribution to our knowledge of the Republic as did the Lynds' *Middletown* in the 1930s. For that matter, a book retailing the final resting places of all the era's frauds would make illuminating and merry reading: the erstwhile firebomber of university buildings now counseling at a day-care center; the revolutionary orator now tending bar and domiciled under the stern eye of a frigid feminist who instructs women in "nontraditional" occupations while he minds the kids; the marijuana prophet now alcoholic and practicing marginal and decidedly shifty law in America's great outback; and the black nationalist whom time has forgotten now whiling away his hours in some seedy Algiers café, waiting for his Stateside broker's monthly check, convinced that the CIA has its eye on him, and wondering if America will ever provide him with fresh opportunities for plunder.

Until a proper historian comes along all we can say with certitude is that not many of the New Age black leaders stayed on top for long. Most burned themselves out, undone by the Liberals' voracious appetite for new thrills. Some, sated by all the astonishing boodle and honors heaved at them by Liberals, probably did waddle into retirement well satisfied. But for every happy ending, there must have been a dozen tragedies: the activist turned welfare impresario nabbed for swift bookkeeping; the activist turned "human rights" specialist nabbed for assault with intent to kill; the progressive Congressman, long an advocate of the politics of compassion, convicted on twenty-nine counts of old-fashioned boodling. This last, of course, is not merely a speculative sketch but an actuality: the Hon. Charles C. Diggs, Jr., founder of the Black Caucus, a civil rights champion who after more than two decades in the House of Representatives resigned his seat and headed for the Maxwell Air Force Base hoosegow, hollering of racism all the way.[10] His fate could have been grimmer. He could have gone the way of a woebegone George Wiley, founder of the National Welfare Rights Organization, who fell from his cabin cruiser and drowned. Hustling the Liberals had been rough work. The day before his death an interviewer asked, "Are you burned out, George?"[11] It was the last question ever asked him. Or there was Floyd McKissick. From 1972 to 1980 he spent $37 million, all coaxed from the Feds, on Soul City, an attempt in the North Carolina wilderness to turn "a poor rural area into an industrial town."[12] The thing was always a bust, though Floyd did raise up a $300,000 manse for his wife, her Maserati, and his son's Mercedes. "Soul City is almost a religious idea. It can't be judged in white man's terms," he would tell reporters as they surveyed the idiot street signs and empty buildings surrounded by the pines and the chiggers of North Carolina's dank backwoods. When the Feds finally booted him from his remaining three thousand acres, all that stood to discommode the local rattlesnakes was thirty-one homes, a partly occupied industrial building, a gift shop, a health-food shop, and Floyd's swell home.[13] Where is Floyd now? Where are the hundreds like him? What ever happened to that Maserati?

For more than a decade the New Age black leaders had sweated through a sociological fandango. Of a sudden one would catch the Liberal eye with a truly great performance; of a sudden the Liberals grew loonier and yearned for weirder spectacles. In 1973 the orator of black revolution Stokely Carmichael could be assured of Liberal munificence and goodwill by notifying the *Newark News* that "Brother Essex," the New Orleans sniper who had just murdered six and injured twelve, "carried our struggle to the next quantitative level, the level of science."[14] Within a few years he could not even get on the *Today* show with such a feeble act.

American Liberals had progressed far into the New Age. They were gaga over dozens of good causes: the black-footed ferret, radiation plagues, the plight of lesbian novelists, the CIA, the bake sale to fund the women's powerlifting team down at the university. I actually attended the bake sale. It was held at a Big Ten cow college, and the cookies were poisonous. By the late 1970s Jim Crow was only a memory—transmogrified but a memory. Furthermore, there was a new black middle class. As William Julius Wilson of the University of Chicago demonstrated in *The Declining Significance of Race*, discrimination no longer kept the black man down.

Under these circumstances the remaining black mountebanks had very few opportunities. There were a few positions on foundation boards available. There were Afro Studies departments on the campuses. But there was simply not much money in any of these positions. I take it as proof of the advanced sophistication and even urbanity of the surviving black mountebanks that in the late 1970s they looked abroad. They turned the remains of the civil rights movement into an international scam. In the annals of American humbug no other impresario—not the late Aimee Semple McPherson, not Joe McCarthy—had ever manifested such imagination, such *audace*. These were not ruffians Mau Mau–ing flak catchers or howling from soap boxes. These were readers of *The New York Times*. They knew that no matter how lost in onanism the New Age Liberals might be, armchair revolution was still in their blood, and the most appealing rumor of revolution now came from the Third World's tin-pot dictators and dovish Socialists.

Soon the surviving holy reverends of "the movement" were flying off to exotic parts, splicing Third World rants into their American civil rights sonorities and emptying sand from their shoes. They were also praying that their aides had not forgotten to pack their hip flasks. The mountebanks, you see, now labored in the lands of Araby. As the Rev. Hosea Williams put it, "They've got the money." But they also had dry laws, and *Playboy* magazine was *malum prohibitum*.

At any rate, the surviving reverends of the civil rights movement now confected for themselves a "foreign policy." As foreign policies go it was a curiosity. Addressing itself hardly at all to Europe or Japan and remaining absolutely mum on the USSR, the world's major slave master, it invested its preeminent interest in the Middle East and rich Arabia. The Rev. Joseph Lowery, head of the Southern Christian Leadership Conference, toured the region and sang "We Shall Overcome" with Yasir Arafat in his Beirut bunker. The Rev. Jackson, known as "the father of us all" by his followers at Operation PUSH (People United to Save Humanity), toured the region even more often than Lowery, and when Israel's prime minister refused him a summit meeting, he unmasked Mr. Begin as a "racist." However, the Rev. Hosea Williams, president of Atlanta's chapter of the Southern Christian Leadership Conference, made perhaps the most memorable junket of all. He went to Libya. There in 1979 he conferred "the Decoration of Martin Luther King" on a smiling Colonel Muammar Quadhafi, just before the colonel's troops began killing multitudes of black Christians in Chad. "Brother Quadhafi and the Libyan people," the Rev reported, "expressed a great desire to ally with the black American in eliminating racism and Zionism internationally."[15] Zionism? How did that get onto the civil rights agenda? Well, in the desert the yokels worry a lot about the Zionist conspiracy. They are in constant need of the Zionist catnip. "I can help your cause, but you have to help my cause," the Rev. Jackson admonished a gathering of Arab businessmen in Chicago. At that meeting, reported *The New York Times*, he picked up a cool $10,000.[16]

Yet as the scam went on these references to Zionism and "the Jews" acquired a creepy tone, vaguely reminiscent of the tone sounded by Harold Cruse in his 1967 book *The Crisis of the Negro Intellectual*. Jews "function in America as an organic part of a distant nation-state,"[17] Cruse wrote, which is itself vaguely reminiscent of earlier poetry, to wit: the yawps of the One Hundred Percent Americans of yore who once howled against Al Smith and "the pope's agents."

What a splendid symmetry! What a gorgeous reminder of mankind's slippery grip on virtue! Here was the remnant of the once noble civil rights movement suddenly stirring with cockeyed references to "the Jews." For thirty years anti-Semitism had been on the wane, but suddenly, as Murray Friedman observed, there came "a rise in anti-Jewish feelings among the best-educated and best-informed members of the black community."[18] The black mountebanks' earlier cockeyed references to the white race could be attributed to playing upon the Liberals' bugaboos, but this Jew-baiting suggested malice and a deep vein of Stone Age bigotry.

Their most noisy occasion for anti-Semitism came when Jimmy finally rid himself of his celebrated UN ambassador. Andy Young was probably the most perfect specimen of an ass ever to serve as an American diplomat. He had appalled the world. Yet when the Wonderboy finally sought his resignation, the black leaders insisted that Andy was a victim of "the Jews." Well, if the term bigot means anything at all, it denominates a person possessed by an invidious absorption with racial, religious, or ethnic differences, especially on issues where these differences are irrelevant. If Andy was a victim of anything other than his own grandiose and stultifying arrogance he was a victim of Liberal flattery. He was a periphrastic maniac, goaded into almost ceaseless idiotic chatter, 90 percent of it trendily antithetical to American interests but perfectly in cadence with the mountebankery of the hour. He performed for the applause of the New Age Liberals and the sheikhs. He was not the American ambassador to the United Nations: he was the conscience of George McGovern the morning after an orgiastic night at an American Legion post. When his long-awaited defenestration finally occurred it was not owing to Jewish treachery but to Andy's own clownish arrogance and deceit. He was caught carrying on the foreign policy of the black mountebanks rather than that of his government, and when confronted with the *corpus delicti* the Rev lied.[19] Blaming "the Jews" was an essay in Jew-baiting dependent for its effect on a deep and primitive bigotry, which suggested that maybe those canards about America's white power structure issued from darker sources than mere mountebankery.

This enterprising racialism soon reached macabre culmination in Atlanta, Georgia. There, in a black neighborhood well insulated from the honky, black children, mainly males, were being murdered; and by the fall of 1980 the murders were making national headlines. No evidence of racial motivation existed. Yet with their usual rationale the frauds soon arrived and set up their tents: Racism! "It is open season on black people," pronounced the Rev. Jackson.[20] "The feeling is that if it ain't the Klan, it's the cops," declared a local operator.[21] Dick Gregory believed that the Centers for Disease Control in Atlanta was killing the children and using them for experimental purposes.[22] Thus tragedy was turned into buffoonery. On came the psychics, the street demonstrations, the concerts, and all the rest of the tawdry symbolism, the newest of which was green ribbons. Even athletes pinned the ribbons on their persons. In world history no crime had ever been solved by such means. It was another first for the New Age. The ribbons were to be worn until a proper murderer was arrested and brought to trial.

When a black Atlantan was arrested and charged the ribbons began to disappear . . . but gradually and, one suspects, with remorse. There had been such great expectations. The oratory swelled and sang. Here was the old cause! Here was oppression! Here was genocide! Astonished cops pleaded for calm. This was a matter of murder, not politics. The oratory and the celebrity were bringing confusion and possibly more murders. Yet the frauds continued to exploit the misery with their fantastic sophistries and green ribbons. Mayor Marion Barry of our nation's capital justified the charges of racism, explaining that had the children "been Jewish, the Federal government would have moved faster."[23] Jewish? Why Jewish? Why not simply white or rich or famous? Atlanta was the sad culmination of more than a decade of sham. "Whether the killer or killers turn out to be black or white," the Rev. Jackson wrote in a letter to *Time* magazine, "black life is not and has never been . . . seen in the same manner as when whites are killed. I regard this attitude as a cultural conspiracy to kill black people . . . the American culture is anti-black."[24]

So maybe those green ribbons never should have come off. Certainly no black mountebank ever said it was okay to retire them. The ribbons just disappeared, and no Liberal felt embarrassment. No one seemed to see anything amiss—though again, in all of American history you would be hard pressed to find anything comparable to the Atlanta spectacle. And if you looked in FBI files on crime in Atlanta you would find that in 1977, 1978, and 1979 black homicides had been solved markedly more often than white homicides.[25] What is to be made of this? My guess is that the Rev. Jackson would consider such statistics evidence of police harassment in the black community or an insult to black murderers. In his actions and his utterances he has continually pushed back the frontiers of the unimaginable.

Had the civil rights movement concluded in abomination?

Did it make the United States of America a laughingstock? In its epistemology, its metaphysics, its theory of law, and its tactics for rousing the rabble, did it shoot great holes into the Constitution and the Bill of Rights? It did indeed. Moreover, it denied millions of poor blacks the worthy leaders they so badly needed, and it conduced to the bungling of the Liberals' other great causes. It allowed all social problems to be politicized by con artists, particularly con artists versed in the Marxist arts. It ushered in an amazing variety of cheap thought, and it allowed America to be portrayed as the world's great villain, our every high-minded endeavor to be denigrated as hypocrisy.

The botching of civil rights in the 1960s and the 1970s was an epochal botch. *In fine*, it encouraged the growth of certain idiotic notions that eventually flummoxed all the Liberals' great causes, introducing unprecedented mountebankery and barbarism into American life. Once Constitutional guarantees had been extended to blacks in the mid-1960s and once measures had been taken to ensure against backsliding, the movement should have shut down its militancy, and allowed all the holy reverends to return to choir practice and evening bingo. Now, having demonstrated all this and in terms that even a sociologist or a Hollywood starlet will understand, we can more speedily dispatch the Liberals' remaining great botches—namely: welfare and the Vietnam War.

2

It is but one of the myriad ironies pelting the Liberal today that though once a critic of materialism, as the years piled up he became obsessed by Mammon's cursed perspective. By the 1970s no problem was judged so stubborn that it could not be solved by a proper Congressional appropriation. No life was considered livable below income levels divined by social science. Did this mean that a hermit in the woods was incapable of a little merriment? Did it mean that the good life could be found only in Palm Beach and similar socioeconomic purlieus? Probably it did. The position of the Liberal cleric was even more whistle-brained. He would thunder imprecations against

American affluence with the utmost fury, and in the same homily he would urge that Zambia be remade in the image of San Diego, California. Not even the prosperity of Bull Snort, Georgia, would be sufficient. Yet whatever the New Age Liberals' public utterances on affluence might be, very few ever peeled off much of their own wealth for the poor, and many actually prospered in their service.

The palmy days of the poverty industry began with the War on Poverty. Lyndon Johnson had personally experienced government's magical power to enrich, and now he would use government to enrich others. Once he had fattened up the welfare budget, Washington became a city full of quacks adept at dispensing the loaves and the fishes, and making a bundle. Aid to Families with Dependent Children! Food stamps! Community action programs! Housing assistance programs! Medicaid! More! In the extravagant spirit of the time they remade the American polity. Frenzy directed their labors. They worked without blueprint. They taxed without mercy. What resulted was not an American welfare state, rationally and prudently constructed, but a blowsy milch-cow state teeming with superparasites: social engineers, welfare counselors, bureaucrats, nutritionists, social scientists, legal-aid advisers, and charlatans of even more dubious repute. Chronicling the growth of this great beast at the end of the 1970s, George Gilder found that its forty-four major welfare teats had throughout the decade grown two and a half times as fast as the GNP and three times as fast as wages. Soon these jugs were pouring out $200 billion to some fifty million persons, with some five million welfare quacks directing the orgies.[26] In the 1970s so terrific had the momentum toward welfare grown that neither the fiend Nixon nor his agent Ford could apply the brakes. To the contrary, under them welfare expanded even more voluptly than under LBJ. Five million Americans had made compassion their meal ticket, and they were still grasping for more when the 1980s crashed down on them, yet the growth did not end even under Ronald Reagan. "With astonishing consistency," Daniel Patrick Moynihan wrote in *The Politics of a Guaranteed Income,* "middle-class professionals . . . when asked to devise ways of improving the condition of lower class groups would come up with schemes of which the first effect would be to improve the condition of the middle-class professionals and the second effect might or might not be that of improving the condition of the poor."[27]

Yet the cost to the middle class had become onerous, and the economy fell upon very hard times. The New Age Liberals had attempted to pay for their milch-cow state through higher taxes and through inflation—that is to say, taxation by surreptitious entry. The resulting squeeze upon the middle class became unbearable. By the end of the 1970s a huge number of middle-class workers had been dragged up into very high tax brackets because of inflation. In the mid-'60s, only about 5 percent of the American taxpayers were affected by marginal tax rates of 25 percent or higher. Now approximately 50 percent of the taxpayers were in these tax brackets. They were in tax brackets theretofore reserved for the very rich, but their incomes were still only middle class. Savings had declined sharply. In the world beyond our shores, the sorely pressed British saved 50 percent more of their incomes than their American counterparts, and America's low rate of personal savings soon caused grave problems in capital formation. By Jimmy's last year in office the rate of productivity growth in the United States was less than 1 percent. The economy was queasy with high inflation, rising unemployment, and an economic slowdown.

Nor did the transfer payments to the poor help the poor all that much. Unemployment among them soared, as did family breakup and every sort of social problem. As more and more middle-class wives had to go to work just to maintain their family income levels, more and more poor people quit work and often broke up their families, thereby raising their income levels through welfare. George Gilder has estimated that by 1979 the average welfare family of four received subsidies of just under $18,000. That was $1,500 more than the 1979 median income.[28] Before all this boodle had been available, poor people, many of whom were only temporarily poor owing to some transient misfortune, might go on the dole for a short while, but once the New Age Liberals had conjured up all the programs of the 1970s, increasing numbers of poor people simply settled into a lifetime of government benefits. It was a simple economic decision, revealing that many of the poor knew more about economics than the welfare quacks, who had all sorts of abstruse notions about how poverty bred more poverty and a handout was all that was needed to turn a pauper into a middle-class American.

Actually, the welfare state was bringing its clients not into the American middle class but at least sociologically into some of the most rarefied regions of the upper class. Once all the therapists, counselors, legal advisers, and other such frauds had had at them, many of America's welfare clients were leading lives similar to those lived in Hollywood, California. Divorce, alcoholism, drug abuse, psychosomatic illness, neurosis, suicide, and the incidence of social problems all increased rapidly in every neighborhood that fell under the ministrations of the welfare quacks. To students of the Beverly Hills–Hollywood axis the grim statistics were all too familiar. It was a garish decline. No wonder that even in the late 1970s, with welfare more munificent than ever, twenty million wary American families still chose to work at or below the poverty level rather than hazard their well-being amongst the teats of the milch-cow state.

The government sent out beaters to drive them onto the dole. With the taxpayers' money it propagandized and promulgated its programs. Almost always it ignored what was slowly becoming known about welfare, to wit: welfare undermined self-reliance, perpetuating poverty and wretchedness. A guaranteed income had become the dream of all Liberals by the early 1970s, but tests of guaranteed-income programs in Denver and Seattle now showed beyond doubt that such a policy reduced work effort by between one-third and one-half and increased family breakup by nearly 60 percent.[29] Daniel Patrick Moynihan, the most energetic proponent of a guaranteed income, came to the courageous judgment that in pushing the guaranteed income "I was wrong."[30] But Moynihan had rarely been stupefied by the New Age. Those who had, gave not a hoot for such findings.

Ever since the civil rights movement went bonkers in the late 1960s increasing numbers of New Age Liberals gave themselves over to extremism. With welfare they moved from propounding financial assistance as a matter of humane policy to propounding it as another of the bogus rights they were conjuring up in the 1970s. They urged militancy among the poor and their champions. Soon they were not even content with establishing an economic floor under the poor. They had moved from urging a guaranteed income to insisting on "redistribution" of the wealth from the haves to the have-nots. They got mad. Then they felt "rage." Ultimately they seemed to desire the destruction of all wealth. From loving the poor they came to hate the prosperous. The moral stigma that ignoramuses of an earlier era had attached to poverty they now attached to prosperity. In their egalitarian hallucination they came to espouse not only the cause of the poor but the virtue of the vicious. So it was that in one more realm, economics, they could not abide reality. They had moved eons away from the immutable truth that that wise statesman of the Renaissance, Francesco Guicciardini, had noted while reading Machiavelli's *Discourses*, "necessity is an ever-present law and stimulus"[31]—without it the poor stayed poor and with the welfare quacks accosting them they grew more wretched.

3

The third of the Liberals' great botches was their embroilment in Southeast Asia, and its consequences were the most spectacularly calamitous of all. As the war expanded and then petered out, the Soviet Union sedulously fortified its strategic force unchallenged until it approached parity with the United States for the first time in history. Possibly it had gone beyond parity. Simultaneously with this buildup a huge propaganda campaign commenced against the United States, leaving it the world's foremost target of abuse. Finally, as its influence diminished, the United States' worldwide alliance system began to unravel, and by the 1980s even NATO was politically decrepit. The war was the occasion for political and social inebriation at home that celebrated an infantile radicalism at the expense of useful customs and institutions. Ultimately, the Vietnam War led to the reign of Pol Pot and the third major holocaust of this century, thus exposing all the New Age Liberals' human-rights arias as so much guff. This final botch was a tragedy of bloody dimensions.

In the early 1960s the Liberals had grown ornate with a combination of Wilsonian fustian and he-man bellicosity. After the previous regime's caution and conservatism under the glabrous old general Dwight D. Eisenhower, John F. Kennedy promised challenge, grandeur, and hair. The administration of government was to be an epic: Unscotchable youth! Sophistication! Grace at one minute to midnight—damn the acidosis! All this would replace fuddy-duddyism on the Potomac. Moreover, the hatless young president brought with him "the New Economics," a magic wand for funding the most highfalutin peacetime foreign policy ever.

Now the great adventure began. In terms of oratory and sheer theater it was prodigious. JFK was one of the weirdest rhetoricians in presidential history, and that his odd oratory actually enraptured the Liberals should have warned us of the bats residing in their belfries. From his inaugural address to the day he was assassinated he enveloped the nation in hot air. "You must wonder when it is all going to end and when we can come back home," the hatless leader chided a cringing audience in Montana. "Well, it isn't going to end . . . because what happens in Europe or Latin America or Africa directly affects the security of the people who live in this city, and particularly those who are coming after." The song was the same the day he died. In Texas, the morning of November 22, 1963, he declared:

Without the United States, South Viet-Nam would collapse overnight. Without the United States, the SEATO alliance would collapse overnight. Without the United States the CENTO alliance would collapse overnight. Without the United States there would be no NATO. And gradually Europe would drift into neutralism and indifference. Without the efforts of the United States in the Alliance for Progress, the Communist advance onto the mainland of South America would long ago have taken place. We are still the keystone in the arch of freedom.[32]

Thirteen years later the scepter had passed to the anile figure of Jimmy Carter, sermonizing vacantly about America's "inordinate fear of Communism" and the "humane ideals" of our Constitution, ideals that could wow the whole Third World. Pol Pot was then slaughtering somewhere between a third and a half of his fellow Cambodians. The North Vietnamese were robbing millions of South Vietnamese and driving thousands to sea in leaky ships. They were using chemical warfare throughout Indochina, and their friendly pharmacist, the USSR, was using it in Afghanistan. Moscow had moved its theater of operations on to Africa, the Middle East, and Central America.

Kennedy had propounded a "flexible response" to Soviet mischief, a mix of diplomacy with military and foreign-aid programs. Notwithstanding its flamboyant oratory, the policy was sound. At times, of course, Kennedy became lost in his rhetoric, passing up opportunities such as the opportunity to neutralize Fidel Castro during the 1962 missile crisis. He even failed to ensure that the agreements with Khrushchev were enforced. Still, beneath the rhetoric there was at least a sober and sensible perception of the modern world. Jimmy Carter's substitute for "flexible response" was to orate like a schoolmarm and to vibrate with good intentions, good intentions that he was sure would stupefy even the vilest dictator.

Jimmy and his yokels believed in the politics of good example. Assistant Secretary of State Richard Holbrooke spoke for the whole imbecilic regime when he asseverated that vast sections of the world were very favorably impressed by "the basic moral force that exists in the principles of our system."[33] Hence grease-paint moralizing replaced military strength and diplomatic steadiness. The New Age Liberal would negotiate any indignity, anywhere, for any amount of time, notwithstanding the fact that as he negotiated his pockets were being picked and his shoelaces tied together. The Vietnam War had so shocked the New Age Liberal that all that remained with him from his days on the New Frontier was the talent for pontification.

In the botching of the Vietnam War the Liberals displayed the same moral bugs that assisted them in the botching of civil rights: timorousness, stupidity, inconstancy, and frivolity. Yet by the 1970s, they had grown so precious that a historic migration had commenced: intelligent Liberals began departing for the conservative camp, often bringing their Liberal values with them. Men like Norman Podhoretz remained friends of the welfare state, but they also became friends of William F. Buckley, Jr. Meanwhile the benighted continued to shed New Frontier principles as they undulated into the New Age: from opposing a Communist takeover of Vietnam they moved toward advocating a coalition government with the Communists, then American withdrawal, then North Vietnamese victory. After this abominable tergiversation they affected a grand scowl and trained it upon every Yankee effort in foreign affairs. They became isolationists transfixed by a vision not of American purity but of American profligacy. Their enemies by the middle 1970s were not so much the Communists as the officials of the American government. One might sympathize had these New Age Liberals now become libertarians or anarchists, but they were still statists, statists living in a dream world of berserk CIA agents and aggrieved Russians.

More than most, the Vietnam War was a fouled-up war. Possibly, it was an ill-advised war. It may have been a prosaically executed war. Truth be known, however, it was the Liberals' war, foul-ups and all.

Entered during JFK's years of adventure, it was brought to a huge boil by LBJ, who conducted the American effort according to the progressive theories of warfare conferred on him by his Liberal assistant presidents. When the enemy did not yield to graduated escalation or any of the other tony axioms of Harvard, the more precious Liberals huffed out of the Johnson White House into the Age of Aquarius. There they juvenesced and met the brave idealists from North Vietnam—"such gentle and simple and beautiful people," observed Ramsey Clark.[34] Clark had been LBJ's attorney general, and here he was speaking on Radio Hanoi. Two years later he would be his party's senatorial candidate in New York, where he would distinguish himself by wearing Levi's and sentimentalizing all social and political problems that were not outright hallucinations of the Leftist mind. His personal ideological metamorphosis was to be repeated by hundreds of thousands of Liberals, who, as their numbers increased, conspired willy-nilly to render the consummation of what had theretofore been Liberal endeavors ever more improbable.

Contrary to the mythology that the peace movement so arduously confected, the American people never abandoned their government. It was the Liberals who absconded, demonstrated—often violently—against it, and were fulfilled when the North Vietnamese—aided by Congress' refusal to resupply the South Vietnamese army—rolled into Saigon. The Liberals' success in shaping the media's perceptions of the war remains one of the era's great mysteries. Even long after the war had ended, they were juggling the facts—creating, for instance, the bizarre legend that the typical Vietnam veteran returned to America despised by his countrymen and ready for the Freudian couch, when in truth it was the Liberals who treated the veterans as war criminals and it was the Liberals who most often were unhinged by events.

The most stupendous myth confected by them was the myth that the war's outcome vindicated their opposition to it. Actually, they were proved wrong within days of Saigon's surrender. The domino theory, long a derisory subject with them, took almost immediate effect as Cambodia and Laos fell to the Communists and Thailand came under increased pressure. Soon the predictions of humane reform under Communism were also unhorsed. Millions of Southeast Asians were butchered, incarcerated, or stripped of their possessions and driven into the sea. The horror persuaded many European opponents of American policy such as Jean Lacoutre and Olivier Todd to recant and admit complicity in the Communist victory. Yet as the bone heaps in Southeast Asia multiplied, the New Age Liberals remained silent; and many ducked into the personal-growth claptrap of the late 1970s. This discrepancy between European recantation and the American evasion was quite startling. During the third great holocaust of the century the moral exhibitionists of America's New Age reposed on water beds, protested smoking in public places, and declaimed against nuclear energy and the enemies of the snail darter.

The most brazen among them insisted that despite the grisly evidence mounting in Indochina, the credenda of the peace movement would replace all the principles that had governed American foreign policy since the late 1940s and be an improvement. America, as the suave Andy Young expounded, would finally get on the right side of world revolution. Negotiation and goodwill would form the foundation of a new era of American diplomacy. In the White House our Snopesian president took note and returned to his maps. As he was to inform *Newsweek*, one of his most exacting tasks since election day had been to master the locations of all the countries of the world plus their capitals![35]

The empty moral posturing that characterized the New Age Liberals as they presided over the farcical culminations of welfare and civil rights was with them too during the last tragic chapters of Vietnam. On September 20, 1977, a record 105 forward-looking nations cosponsored Vietnam's successful application to the United Nations. On September 26, the world's newest gulags now in place, the boat people now a matter of record, the New Age Liberals of the peace movement strutted into New York's Beacon Theater to celebrate Hanoi's admission to the brotherhood of peace-loving nations. Passing through a demonstration by anti-Communist Vietnamese refugees, Ramsey Clark exulted in the peace movement's achievement; Sam Brown too passed through the sad anti-Communist pickets and joined the happy throng. It was probably the only picket line he had ever crossed, at least when journalists were about. Brown was the Carter administration's director of ACTION, the federal agency charged with coordinating such Kennedy-era programs as the Peace Corps. He had been a giant of the movement, an organizer of the Vietnam Moratorium, and he was weepy with happiness. His whole life had now been redeemed. A Vietnamese government spokesman vilified American imperialism and panhandled for reparations from the whipped Yanks. The assembled applauded. Six days before, Ambassador Young too had rejoiced in the purr of labors justified. He had put on his unseemly display right in the General Assembly, where he remarked on how fitting it was for him, once a peace demonstrator himself, to be there on the day of Hanoi's final triumph. He stepped from the rostrum to shake hands with the entire Vietnamese delegation. At times New Age Liberals could become very emotional. It was another of their little indulgences. From the war's earliest days they practiced very little restraint, so confident were they of their superior morality. Not once in any protest or public utterance had they committed a reproachable act. Such was the self-congratulatory consensus of 1977 which covered so many of their discreditable deeds.

The excesses were amazing. In the early 1970s after shmoozing with the North Vietnamese and spreading their propaganda, Jane Fonda boldly described our returning POWs' claims of torture as the statements of "hypocrites and liars."[36] In *The New York Review of Books*, the scholarly Noam Chomsky esteemed America's conduct of the war "an indescribable atrocity."[37] Blubbered John Leonard in the February 1977 *Esquire*: "If everytime I think of Vietnam I can manage at the same time to think of Mary Tyler Moore, I can also manage to feel not so bad about being an American."[38] If it took an apparition of the innocent Mary Tyler Moore to make Leonard feel better about his citizenship, imagine what it would take Fonda or Chomsky to cheer up. Eventually this diabolizing of the American military effort in Southeast Asia became the current wisdom, as Christopher Lehmann-Haupt demonstrated in a 1981 *New York Times* review of two books on the war. "Alas," he repined, "we have read it all before . . . the reports of wanton rape and murder by American soldiers driven mad by the elusiveness of the enemy."[39] Now, ask yourself, just how many "reports of wanton rape and murder" were there? The war had become an occasion for baby talk, fantasy, and extraordinary rancor against America.

Far more suggestively, it became an occasion for denial. To begin with, the members of the movement had denied the aggression of the North Vietnamese. Furthermore, they had denied the aggressors' brutality despite the reality of some 50,000 Vietnamese peasants having been executed when the Communists took over the North. They denied the reality and significance of some 3,000 to 5,000 South Vietnamese civilians who were butchered when the Communists overran Hue in

1968, to say nothing of the thousands of South Vietnamese village chiefs who, often with their families and friends, were tortured and murdered whether they were combatants or not. As Jane Fonda reveals, the movement even denied the reality of the POWs' scars. Finally, of course, the members of the movement denied the clear evidence of holocaust in Cambodia.

Throughout the whole bloody conflict the New Age Liberals' treatment of the war had been an act of denial. Denying the ferocious nature of the Communists had been their especial art. So polished had they become at this art that even in the last weeks of the war, as stories of Communist atrocities multiplied, the gifted Anthony Lewis could look up from the grisly proceedings and invoke an article of New Age faith one more time. In the final days of free Cambodia, as President Ford sought emergency military aid from Congress to prevent a Cambodian bloodbath, Lewis announced, "Some will find the whole bloodbath debate unreal. What future possibility could be more terrible than the reality of what is happening to Cambodia now?"[40] It would take years of horror to bestir this elegantly preened public conscience to face his own ill-timed question. Frankly, I doubt he ever faced it.

How was it that people like Lewis failed so miserably to observe the luridly observable? When he wrote the above lines there was already abundant evidence of Khmer Rouge barbarism. Then, just hours after Phnom Penh's fall, gruesome stories were seeping from Cambodia telling of a forced evacuation of the city. Cambodians, regardless of condition, were ordered to drop everything and march into the jungle. Patients were wheeled out of hospitals, some with insulin bottles dangling above them. Bewildered children were whipped into the lengthening lines. Stragglers were shot—even mothers with babes at their breasts—by black-clad barbarians. Soon Freedom House was comparing the condition of the Cambodians to the annihilation of the Jews. Secretary of State Kissinger spoke of a mounting death toll. Anthony Lewis was unmoved. On May 12, 1975, he explained that there was bound to be a little rough stuff. Responding to reports of the forced evacuation of Phnom Penh, he scoffed at "our cultural arrogance, an imperial assumption that by superiority or sheer power our way of life must prevail."[41] And then he fell silent. His attention turned to Chile.

Rancor, vehement beyond all provocation; denial, blind to the most terrible realities—does one need any more evidence that as time wore on the so-called peace movement was overtaken by psychosis? The historical record has made a statement; the New Age Liberals by the late 1970s had simply gone round the bend. Their violent demonizing of a nation that despite its frailties was still one of the world's most decent, and their simultaneous rhapsodizing of a nation that was by almost any standard one of the world's most barbaric, was, *in fine*, an act of insanity. Reflect again on the *corpus delicti*: during years of the most horrible suffering for the people of Cambodia, Laos, and Vietnam, the members of the movement were more inflamed about human-rights violations in Chile. They attended movies on the subject. There were bake sales!

This mass psychosis took on the most ludicrous dimensions: Richard Dudman of the *St. Louis Post-Dispatch*, returning from Cambodia in late 1978, writes that Pol Pot's associates are not fanatical madmen: ". . . Cambodia is in the midst of one of the world's great housing programs";[42] William Shawcross is celebrated for *Sideshow: Kissinger, Nixon and the Destruction of Cambodia*. By the time of its publication Pol Pot had murdered something like a third of the Cambodian population. The country's middle class had been deliberately exterminated, its culture almost extirpated. Nothing like this had happened in modern times. Yet Shawcross's demented theme is that those responsible for the holocaust are the men who tried to prevent it, the villainous Kissinger and Nixon. The New Age Liberals whooped it up and celebrated above all else the book's *scholarship*. Naturally, its scholarship was soon exposed as the utmost poppycock.[48] Kissinger's aide Peter Rodman performed the unmasking in the March 1981 issue of *The American Spectator*. Still the Liberals of the New Age clung to their delusion. They simply denied Rodman's revelations. Not until the horror of Cambodia was being pointed out even by the Communist Vietnamese did the New Age Liberals reform their denials; and now they simply denied that there had ever been earlier denials.

The madness of the movement grew invincible to reason. The New Age Liberals' maniacal faith in the efficacy of negotiations made foreign-policy debate futile; and when the Carter administration adopted this faith in negotiations it made US foreign policy futile, allowing the United States to become ever more widely reviled, the Soviet Union ever more influential across the Third World, world politics ever more remote from American influence. In every foreign ministry on earth, diplomats beheld Jimmy Carter sermonizing loonily and either cringed or guffawed. Yet in Washington there was no sobering up. American diplomats were being killed, American citizens mauled, American property and interests abused. Nonetheless Jimmy bragged that during his presidency no American soldier had died fighting. He neglected mention of the murdered diplomats, the dead embassy guards, and the lost influence. To penetrate such derangement what was needed was not syllogisms or facts but an equally balmy leader, and the Lord God provided the requisite wails and gongs somewhere in the swaddled dome of the fabulous Ayatollah Ruhollah Khomeini, D.D.

It took the Rev. Khomeini and his dirty-necked galoots to undo the wisdom of the peace movement. The movement's dogmas were revealing their futility during the boat people's exodus. They lost still more magic with the Russians' invasion of Afghanistan. In both cases negotiations were not even begun. For the Communists there was nothing to negotiate. But when American foreign service personnel were kidnapped, abused, and held ransom for 444 days, Jimmy's New Age diplomacy revealed itself not only as futile but also as dangerously provocative. His servility doubled the ancient holy man's rage. Jimmy's policy of righteous guff and disarmament had made the world more dangerous, the tyrants more bellicose. In the end ordinary Americans discovered that shaky though our prospects in this modern world might be, power was preferable to piety feigned.

From the serene plateau of historical hindsight, then, we see the Liberal scudding balmily into the New Age. With crackpot gogues counseling him and ravening activists keeping the heat on, he has repeatedly redefined society's problems until finally life has lost all definition. All thought has been rendered meaningless. What is peace? What is democracy? What is freedom? What is the good life? For fifteen years the answers grew more esoteric and preposterous.

By the 1970s even sanity was no longer definable, and so in all the advanced outposts of the Liberal crusade bedlamites were simply released from their asylums.

"Our handling of the mentally ill has never seemed in such a mess," *The Wall Street Journal* editorialized.

> Medical advances have made possible the treatment of most forms of mental illness, yet thousands of obviously disturbed people sleep in alleys and idly roam the streets of most major cities. This is a failure not of our mental institutions but of our political institutions.
>
> Take the case of New York City, where the sight of "shopping bag ladies" is all too common. A class action suit was filed recently against the state on behalf of an estimated 6,000 homeless ex–psychiatric patients who now live on the city streets. The suit seeks a court order for the state to provide residential housing for these people.[44]

Onto the streets they came, the true heirs of Liberal progress. Some were instantly slaughtered, set upon by wolf packs of those other beneficiaries of Liberal progress, the common brutes. Others perished from exposure. Yet some of the recently liberated bedlamites triumphed over the false pieties of progress, at least temporarily. In the late 1970s, on Park Avenue, on Central Park South, in all the haunts of the fashionable and the modern, one could see them jeering, flapping their ragged limbs at pedestrians and giggling lewdly—strutting loons ridiculing the lunacy of the New Age.

3

The Environmental Enthusiasm

With the Credo of Wholesome Progress Come the Fantasy and the Gloom

THE New Age became a breeding swamp for exotic enthusiasts, each following his own incandescent agenda, each growing ever more fanatical and incapable of compromise or of composing himself within the old Liberal consensus. Soon the old consensus was no consensus at all but a madhouse throbbing with rioting monomaniacs. Not since 1968 has a normal American pol made his way through a Democratic convention, and in 1968 the party's fanatics saw to it that the convention was such a carnival of zealotry that Hubert Humphrey was doomed before he left Chicago.

Thus to analyze the crack-up of American Liberalism we must make a scholarly expedition into the fever swamps of American politics and come back with these bugs. We must study their enthusiasms and appraise the damage they have done to the Great Republic, for Liberalism was not all that suffered from their rampage. In the 1960s and the 1970s they emerged and swarmed forth toward America's centers of power and influence. In prior times such pests were swatted smartly before they could spawn. Now the Republic's bug swatters hesitated. They listened to the bugs' side of the argument. Anon, there were more bugs.

One of the most fantastic of these bugs was that friend and ally of all bugs, the environmentalist—not the simple, unadorned conservationist but the *environmentalist*! The denomination is sonorous, suggesting a grasp of science, arcanum, and progress. Actually, of course, this gasbag term is another of our era's pretentious titles. Any clod can qualify as an environmentalist; all that is necessary is that he adhere to the American Credo of Wholesome Progress, be somewhat radicalized and sozzled by the ludicrous pantheism so often observable among those of the maudlin left. A prime postulant to environmentalism is the schoolgirl who falls for every stray dog in the neighborhood and goes to pieces over the poetry of Rod McKuen. In an earlier era she would have been sucker for Edgar A. Guest, whose collections include *A Heap o' Livin'*, *Just Folks*, and *Life's Highway*.

At this point, let us digress for a moment to discuss the American Credo of Wholesome Progress. Every group absorbs a set of defining beliefs, some by osmosis, some by conscious intellectual effort. The Cuebo of the Colombian wilds have their beliefs; the members of the American Institute of Physics have theirs. In terms of sophistication the American Credo of Wholesome Progress falls somewhere in between—though no adherent of the Credo would ever proclaim his beliefs to be in any way superior to those of the Cuebo; the physicists' possibly, but not the Cuebo's. The Credo of Wholesome Progress composes an amalgam of highly sophisticated and sensitive ideas or principles—often changing, always tentative, yet somehow always enunciated with the utmost confidence, as a child's knowledge of fairies is declaimed with confidence.

Like a huge glacier, the Credo has moved through America during the last three decades, smoothing off the craggy salients of American temperament, filling in the depths, leaving every province through which it has passed abundant with smooth oval-shaped Americans, fatuously comprehending, reflexively platitudinous, derisible beneath their Pecksniffian purr. Originating decades ago in those enclaves where the intelligentsia fancied its contents progressive and exciting, the great glacier has now reached into suburbia, the corporate world, the bureaucracy, even the boondocks. No sector of American life has remained wholly untouched by its transforming ice. An indigent, a lawyer, a housewife, a professor of Elizabethan drama—all Americans when interviewed are apt to recite snatches of these dogmas; though the New Age Liberal is most affected, which is as it should be. The Credo is mostly his creation; and where he does not share its values it is only because he has opted for even more advanced thoughts—say, that trees have souls or eloquent conversations among their peers.

Just as the character of 1920s Ku Kluxism owed much to the intellectual groundwork laid by the debased Christianity that preceded it, so too the character of the Credo of Wholesome Progress owes much to the debased form of higher education that spread through the Republic in the post–World War II period; and, come to think of it, the grim educators who did the spreading were not all that much different from a turn-of-the-century Methodist howling for the Anti-Saloon League. In modern America the cheap cachet of a college degree became a license for stupidity, and by 1972 nearly twelve million American youths were incarcerated in these dreadful institutions annually. Only a minority ever progressed beyond semiliteracy, yet the majority's wretched state of learning was adduced as evidence that still more of the national treasure must be dumped into the greedy hands of the educationists. Expenditures grew from $5½ billion in school year 1959–60 to almost $51 billion in 1978–79 with no discernible educational improvement. Had this gigantic growth in what the educationists are pleased to call higher education not taken place it would have been impossible for the Credo of Wholesome Progress to gain such wide purchase on the American mind. Never having been stunted by the years of propaganda that constitute higher education, too many Americans would be free of its bugaboos.

Research data on the Credo remain scarce. Not even the Soviet Union's Institute of USA and Canadian Studies examines it comprehensively. The Credo's adherents actually discourage intellectual inquiry, notwithstanding the fact that many are themselves intellectuals and some are quite accomplished. When the interested scholar seeks data on them they grow hostile and confused, often believing the scholar to be a book-burner, a McCarthyite, or some other disagreeable phantasmagoria. I myself have been exposed to their effronteries even on college campuses where my only offense was to seek clarification about a young prof's anxious insistence that America is full of Nazis. That grim episode puts me in mind of one of my most unshakable beliefs. The most important divisions in this world are not between Communist and capitalist, rich and poor, conservative and liberal, man and woman. Rather, the important division is between the intelligent and the unintelligent, the sensible and the irrational, the laughers and the laughees. All other divisions recede into picklewash.

Essentially, the Credo is a combination of humanistic pieties, interlarded with some scientific findings, some social-science legends, some Freud, some Marx, Rotarian optimism, and YMCA flumdiddle about how to be good. I have been assiduously collecting and analyzing these droppings for years, with the fond hope that I might someday have the opportunity to present a monograph to one of the learned societies —say, the American Political Science Association or the American Sociological Society. Possibly I might impress them and so secure refuge and a livelihood on a university faculty once the oxygen ceases to flow unimpeded to my brain. Sad to say that at this writing no learned society has admitted me to its conventicles, though ludicrous windbags now hold forth on all manner of hysteria, and though I have solemnly promised to drink only from my own flask. In 1978, I was voted one of the Ten Outstanding Young Men in America, and shortly thereafter *Time* magazine wrote me up as one of the fifty future leaders of the Republic. Still the telephone has not rung. If I ever do attain a leadership position, and it is commensurate with the rank attained by Peter the Great or by Woodrow Wilson, it will go hard for those who have snubbed me.

A comprehensive catalogue of the Credo's ideas and first principles would run into many pages, but from a small sampling it is possible to convey the average environmentalist's habit of mind:

#28—That the world is in the earliest stages of a general warming trend, which, if it is not somehow abated, will melt the polar caps, causing a rise in sea levels that will force inhabitants of coastal cities like New York to make enormous changes—for instance, raising their homes onto stilts.

#78—That coitus if pursued diligently prevents heart disease and has a highly salutary effect on the lungs, similar to the effect of wind sprints.

#193—That the light bulb is a poor substitute for sunlight and probably over the long run has impaired human vision.

#262—That the stifling of strong urges such as the urge to shout or to cry is not good. Research shows that it is a contributing factor to gastrointestinal disorder, cardiovascular malfunctions, and nerves.

#340—That the rich harbor lewd thoughts toward house servants, some of whom, usually women, still have to wear short black dresses.

#490—That the use of hallucinogenic drugs is as dangerous as the martini, though drug users probably do gain new insights into art, especially music.

#556—That homosexuals are more apt to understand the sad side of life than, say, a worker in a Chinese hand laundry.

#700—That blacks are good dancers, enjoy life more than whites, and jump higher, owing to the unique presence of a small bone at the lower end of the tibia.

#730—That the world is in the earliest stages of a general cooling trend, which, if it is not somehow abated, will send new glaciers down across the Republic.

#786—That Vitamin C, taken in sufficient doses, prevents colds.

#787—For that matter, that there are many vitamins which are useful in the treatment of disease, but that doctors are pigheadedly ignorant of nutrition. Taken in large enough doses, vitamin supplements could prevent most disease; all disease is nutritional in origin.

#835—That astrology is often the province of quacks, but it is still not wholly to be written off.

#836—That if you step on a crack you will break your mother's back.

Admittedly, as the New Age Liberal grows in years and in experience #836 appears somewhat dubious to him, and once middle age sets in, #836 begins to lose the cogency of other entries. I include it, however, because our present topic is environmentalism, and large numbers of environmentalists can never quite shake the logic of #836: "Oh, sure, what possible harm could it do to step on a crack? But then, after all, avoiding cracks is not a difficult matter. And if it will prevent serious misfortune to Mother, well, why not?" And so, carried along by concern for his mother's back the environmentalist in his heart of hearts comes to believe that the world would be a better place if laws were passed prescribing criminal punishment for crack-steppers. In due course the National Wildlife Federation comes up with the law. This is the mentality of those who speak movingly of the furbish lousewort.

Emerging from the American conservation movement, environmentalism distinguished itself by its sense of hysteria and its absorption with a series of political reforms that, were they implemented, would bring the American economy down to a condition similar to that of the Chinese economy during the late Cultural Revolution. Not content with the conservationist's reasonable desire to preserve what is properly called the natural environment, the environmentalist was transformed by the sublime events of the 1960s and 1970s into a Luddite, well born and driven by an endless cycle of idiot preoccupations: a love for things furry and wet, a resolute hostility toward the throwaway bottle, an insistence that resources remain in their natural condition, plus unrelieved premonitions of catastrophe. The superstitious fears and longings accumulated at an amazing pace, as did the crackpot therapies that the environmentalist wishes to bring down on the citizenry.

Environmentalism united the headaches of the late Thomas Malthus of Haileybury, England, with the tendency toward pantheism that Tocqueville spotted among the mob-minded more than a century ago; but for the purpose of observation it is helpful to categorize environmentalists as catastrophists or nature lovers, neither group being exclusive of the other. The catastrophists see the great orb earth as a gigantic spaceship, rapidly falling into disrepair and soon to be mere space garbage, uninhabited and uninhabitable. The nature lovers keep a deathwatch over every living thing on civilization's hit list. The noble snail darter, the furbish lousewort, the black-footed ferret, *Staphylococcus aureus*—these and other doomed life forms all bring out the Florence Nightingale in the nature lovers. Counseled by the Credo of Wholesome Progress they believe that all living things have rights: orangutans, trees, gnats, artichokes, everything. Possibly all living things should be allowed to vote. To the environmentalist it makes sense. After all, it is in this direction that democratic progress has marched since the days of Plato.

The first great environmentalist was Theodore Roosevelt. A prodigious composite of brains and energy, this patrician reformer from New York City also had a forcefulness about him that made him a man of very large moment in New York and in Washington at a very green age. Roosevelt reverenced the great outdoors. As a boy in the 1860s he had been deeply interested in natural history. Wherever his father's travels took him, across Europe or through the Middle East, the young TR collected specimens of the flora and the fauna. Always he lugged the debris back to Roosevelt *père*'s Manhattan mansion, there to be stuffed and studied and hidden from servants of delicate sensibility. While still a teenager TR had become a respected ornithologist, which could not be said of many Manhattanites then or now.

Eventually Roosevelt became the country's first and most powerful champion of the environment. He was the founder of the Boone and Crockett Club, perhaps the world's earliest conservation organization. The club helped create the National Zoo in Washington; the Park Protection Act of 1894, which saved Yellowstone from debauchery; and many zoological gardens. TR helped edit and publish such volumes of wilderness lore as *Trail and Camp-Fire*. Once in the White House he kept conservation near the top of the national agenda.

Through all these years he remained an ardent outdoorsman. He had purchased land in the spacious and unspoiled South Dakota Badlands in 1883. Working with a few hired hands, he created one of the area's first ranches. There he would repair from the reek and clatter of urban life to sniff the pristine air, to listen to the sounds of nature—and to hunt.

The late summer of 1883 was the occasion for one of TR's most amusing expeditions. Between August 19 and September 17 he sojourned in the region of the Big Horn Mountains. "My battery," he wrote sister Bamie, "consists of a long .45 Colt revolver, 150 cartridges, a no. 10 choke bore, 300-cartridge shotgun; a 45-75 Winchester repeater, with 1000 cartridges; a 40-90 Sharps, 150 cartridges; a 50-150 double-barrelled Webley express, 100 cartridges."

The battery was tested to the fullest. In those twenty-nine glorious days he executed sixteen grouse, twenty prairie chickens, five blue grouse, two sage grouse, two doves, two teal, and one ill-starred red rabbit. He also hooked fifty trout and blasted hell out of two whitetail does, one blacktail buck, and six elk. On the day he shot one of the elk he also "knocked the heads off" a couple of grouse. And by the time he returned home, he had finished off three grizzly bears: a mama bear, a papa bear ("through the brain"), and a baby bear ("the ball going through him from end to end").[1]

By the 1970s the heirs of TR had laid down their artillery. The ferocity, however, remained, and now it was turned not against the lower orders of life but against the higher orders and against civilization in general. Some ninety years after TR's massacre in the Big Horn Mountains, William O. Douglas, long a stalwart friend of nature, pronounced that in the struggle between mankind and Animalia, specifically the birds, he was taking the side of the birds—and he was not alone.[2]

Alarmed in the 1960s by civilization's advances against the last strongholds of indigenae, the environmentalist was moved to fulminate and to rage, and the range of his ire has been stupendous: DDT, aerosol cans, research into recombinant DNA, the flush toilet, the Concorde supersonic passenger plane, and an array of animals, insects, and flora that would astound the city slicker.

There the newly aroused environmentalist would sit monitoring the evening TV news, his eyes filling with tears as he heard the grim toll: automobile production up 4 percent; oil consumption up 11 percent; steel production up 2 percent; farmlands, forests, and mines all producing at an insane rate.

Each increase in the Gross National Product was a stab in the heart of every sentient environmentalist. Yet during the recessions of the 1970s and 1980s, when the GNP ceased to grow and depression was rumored, was there consolation over at the Audubon Society? Not likely. The catastrophists and the nature lovers were too burdened by awareness of that immense dilemma that modern life has brought down on us.

Of all the fanatics of the New Age—the feminists, the socialists, the anti-defense demonstrators, the multitudinous liberationists, and so on—the environmentalist was one of the gloomiest and most given to hysteria, for he was shadowed with a sense of hopelessness. Modernity and affluence were two of the large hostile forces arrayed against him, and not even recession or depression was sufficient to assist in preserving the natural environment. Every serious environmentalist understood the need for more specific measures—for instance, laws. But laws, no matter how enlightened and coercive, had only limited influence. Owing to the United Nations' failure to become an effective world government, environmentalist legislation could influence only a small group of nations: the imperialists and neocolonialists, curiously enough, of Europe and North America. International law was without force in the Third World, to say nothing of the Socialist paradise. Pollution and the rape of the earth is a worldwide problem, but a worldwide poultice remains undiscovered. Closing down nuclear power plants in America, or at least making their construction intolerably expensive, is not easy; but influencing the Brazilians or the Iraqis to do the same is almost inconceivable.

How to apply wholesome environmental laws to disparate lands remote from Audubon has thus been environmentalism's most vexing problem. The United Nations has proved to be impotent, and practically every Third World nation has actually been avid for the fruits of what the environmentalists call "overdevelopment": international airports, superhighways, parking lots, malls, Coke in aluminum cans, the works. Many insist on hospitals full of hexachlorophene and other of science's monsters. Only Albania is really on the side of "environmental sanity," and what can little Albania do? In Africa the post-colonial regimes have often been very abusive toward the natural environment. In some countries local armies slaughter wild-game herds more ardently than missionaries. Thus on June 7, 1981, when the Israeli air force turned an Iraqi nuclear facility into a junkyard, you can be sure that many American environmentalists had little light bulbs illuminate their cranial vaults: War! World Conquest for World Health! World War for World Ecology! But is Washington a prudent place from which to further such a good cause? Can the Pentagon be trusted to make the world safe for malaria, beriberi, and sea turtles?

Alas, war is no solution to the environmentalists' impotence in the Third World. Writing in the March 1982 number of *Audubon* magazine, the learned Peter Steinhart explained: "Since nuclear war is likely to aim at the destruction of industrial capacity, and since industrial capacity is built at the expense of nature, a large-scale reconstruction effort would be unthinkable. . . . How long would African game reserves last once war-ravaged northerners stopped arriving as tourists? Who would speak for elephants when human life was in doubt? What would become of the forests of the Amazon if a reconstructing world displayed an insatiable demand for timber? . . . There is hardly any doubt that the aftermath of war would see mankind abandon its commitment to ecological sanity."[3] So police action is out.

The champion of ecological sanity thus lives with anguish, his power to do good forever impeded. Restricted to lands under Western suzerainty, he has only one option: to make the United States and Western Europe ecological exemplars. Yet as he devotes himself to this task deep within the *sanctum sanctorum* of his conscience, he knows that every passing moment knells death for a Ugandan elephant, a Brazilian balsa tree, an Egyptian marshland, or one of those ancient pools of crude oil that innocently lie beneath some Saudi prince's swaddled arse. Moreover, he knows that very few of the world's forward-lookers admire the USA and not many respect Europe either. Thus even if America and Europe are repristinated, will it matter? Will anyone in the progressive Third World or the Socialist bloc care?

The environmentalist is, then, not a happy warrior. Frequently he is driven to desperate measures. For instance, when he and his colleagues visit zoos and, in particular, porpoise aquariums they have to be watched. A capacity for violence is always just beneath the surface. Some are merely cage-openers, but others become more aggressive. By the 1980s, some had actually become terrorists. The April 19, 1983, issue of *The Wall Street Journal* reported in an article on political terrorism that thus far in that year something called the Animal Rights Militia was suspected of having set off thirteen bombs and incendiary devices in the United Kingdom alone.[4] In the summer of 1983 a contingent of whale lovers from Greenpeace even invaded the Soviet Union to disseminate anti-whaling propaganda. Illustrative of these progressives' unique fanaticism is the fact that at about the time they invaded the USSR, reports spread of a wide-scale practice of infanticide in the People's Republic of China. Imagine the furor if those little Chinese had been little whales. The lovers of life at Greenpeace would be on their way to another Socialist showcase, and chop suey would be off their menus forever.

Along with the environmentalists' fanaticism have come prophecies of catastrophe, almost all of which already stand revealed as fictions. "We must all realize," Norman Cousins, chairman of the New York City Air Pollution Task Force, declaimed in 1970, "that the human race is operating under the starkest of deadlines."[5] He was dismayed by a recently proposed three-year environmental study of Long Island. Three years? Cousins was not sure that Long Island had three years! In that same year *Life* magazine prophesied that by 1980 urban dwellers would probably have to wear gas masks, and Edwin Newman notified an NBC audience that by 1980 the nation's rivers "would have reached the boiling point."[6] Three more decades and they might evaporate! The marvel would be brought about by the "thermal pollution" of nuclear power plants.

Gruesome warnings of the above voltage have been sounded countless times during the environmentalists' epoch, only to go poof at deadline time. Some were issued in bald contradiction of well-known facts. In the case of air quality, the US

Council on Environmental Quality has found the air to have been steadily getting cleaner since the 1960s. In the case of water quality, the US Geological Survey has found water getting cleaner since 1961.[7] No astrologer, no psychic in the Great Republic with such a record for defective prophecy could remain free from the hoosegow. Consumerists would be hollering for the wretch's blood. That the environmentalist is the consumerist's next of kin obviously counts for something.

The environmentalists have long been given to holding wakes for those of their furry or slimy friends deemed too stupid to get out of civilization's way. Their solicitude for the snail darter held up the Tellico Dam for years, an act of Congress being required to renew construction.* The list of endangered species begins with forms of life that are little more than noxious bacteria and runs the gamut to truly ferocious beasts like the wolf and dreadful pests like the whale.

In the case of the whale, environmentalists would have us believe that it is a vanishing species, harmless and endearing. The evidence suggests an alternative conclusion. These ancient prototypes of mammalia are, in truth, so plentiful that they often spill out onto beaches or into tide pools. There they become intolerable health hazards and a burden to local treasuries. When an oil tanker bringing energy supplies to millions of Americans accidentally breaks up, the environmentalists howl for reparations and an end to such infamies; but when a herd of berserk whales slams into a shoreline they weep and curse fate.

Why not take action to limit the population of these aquatic oafs? We are doing it with humans. Whales are no friends of the environment. The average blue whale weighs 150 tons and devours 4 tons of helpless krill per day during its gluttonous 120-day feeding period. This slob's relative the killer whale slaughters baby seals and penguins in the very presence of their mothers. What is more, the blue whale excretes as much solid, untreated waste into the ocean per day during feeding season as all the inhabitants of Martha's Vine-

* In the 1980s snail darters turned up elsewhere, and in such profusion, that they could be taken off the endangered-species list altogether.[8]

yard combined on a Monday morning at high season. Nonetheless, so far as I have been able to detect, there has been very little constructive talk about controlling them, not even at the United Nations, where such debate would be a very salutary respite from the usual rattle about prospective ways and means for the Third World to fleece the developed nations further and otherwise mop up what remnant pockets of civilization might exist beyond the borders of Europe, North America, and Japan.

In point of fact, environmentalists have organized a worldwide pro-whale party whose members serve no higher purpose than to abuse the hardworking Japanese whaler and his Soviet rival. Think of it! The Soviets have wiped out many times more Afghans than whales in the New Age, often using ghastly chemical and biological weapons, which kill far more painfully than do harpoons. Still the environmentalists organize no protests against this form of Soviet barbarity. Their humanitarian juices flow only when subhumans are imperiled.

Along with all their inaccurate prophecies and their funerals for endangered pests have come quack remedies, hundreds of them, perhaps thousands, all sublimely asinine and some pernicious; for they have actually been smuggled into the legal code, where they make the life of the freeborn Americano unnecessarily expensive and occasionally hazardous. As the quack remedies have multiplied they have grown increasingly weird—so much so, in fact, that the intelligent observer is left with the inescapable question of whether the remedy in question is the work of a jokester or of someone clinically insane. The only other possible alternative is that one is facing the work of an idiot.

Consider two environmentalist responses to a pair of life's most fundamental imperatives, the need to procreate and the need to evacuate. Take the first. A major worry for most environmentalists is that if the Republic's unregulated fornicators do not stifle themselves the nation will someday be left with standing room only. For most, simple birth control is not enough. Such is the extent of their claustrophobia that they have actually suggested *gendarmerie* for the bedroom. I first encountered the plan as it was unveiled on the op-ed page of the December 15, 1970, *New York Times* by none other than Dr. Edgar Berman. "The ultimate necessity of legislation and guidelines for a strong population policy must be faced," he wrote, for "Elected officials can no longer evade debating the ideologic [*sic*] issue of whether the individual right to pro-create, to the detriment of society, is a basic human right and a fundamental freedom and whether it can be legally halted without damaging the fabric of freedom. The limitation of family size by law seems less an infringement than a boon to individual civil liberty."[9]

Well, was Dr. Berman serious? Some of us know him to be an accomplished farceur, a man devoted to sending up the women of the fevered brow at every opportunity. For my part I would have thought that he was on a lark, making some lib-ertarian point through Swiftian extravagance. Yet Paul Ehr-lich had made a similar case two years earlier, demanding population control "by compulsion if voluntary methods fail";[10] and such is Ehrlich's claustrophobia that he would never laugh about such matters. Moreover, Dr. Berman's piece was on the *Times*'s op-ed page. No one cracks jokes on that dolorous page except, possibly, Georgi Arbatov.

Or consider a Miss Mary Louise Weber's remedy for the toilet. All conscientious environmentalists believe that one of the most hostile threats to America's water supply is the flush toilet. The Hon. Jerry Brown, while governor of California, actually ordered a state-sponsored inquiry into the toilet's en-vironmental costs, and ever since then hundreds of thousands, perhaps millions, of sensitive environmentalists think twice before moving their bowels. They flush as rarely as possible. In point of fact many do not flush at all; and having them as house guests can be complicated, especially if one's daughter is home from finishing school.

At any rate, this apprehension over the flush toilet occa-sioned a long essay from Miss Mary Louise Weber which memorably illuminates the environmental movement's grow-ing repute for quackery. In the April 14, 1979, issue of *The New Republic* Miss Weber divulged her plan for reworking the indoor plumbing of every domicile in America. The plan is characteristic of the remedies that environmentalists admire most—that is to say, plans that dwell almost sensuously on grim trends, hysterically reproach the bourgeoisie, and ultimately prescribe a maximum amount of social upheaval and government coercion.

According to Miss Weber: "The main feature of a more sensible design would be that one toilet per house would be connected to the main sewer line. This toilet would be used for bodily disposal other than urination. The other toilet's pipes would be redirected to a large underground tank in the back yard. These toilets could be used only for urination. The accumulated mixture of water and urine (approximately 90 percent and 10 percent respectively) would be filtered through a layer of organic substance and then piped back through the house into the showers." The extravagance of the present system would end and American hygiene would improve. "Water-urine showers are healthier and less frequently necessary than normal bathing." Urine is a natural moisturizer, thus eliminating the need for "costly lotions."

In time, Miss Weber predicts, the citizenry will become accustomed to the somewhat acrid fragrance of urine, and perhaps even acquire "a liking for the scent. This could eventually open up an entire market for urine-based soaps and colognes." Diet too would improve. "Various kinds of food and drink can produce substantial differences in an individual's urine. Healthy, wholesome foods and a large quantity of water work most effectively to produce beneficial acids in the urine." Families will "return to well-balanced diets."[11]

Once again we are left with the perfectly understandable question, what was the writer's intent? Was she in earnest or just having a few laughs at the expense of the credulous? It now turns out that the editors of *The New Republic* were cutting up. There was no Mary Louise Weber. Her cerebrations come under the classification of comedy. Yet no one laughed aside from those of us who always laugh when the environmentalists are at work. So accustomed had the citizenry become to this sort of quackery from the environmentalists that all considered it yet another high-minded communiqué from the Friends of the Earth and the Enemies of the Toilet.

The oratory and images of these enthusiasts were, however, something new for America. There was something so very dramatic and infantile about each of their anxieties. This was not just a reform movement as of old, led by pamphleteers, sages, demonstrators, and the occasional bomb thrower. In style, substance, and expanse of concern these were radicals indigenous to the New Age, and so I shall digress briefly to dilate on a modern development that explains, at least in part, the New Age enthusiasts' break with public nuisances of the past.

By the late 1970s the enthusiasts of the New Age, and for that matter millions of normal Americans too, had had their perceptions of reality almost wholly shaped by the photograph, the motion picture, and television. They conceived reality in terms of fantasy presented to them in pictures and films. No other generation has had so much of the world conveyed to them in living color, dramatically filmed through a multitude of distorting lenses and artificial lightings. Always volupt music accompanies the sham. These people are unaccustomed to seeing the world as it is. Reality is a letdown. They turn to TV for authentication much as a dripping-wet Cro-Magnon man once turned to his corner wizard for an authoritative statement on the morning's thunderstorm.

As Malcolm Muggeridge is fond of observing, the camera in the hands of a dramatist has become the age's great falsifier of reality. Many Americans who might once have been readers and careful thinkers have become spectators, accustomed to seeing dramas with beginnings, climaxes, and endings. The environmentalist is one of the most egregious examples of these addicts to vicarious experience. Through all their tirades few have ever shown much understanding of the reality of nature: its complexity or resilience. The modern environmentalist has not even shown much awareness of nature's beauty. If there is an environmentalist artist who has ever manifested an affection for nature's charms comparable in discernment and beauty to that shown by Wordsworth or Blake,

Schubert or Mahler, I am unaware of him. Send me his art. An environmentalist's song to the earth? Bah! I cannot even recall a bad poem. Instead there are ill-conceived political positions and graphic renderings of nature for vicarious consumption. Ehrlich has been environmentalism's Walt Disney, all his bogus pronouncements and tendentious facts being conveyed in images congenial to the modern picture-oriented mind.[12]

It is Prof Ehrlich who dramatized nature's supposed fragility by depicting the planet Earth as a "spaceship" dependent on ecological systems, or "ecosystems." If any of an ecosystem's components degenerate—even, Prof Ehrlich warns, "tiny bacteria, protozoa, and fungi"—"the danger of large scale malfunctions of the life-support systems of the planet is increased." Today the danger is just at the water's edge; "Suspicious signs of such malfunctioning are already apparent in our lakes, rivers, and even in the oceans."[13] Soon, he tells us, they will creep ashore.

Prof Ehrlich is the author of many volumes, such as *How to Know the Butterflies,* and as his thought has deepened, tinges of purple and black have slipped into his judgments. Optimism fades with every tome. In *How to Be a Survivor* he notes that such infamies as paved roads and one-crop fields have perilously "reduced the complexity of the ecosystem." Precisely when the spaceship *Earth* will be brought to foozle he will not say, but with the *kapitalists* bashing hell out of those benign bacteria, protozoa, and fungi, "we can guarantee that . . . sooner or later it will break down. Preliminary signs make 'sooner' seem more likely than 'later.' " Prof Ehrlich writes for the New Age, and across his readers' wide-screen minds there appears the brave little spaceship *Earth* sputtering, then smoking; then it slips from view!

Who would have imagined it? Eliminate a bit of fungi here, blot out a little bacteria there, and suddenly the ecosystem begins to blow fuses. Things are out of control! The infernal process could be in motion right now. Some nitwit farmer scratching out a new cornfield somewhere in Iowa goes too far, and the fuses of the ecosystem start to blow. Do you think the environmentalist does not worry? Prof Ehrlich's drama can apply to the environmentalist's own program of personal hygiene, which you can be sure is very rigorously maintained. Consider an otherwise simple matter, to wit: nasal cleanliness. Any environmentalist aware of Prof Ehrlich's thesis on the fragility of the ecosystem must know that in cleaning his nose he hazards irreversible destruction to his personal ecosystem, for there is always the chance that one might destroy valuable substances; for instance, those substances that had theretofore regulated the moisture and velocity of oxygen passing through one's nasal hair en route to the pharynx. The consequence is catastrophe: the ecosystem suddenly goes haywire. Huge gusts of air rush into the lungs. Alveolar cavities rupture! Massive tension pneumothorax ensues!! Presently the environmentalist is an angel!!!

Mark it down as but another sign of Christendom's decrepitude that despite the manifest suffering of so many of America's environmentalists no member of the holy clergy has taken it upon himself to establish a special apostolate for these wretches. There are priests who minister to alcoholics and to dope addicts. There are others whose ministry is to the poor and to the low-down. These are the easy cases; they have been Christianity's prey for centuries. But let us have a Saint Francis for the casualties of the New Age, among whose throng the most sorely pressed must be the lonely, hollering environmentalists plodding their anguished paths without benefit of clergy and without hope. Even the shrinks have not stepped forward to assist, and that is very surprising, for many an environmentalist is very well heeled.

Even government has failed to soothe these worrywarts. In fact, government has exacerbated their fears—as might have been expected. Keeping the environmentalists' bugaboos healthy and growing makes good sense from the point of view of the government bureaucrat, for environmentalists turn to government at every opportunity for relief from civilization's polluting hand. Most of the nostrums issuing from the environmentalists call for more government bureaucracy, more government regulation, and increased governmental power. This is true notwithstanding the revelations of scholars like John Baden and Richard L. Stroup, who have demonstrated that government bureaucracy is a most slovenly custodian of the natural environment. They argue convincingly that the privatization of resources under intelligent legal supervision is the most prudent method of preserving the flora and fauna.[14] With enemy forces like this arrayed against the bureaucrats it is understandable that the bureaucrats labor to keep the environmentalists enflamed. Moreover, there is a growing body of data suggesting that the fears of the catastrophists and the nature lovers are passé.

By all odds the most stupendous effort to keep the environmentalists' hairs on end was the *Global 2000 Study*. Unveiled during the Carter administration, it certified the environmentalists' most defective prophecies. Directed by the Council on Environmental Quality and by the State Department, the study dragged in eleven other federal agencies including the CIA, and came to the judgment that "if present trends continue, the world in 2000 will be more crowded, more polluted, less stable ecologically, and more vulnerable to disruption than the world we live in now. Serious stresses involving population, resources, and environment are clearly visible ahead. Despite greater material output, the world's people will be poorer in many ways than they are today."[15]

The "Global Two Thousand" yell could not have come at a more exigent hour in the life of environmentalism. The water and air were steadily becoming cleaner. Babies were no longer arriving at the hospital with such alarming frequency. Moreover, people were beginning to notice that after ten years of doomsaying the environment was still out there pollinating. Contrary to the prophets, the rivers never did heat up in 1980. Gas masks were not even being worn by the citizens of Gary, Indiana. A growing body of statistical data indicated that resources were becoming more available. For instance from 1950 to 1970 of our known reserves of tungsten, tin, manganese, zinc, lead, copper, bauxite, oil, chromite, iron, potash, and phosphates, all increased between 10 and 4,430 percent— except tungsten, which declined. By the time the Carter administration's Study came out even the Club of Rome had recanted the gloomy forecasts it had handed down in its worldwide-best-selling jeremiad *The Limits to Growth*. The movement's hysteria needed a boost and the *Global 2000*

Study provided it. Today it epitomizes the movement's bogus arcanum.

In reviewing the Study, Julian L. Simon, professor of economics and business administration at the University of Illinois, has judged its conclusions "baseless," though he adds that "I am not saying that all is well now, and I do not promise that all will be rosy in the future. . . . What I am saying is that, for most or all of the relevant matters I have checked, the trends are positive rather than negative."[16]

Simon's writings have been a bracing antidote to the environmentalists' fears. The explanation for the catastrophists' hellish visions is that they fail to take into account what Simon tells us is "a reasonable rule of prediction in economics (if not everywhere) that experience is to be preferred to pure logic as a policy guide" assuming "plenty of experience is available and there is no obvious discontinuity." The catastrophists working on the *Global 2000 Study* and in all their cells throughout the Republic rely on "technological modes of analysis even when contradictory historical evidence is available."[17] Human beings, at least throughout the long history of the West, have used their intelligence to adapt to changing circumstances and to turn to different resources or to technological advances when a resource becomes too dear. The process is called progress, and it explains why most of us no longer live in caves.

The catastrophists' second error is to ignore the law of supply and demand. They apparently are incapable of understanding that when prices rise consumers begin to seek alternatives even as suppliers seek to serve their customers either with more of the resource in question or with alternatives. One scholar who has written thoughtfully on the environment for years, Petr Beckmann, points out that to say that something is nonrenewable is not to say that it cannot be replaced. One communications satellite can take the place of thousands of miles of communications lines and so serve as a superior substitute to the copper that would be used in those less desirable communications systems.[18] Thus, overlooking "replacement" is the catastrophists' third great error. Moreover, there may just be one resource that is infinite: human intelligence—though the environmentalists have shown that it is certainly not distributed evenly.

Environmentalists have continually been wrong about world trends. In his authoritative book *The Ultimate Resource* Simon puts the kabosh to prophecies of worldwide famine, demonstrating that the world is becoming better fed and that world food production regularly outpaces population increases. Some of the environmentalists' imbecilities have passed beyond the limits of the plainly stupid and into the realm of the deceitful—for instance: when the *Global 2000 Study* blunders into saying that "The life expectancy of a population is the most all-inclusive and widely measured indication of a nation's environmental health. . . . The rate of increase of life expectancy has slowed."[19] Unfortunately for the Republic's morticians, these judgments are untrue. In the United States life expectancy is increasing at an increasing rate, a gain of 2.6 years from 1970 to 1976, compared with a gain of only 0.8 during the entire 1960s. What data the Study can marshal actually contradicts its conclusion! When the Study predicts "serious stresses involving . . . resources" it does so in bold contradiction of history's trends, trends the Study claims to have studied. As Simon demonstrates in *The Ultimate Resource*, "the costs of natural resources in human labor and their prices relative to wages and to other goods—all suggest that natural resources have been becoming *less* scarce over the long run, right up to the present."[20] This relative drop in the price of raw materials probably understates the positive trend, for humans have learned to use less of some raw material for certain purposes and to use cheaper substitutes for the same service. Humans have, in other words, adapted to changing conditions. Contrary to the assumptions of the catastrophists, humans do not wait for resources like oil to run dry. They note the increased scarcity and develop alternatives.

In the environmentalists one sees the same massive collapse of intelligence that is observable in so many of the other New Age enthusiasts. Bawling maudlinly about the rights of bacteria, weeds, fish, and mammalia, they attempted to raise onto the agenda of politics what amounted to childish infatuations. Where they were successful they trivialized political discourse while costing the citizenry a bundle in higher utility costs, slowed economic expansion, and lost jobs. As Roger Starr has observed in *The American Spectator*: "Much more than enthusiasm is needed to resist degradation of the natural world . . . Conservation requires professionally trained specialists capable of distinguishing between important and trivial dangers. It requires the patience to make difficult distinctions carefully and the wisdom to establish goals that harmonize the values of the environment with those of the economy. While professionals can make these judgments, the money and zeal that drive their organizations come from members who perceive wildlife as benign, noncompetitive, and undemanding. The childlike sentiment makes it difficult for them to agree to accept the loss of any part of it in order to achieve a saving which they cannot see."[21] Starr then proceeds to discuss examples of zealous environmentalists' holding up utility and industrial development at enormous cost all because of the environmentalists' apparent belief "that any other creature is man's moral superior."

The poor of course are always the ones least able to absorb the increased costs. They do not have the large layer of discretionary income to pay out for higher bills. They are the ones in need of the growing job market. Unfortunately they are not snail darters or Tecopa pupfish and so as the forces of Audubon sweep forward with their balmy crusade, the poor are left behind. Putting them on welfare is the solution of the Friends of the Earth. Here is another of the environmentalists' quack remedies. William Tucker, in his splendid study *Progress and Privilege: America in an Age of Environmentalism*, has equated the environmental movement with privilege; the privileged want clean air and furry friends. Cost is no problem, nor is the pull of experience or reality.

4

The Anti-Nuke Enthusiasm

Masked Politics, False Prophets, The New Age Politico

FOR the New Age Liberal, reality came to be that which tinkled and crashed and declaimed in his head—not what was humming or sprouting around his feet, not life. The hypothetical, the academic, the messages on the bumper stickers, all these took precedence over what is. When, in the late 1940s, nuclear energy was but a castle in the air the Liberals were for it. Three decades later, when the thing was actually heating homes and driving industrial plants, through Arab oil boycotts, coal strikes, and some of the most arctic winters since the last Ice Age, they conferred the taboo upon it. Fear of the unknown is an ancient human weakness; fear of the known and useful is comparatively modern. Yet this is just the bizarre kind of fear that the New Age enthusiast developed for nuclear energy, and one is left wondering why. How did an energy source that had moved from the drawing boards to the operational stage during three palmy decades suddenly become a terror despite having a record as clean as that of aspirin and being a lot more powerful?

Whether or not to adopt nuclear energy is, one would have thought, a technical question best left to scientists. The citizen asks, is nuclear energy safe and useful? The scientists supply the answer. A decision is made *démocratiquement*, and we pass on. Ah, but things do not move so smoothly in contemporary America. There are too many anxious people at large, and they know where to take their anxieties. They present them to the media, to the judiciary, to government bureaucracies, and to eminent politicos; hesto presto, what was once a question of practicality is now fraught with political considerations and vexed beyond reason or resolution.

Consider this 1979 report: "Rock stars organize antinuclear benefits; poets churn out antinuke poems; demonstrators plot antinuke demos; foundations fund antinuclear activists; housewives neglect their hubbies in favor of antinuke Washington lobbying; Quakers soothe interantinuclear factions; the bishop of Detroit celebrates a two-hour antinuke mass on the Catholic Church's Day of Peace; and from Oregon, Austria, Australia, France, Westchester County, and Turner's Falls, Massachusetts, 'leftover hippies' invade my office and clog my phonelines with news flashes and rumors and analyses of the E situation that would put the well-placed energy expert to shame."[1]

This bustling scene! This saturnalia of concerned citizens! This chaotic office! What was it all about? Well, this is America in February 1979 as seen through the eyes of Miss Anna Mayo, *The Village Voice*'s resident nuclear scold. Is her account accurate? I suffered no clogged telephones that month. Nor did I hear any news flashes from Turner's Falls, Massachusetts, or even Westchester County. Miss Mayo's fidelity, however, is not the point, is it? Her dithyramb is of value for what it tells us about those who in the mid-1970s suddenly snapped to as if from a deep sleep and lurched into battle against the atomic-energy industry. To come to the point, they were excitable.

After the Vietnam War and the exhilaration of Watergate, life in America had quieted down. Months would go by and all that was to be heard was the thunk-thunking of Jerry Ford's pate hitting some equally hard object during a maladroit exit from a presidential limousine or aircraft. Then were heard weird potherings from the populist messiah and his Moon Pie Mafia. For the most part, however, there was the gentle sough of normality. In the course of time, however, word was received that nuclear power plants were bringing death to the gentle clams (of New Hampshire), to the harmless abalones (of California), to the laid-back catfish (of Alabama)—every day the list acquired a new victim. The problem was a deadly effluent: *warm water!* Pickets were mustered. Demonstrations were auspicated. Letters-to-the-editor were received, and from academe came the learned disquisitions: "Split Wood Not Atoms"; "No Nukes Is Good Nukes"; "Better Active Today than Radioactive Tomorrow."

What was going on? An important chapter in the New Age was being written. The narcissists, the hypochondriacs, the nature lovers, the catastrophists, and the members of the hard left were coalescing. Other New Age enthusiasts were getting the message. All were becoming aroused by what the venerable *Nation* felicitously dubbed "the Nuclear Colossus"—a huge but covert transcontinental conglomerate of bankers, utility magnates, nuclear physicists, engineers, and sworn enemies of the natural environment, all intent on advancing nuclear power where, but for human greed, windmills would be perfectly adequate.

Overnight, Miss Mayo's readers and thousands of other hypochondriacs rose to their feet in reproach; and the Colossus was duly flattened. Artfully massaging the bureaucracy and the courts, they brought an entire industry to a standstill. How did they do it? What foul *corpus delicti* had they come across three decades into the nuclear age, and why did the French not get wind of it? France was building nuclear power plants as fast as De Gaulle had once built nuclear weapons. By the 1980s 33 percent of its electricity came from nuclear power plants, and the French hoped that by the next decade that figure would rise to 54 percent.[2] The Japanese were also avid for nuclear power, as were the Swiss and the Swedes. Had these great nations been subverted by their own Nuclear Colossi, or was it just that they were without a Miss Mayo? The American anti-nuke campaign was one of the historic successes of the New Age; and if on some dark and chill morrow, when the Republic is abundant with abalones and clams but when Arab oil is unavailable and the windmills are becalmed, you might want to remember France, Japan, Switzerland, and Sweden as possible outlets for your electric yogurt maker.

At the outset I too had been fetched by the anti-nuclear complaint. Surely I thought, nuclear energy is dangerous stuff, and in preparing to analyze the issue I was stirred by the thought that for once I might find myself on the fashionable side of the barricades. I made the error, however, of reading beyond the bumper stickers and the news reports of Three Mile Island, and thus made the unhappy discovery that the anti-nuke enthusiasm, like so many of the New Age enthusiasms, was bunk. Compared with practically every other energy source, nuclear energy is safer albeit more awesome—even as, compared with its competitors, jet travel is safer albeit more awesome. The anti-nuke jeremiads were quite fanciful. The scientific learning was sham. Nonetheless the campaign was a huge success. While exploiting well-tried themes of science fiction, the anti-nuke movement adroitly summoned all the techniques of the New Age polemicists: the prophecies of catastrophe, the quack remedies, the disguised radicalism, the songs, and the poetry. Soon what had begun as a proper concern for health and the environment took off into realms of science fiction, thence into the screeds of battle-axes like Miss Mayo and the poetry of Allen Ginsberg.

Ginsberg's anti-nuke poetry is worth noting, for its grandiosity and stupidity characterized many of the cranks in the movement. Here you have a literary prankster whose body has been a test tube for every imaginable narcotic, yet he mounts the stage and advises the morally upright on matters of health and safety. Phew! When he read his maudlin hooey to anyone with any knowledge of nuclear fission his pants fell to the floor. Take his "Plutonium Ode." It had been a source of great sadness, he notified Miss Mayo. Not only did the lugubrious message make him blue, but, well, he feared that the poem was so technical that it would be read only by "a few scholars."[3] Spare me—his stupidities began with his title, which he arrived at under the impression that plutonium was named for "Pluto, the god of Hell." Actually, it got its name because just as Pluto is the planet beyond Neptune, plutonium is the element beyond neptunium. Moreover, to call Pluto the god of Hell is to reveal as much ignorance of the Greco-Roman conception of Hades as the poet has already revealed about the origin of the word plutonium.[4] This maudlin doltishness pervaded the anti-nuke movement.

The best vantage point for watching the anti-nukers in all their dunce caps was while sitting in Miss Mayo's audience. She reported every nuclear horror, and she believed with the intensity of an Iranian galoot in holy Qum. I became her attentive follower, reading every tirade with that singular relish one reserves for the public utterances of George Mc-Govern or for the personals in the back of *The New York Review of Books*.

Miss Mayo brought an almost primeval violence to her reportage. She bashed logic. She trampled grammar. She hammered the facts. She was always very amusing. My suspicion is that even the Rockefellers, even the rascals planning our demise from the boardroom of Consolidated Edison, even the most fervent, blood-and-gore partisans of immediate, universal, twenty-four-hour-around-the-clock nuclear holocaust could have read her with amusement. The show was that stupendous. Yet it is my melancholy conviction that the majority of her customers were not amused. Like her they lived in fear of the Nuclear Colossus. Every time a new nuclear power plant sprang to life they cringed and awaited the great *ka-boom*. When they did not hear it they turned to Miss Mayo more desperately than ever. What the hell was Con Ed up to this time? They needed facts, man; and as they gathered in health-food shops and drug-rehabilitation centers to ponder and whimper Miss Mayo provided the facts.

Was it, indeed, true that in remote Western towns, near abandoned atomic-test sites, babies were being born with misshapen feet? It was. Had Scholastic Aptitude Test scores, in fact, dropped in the 1970s because of atmospheric tests in the 1950s? They had. Will future generations of Americans no longer have that human form that so many of us have come to know and, at regular intervals, to love? Yes. Well, what shape will they have? Will they take the shape of cabbages? How about eggplants? Anyone familiar with Botticelli's nudes will tell you that an undraped lady shaped like an eggplant is not without charm; in point of fact, had he his preference, the typical Renaissance artist or nobleman would have nothing else. Yet how effective would a crowd of eggplants be at the sit-ins of the future? The cops could just drive up and roll them away, or perhaps leave the whole business to an unscrupulous vegetable vendor.

With the exception of my speculations on the future of the human shape, all the aforementioned matters were discoursed upon in Miss Mayo's column, and had I ever written up my eggplant speculations unquestionably they too would have appeared there. She was open to all possibilities. The link between declining SAT scores and atomic tests had been discovered by Dr. Ernest Sternglass, one of Miss Mayo's favorite men of science; and when *The New York Times* ignored his discoveries Miss Mayo was there conscientiously hollering against this conspiracy of silence.[5] She also apprised us of the impending change in our human form, which perhaps explains why so many of her readers had simply let their wardrobes go to hell. The original research on this one had been undertaken by Dr. Helen Caldicott, author of *Nuclear Madness*. When this inflamed little monograph appeared, Miss Mayo saluted it solemnly, adjudging its publication "a major human event." "If we ever manage to recover from our collective nuclear psychosis," Miss Mayo concluded, "it will be in large part due to the effort of these 'physician-activists.' "[6] In time, Dr. Caldicott and her fellow "physician-activists" broadened their nuclear concerns. She presided over another of the era's pretentiously named groups, "Physicians for Social Responsibility," and emerged as a leading activist in the anti-defense movement. By then she was being extolled not only by Miss Mayo but also by *Pravda*, which on December 1, 1980, quoted her as having told the Soviet citizenry that "The USA has now accumulated an awesome quantity of nuclear bombs, but the Pentagon continues their production . . . Our politicians have long ago turned into obedient puppets of the military-industrial complex. . . . The noisy jabber about the 'Soviet threat' begins every time the Pentagon adopts a new system of mass annihilation into its arsenal."[7] In the anti-nuke movement, as in so many other New Age enthusiasms, people were always growing, experiencing, "going through

changes," as the phrase had it. Always the change was toward
the left and at a goose-step pace.

The Village Voice became a showcase for the New Age. Its
columns, its departments, and even its advertisements minis-
tered to every new enthusiasm and offered helpful informa-
tion not only for combating the Nuclear Colossus but also for
surviving other modern ordeals. How well I recall the issue in
which Miss Mayo informed us of Dr. Caldicott's breakthrough.
That column was surrounded by sixteen ads for unisex hair-
cuts: "February Special: For Men & Women, Perm, Cut, Blow
Dry $25." Bordering it, there were also three ads for diet con-
trol, one ad for acne control, and one for a $35 YMCA course
on mastering lower-back pain. There were two ads for classes
in hypnosis: "The Health class teaches self-hypnosis for smoking, headaches, insomnia, creativity blocs, stage fright . . ."
And there were four ads proclaiming the most scientific advances in personal beautification: "Men—Electrolysis & Skin
Rejuvenization for Every Type of Color & Skin—Hair Removed Permanently, Acne & Discoloration Controls, Skin
Exfoliation [A New Skin Process], Ingrown Hair Eliminated,
Body & Leg Waxing, By Appointment Only."[8] These were the
idiots who were to have the last word on US energy policy!

Nuclear energy had not always been such a vexed question.
After the Second World War people viewed the atom expan-
sively. It was a miracle of science, a source of endless and
inexpensive power. Admittedly there were dissenters—namely,
those pacifists in the "Ban the Bomb" movement; but they
remained without influence, and their policy suggestions were
plainly implausible given the inescapable fact that once the
Soviets had heard of the atomic bomb's wondrous uses they
were ravenous to develop one of these beauties and to make it
even better. Furthermore, the bomb was not the whole of the
atomic age. There were also "the peaceful uses of the atom,"
uses that pleased even the Ban-the-Bombers.

Yet in the 1970s, just as stillness gentled the land the atomic
age suffered a mysterious apodiabolosis. Hypochondria and
visions of doom were spreading throughout the Republic.
Calumniations were being filed against the staples of Ameri-

can life: eggs, milk, sirloin tip, Wonder Bread, Twinkies, fast food, the whole smash. Finally, atomic energy appeared on the list; but it had now been renamed. Suddenly it was rude "nuclear," as manliness had become rude "macho."

Critics of nuclear energy had formed a movement; and, as Americans were learning, against a movement the democratic process is practically helpless. So too, apparently, is intelligent discourse. Policy discussions became bitter shouting matches. Policy alternatives, nuance, and compromise were heaved overboard. This was the unlovely course that the nuclear-power debate followed. Fanatics and simpletons gained the upper hand, and against them intelligent thought is always futile. The members of the movement moved into the streets, took to the courts, congealed the bureaucracy.

All the extremism and disingenuousness of New Age politics were to be seen in this historic struggle. The opponents of nuclear energy did not seek merely to regulate nuclear energy: they sought to abolish it and nuclear science as well. Think of it: here were the very same Americans who at the beginning of the 1970s had been yelping about American arrogance. Now brief years later they were notifying the world's nuclear scientists to shut down an entire branch of scientific inquiry and to prove instead the energy potential of windmills, waves, cow manure, and other still more dubious power sources. Along with the extremism came the sham: it was not simply wholesome energy that interested the movement. Thorough scrutiny of the anti-nuke movement reveals diatribes against bankers, corporations, utility companies, private enterprise, the Pentagon, the State Department, plus almost anyone not made hysterical by an electric toothbrush. In time, the anti-nuke movement implicated millions of Americans—"our collective nuclear psychosis," as Miss Mayo put it.

The anti-nuclear movement was, then, another profoundly radical assault on bourgeois America, though the movement's strategists were coy about admitting it. Instead they resorted to an expedient increasingly popular with New Age liberals— to wit: masked politics. As their causes became ever more extreme with consequences ever more repugnant to ordinary Americans, New Age Liberals began concealing their true identities and purposes behind the masks and fancy costumes of idealistic endeavor. Feminism, civil rights, environmentalism, all were the costumes of the masked politicians of the New Age; and when the political scientists of the future discourse upon this unedifying innovation I hope they will point out that it is even more devious than the perfidies of traditional politics. Most pols will at least admit to being pols. The masked pols would not even admit to this. Rather they insisted that they were simple humanitarians, environmentalists, civil rights activists, and worse. Pishposh; one need but glance at their voluminous pronunciamentos to comprehend their power-hungry extremism.

In the manner of the age the New Age Liberals' harangues would fuse different fanaticisms, presumably to lure the largest number of half-wits, though in some cases the scrambled harangues were simply the consequence of the New Age Liberals' famous loquacity. They were veritable magpies. Typically when the anti-nuke haranguer piped up he was soon all over the lot. For instance, at a 1978 powwow for the Clamshell Alliance, Laurie Holmes, whose memory time has obscured, declaimed that "The struggle against the rape of the earth by rich, white males is the same struggle as the struggle against the rape of our bodies and the rape of our lives."[9] And Jim Haughton from something called Harlem Fightback found a causal relationship between nuclear energy and racism, nuclear energy being "the logical extension in the area of technology of American racism," for "By supporting and maintaining the oppression of blacks and other third world people, people become dehumanized by virtue of their own racism and can't perceive their own interest."[10] Haughton feared that in time these dehumanized racist zombies would become easy pickings for the nuclear tycoons. Thus the anti-nuke dithyrambs would go. Within the anti-nuke bouillabaisse one could find testimonials to decentralization, participatory democracy, alternative sources of energy, homosexuality, organic foods, abortion, malls, fruit-juice enemas, the ERA, and a multitude of other good things that one might not have expected from a movement ostensibly concerned with that which heats a nation's homes and turns its turbines.

Through all the wild vaporings, however, one stupendous desideratum loomed: the legend and science of socialism. As Michael Harrington, national chairman of the Democratic Socialist Organizing Committee, put it with unusual forthrightness, "the resolution of the current nuclear crisis requires a defeat of the corporate power that has dominated energy policy from the very beginning."[11] Yes, behind all the poetry about our happy valley and the spaceship *Earth* was The Cause, Socialism! "Stopping these reactors means battling the most powerful corporations in the world," one Harvey Wasserman sang. "It means revolutionizing our industrial economy. It means transforming our autocratic energy system into a community-owned, democratically operated system."[12] Thus the anti-nuke movement set out, as the eloquent Mark Hertsgaard proclaimed, to "sway broader segments of the middle class away from the mistaken belief that their salvation lies with private enterprise. For so long as the economic system remains in place, critical social decisions will ultimately be settled in a way that preserves the system . . . such a solution in the case of nuclear power could be catastrophic for us all."[13]

Surely if socialism were the science it is passed off as it would have been tried first on animals; but it never was, probably because the New Age's enthusiasts had too much affection for animals. Mankind, on the other hand, always dismayed them, inspiring many curious outbursts. "It would be little short of disastrous for us to discover a source of clean, cheap, abundant energy because of what we might do with it," wrote Amory Lovins.[14] What might that be? Dr. Paul Ehrlich provided the grim answer: "Giving society cheap, abundant energy would be the equivalent of giving an idiot child a machine gun."[15] Anyone who has read Dr. Ehrlich's *The Population Bomb* knows that this is not a happy scenario. In his world-view children—even unarmed, moderately intelligent children—are a portent of catastrophe. By the way, *The Population Bomb* inspired the faithful back in 1970 to wear buttons prophesying "FAMINE '75." It was but one more of the era's prophecies of catastrophe that never made good.

More than any other New Age enthusiasm, with the possible exception of the peace movement, so-called, the anti-nuke movement was under the control of the old placard-waving, boycott-launching, fist-in-the-air hard left—very grim characters indeed. They adored tidiness. They loathed the easygoing materialism of the free society. These were the American champions of proletarian materialism: new clodhoppers for all! heaps of potatoes at *reasonable* prices! For decades these armor-plated faces had shown up at rallies and lectures booming some of the most gruesome tyrannies on earth. Of late they had been lying low, their last good cause, "Victory for North Vietnam!", having turned out rather appallingly. Now, as word arrived about the unhappy abalones, the clams, the catfish, and dozens of distressed mammalia, their old juices began to flow once again.

What is more, they were surrounded by fresh yokels: gay liberationists, vegetarians, wearers of Earth shoes, and thousands of flora and fauna worshipers from the Sierra Club and allied mafias. Yet the left-wingers maintained firm control of the proceedings. On one notable occasion they actually banned a group of anti-nukers from a demonstration because the group also opposed abortion. Protest had become a popular American lifestyle, and growing numbers of moral hams were lining up to join noble causes. Serious activists were under increasing pressure to keep their movements sober; and whatever else one might say about the hard leftists in the anti-nuke movement, they were deadly serious.

From the early 1960s to the late 1970s America had changed. What James Madison had called the genius of the people had been under pervasive assault. The old prejudices—some benign, some not so benign—had been hammered out of the average Yank: color photographs of male and female genitalia, and forget not anuses, were displayed and merchanted at the corner drugstore. Any belief that viciousness might be encouraged by the trafficking in such stuff was scoffed at, as were manners, standards of dress, and customs of deference; so too were the work ethic, military preparedness, religion, the family, heterosexuality. For that matter all the core values of Western civilization were being battered. Cranks were on the march and the Credo of Wholesome Progress revealed the success they had achieved. Not one of the Founding Fathers would have read it without guffawing. In all the pothering the once auspicious nuclear age was easily transformed into the Nuclear Colossus.

Twenty years earlier right-wing cranks had attempted to diabolize fluoride in almost the same way that the anti-nuke movement was to diabolize atomic energy. As municipalities began injecting the stuff into their water supplies to prevent tooth decay, the right-wingers stepped forward with vast quantities of worrisome statistics. According to them, fluoride rotted the brain, leaving its victims with perfectly hollowed-out gourds. Sure, their teeth would be spotless, but so would their cranial vaults! It was a giant collectivist scheme to enslave the freeborn Yank. Unfortunately for the right-wingers, Americans in the 1950s and early 1960s were not yet obsessed with weird diseases. The media did not defer to the crackpot right then as they were to defer to the crackpot left in the 1970s. American culture was still free of bugs and the ideological jinni. Hence when the anti-fluoride activists began rumbling about the machinations of the authorities, the bankers, the men of science, there were no solemn editorials in the *Times* and no frightening presentations on the *Today* show. Twenty years later things had changed; the hard left prevailed, playing on almost the same fears. Only the fluoride was missing.

Great advances had been made in the propaganda arts for which the left could be very grateful. It would take the most gifted propagandists to fumigate the amazing *volte-face* that was being made, for the left had once been one of atomic energy's most ardent supporters. Now, with the word out about the atomic age's complicity in bourgeois mischief, the left changed sides, and with a rapidity not seen since the Hitler-Stalin Pact.

So the historic reversal took a huge amount of effort. Songs had to be rewritten, slogans recast, and dozens of futuristic pronouncements banished from memory. Back in the 1950s Pete Seeger, the left-wing folksinger, had devoted his art to the marvel of the atom. "When nations build the Aswan dam so deserts turn to green," he would sing, "And atom power builds a world the likes we've never seen . . . Then we'll have peace."[16] His friends in the American Communist Party went even further. They adorned their famous hammer and sickle with a tiny atom.

The youthful members of the New Left had been especially rapturous over the atomic age. In the Port Huron Statement of the Students for a Democratic Society one finds such happy thoughts as "With nuclear energy whole cities can easily be powered, yet the dominant nation-states seem more likely to unleash destruction."[17] Insert "solar" in that line where "nuclear" now appears and the thought could have been uttered by Tom Hayden in the 1970s. In fact, the original probably *was* uttered by Tom. He had drafted the Port Huron Statement, but now in the late 1970s he too abjured the atomic age and joined the chorus for "alternative energy sources," solar being one of his favorites.

I should like to have been with Tom the day he found out about the new party line on the atom, though being with Tom in recent years can be hazardous. He has married Jane, who can be difficult at the best of times, and he has nearly wrecked the house with his solar paraphernalia. How do you suppose Jane took it when, after he had placed a solar collector overhead, its water reservoir burst deluging Jane's living room? Or what about the time he installed solar collectors at his Santa Barbara ranch house and was nearly blown from the roof as he scrambled around trying to get the dratted things to face the sun?

Since the fall of Vietnam, life had lost much of its gusto for left-wing activists, a surprising number of whom had rushed into Me Decade enthusiasms and been mellowed to the point where all they ever did was smile and coo. The rest remained on guard but in pain. At first they doubted that the war was really over. Was this another of the CIA's ruses? They awaited word of renewed hostilities. "When are they gonna end the goddamn war?"—that popular question of all *Jugendkultur* in the early 1970s was still ricocheting through their stricken brains. Then word filtered in about brutal tyrannies being brought down on the supposedly liberated inhabitants of Indochina and about the Cambodian holocaust.

At first the left refused to believe these reports. Men like

William Kunstler and David Dellinger scoffed at them and at any erstwhile ally who might find them creditable. Others tried to explain them away: "How many recall that after our Revolutionary War," Robert Richter queried in *The New York Times* in 1979, "Tories in the 13 Colonies went to Canada or back to England? Or that after the Civil War many slaveholders fled to South America and thousands of ex-Confederates roamed the West before finding a new life? The point is, although the parallels may not be entirely accurate, that the situation of the Vietnamese 'boat people' is a cruel but perhaps inevitable aftermath of a terrible revolutionary and civil war. . . ." Explained Richter, "Vietnam has an enormous food problem, and I believe it has much to do with the boat people's tragedy."[18] So there you are. When Joan Baez urged criticism of the North Vietnamese for their cruelty, her old left-wing colleagues identified her as a tool of the CIA.

For all these old peaceniks the news of the hard-pressed clams living near New Hampshire's Seabrook nuclear plant came as glad tidings. As *Newsweek* observed, the anti-nukers' movement was entering "a new phase of mass public protest and civil disobedience reminiscent of the early days of the civil-rights and antiwar movements."[19] There was good reason for *Newsweek* to be reminded of the anti-war movement. This *was* the anti-war movement with very few additions, and it was as impatient with democratic process as ever. In a Delphic humor Ralph Nader warned that civil disobedience "will spread all over the country as needed. It will be used if there is no formal way to protest."[20] The prospects for finding that formal way to protest were not cheering. "We're feeling very disillusioned about the legal and legislative channels for stopping nuclear power," lamented a strategist for People Against Nuclear Power in San Francisco. By a 2-to-1 vote Californians had recently interred an anti-nuke referendum, and so the movement settled on a new method: "Our new method is disciplined, nonviolent direct action."[21]

Now, there are in the Great Republic those who will say that in a democracy one side wins and one side loses; the side whose referendum wins 2 to 1 is the side whose policy should be implemented. The members of the anti-nuke movement obviously did not agree. Energy policy was, for them, another of those crucial matters whose urgency quite transcended democratic process and tolerance. They stood with Miss Mayo. A few more nuclear power plants and our human shapes might slip away forever. Then again, a few more antinuclear referendums like the California referendum and the anti-nuke movement might have slipped away too. Hence the "disciplined, nonviolent direct action" had to become really bellicose. Naturally the media covered and magnified every spectacle of "direct action." Every anti-nuke charge was broadcast. The scientific community, realizing the value of nuclear development, protested. Nobel laureate Hans Bethe gathered the signatures of thirty-four scientific leaders—eleven of whom were also nuclear physicists—on a petition advocating continued nuclear development.[22] But the pop science of fabulists like Amory Lovins and Ralph Nader was more comprehensible to the ignoramuses covering the anti-nuke movement—and remember, in the years following the civil rights movement, such was the slovenliness of thought pervading the media that almost any human assortment calling itself a movement somehow captured the intellectual and moral high ground. Had the nuclear-energy industry called itself a movement rather than an industry, its scientists and executives all showing up at government hearings wearing work shirts and chanting slogans, it is entirely plausible that the media would have presented it in softer, warmer hues and that nuclear energy would never have suffered the steady erosion of support that it experienced in the late 1970s.

Then the Republic was visited by an accident at Pennsylvania's Three Mile Island nuclear power plant, and the media's ignoramuses, their eyeballs spinning in their poor vacant cocos, became screaming meemies. They transformed a minor accident less perilous to life and limb than a fall into poison ivy into a horror story more frightening than the Chicago Fire. Years later the media and the cynical politicos of Pennsylvania who exploited the accident would all be duly criticized for their irresponsibility, which featured such mawkish performances as Dr. Jimmy Breslin lamenting in the New

York *Daily News* that "steam drifted out of the tops of the four cooling towers and ran down the sides like candle wax. [Steam descending? steam metamorphosing into wax?] The steam was evil, laced with radiation."[23] (Gangway!) A special inquiry group appointed by the Nuclear Regulatory Commission and a presidential commission both found that the accident had presented negligible danger to the public. What is more, even in the immediate aftermath 89 percent of the country's energy experts favored proceeding rapidly with development and construction of nuclear energy plants; 92 percent of the nuclear experts favored rapid development. Unfortunately the public knew only what sages like Dr. Breslin were telling them. Their approval for the construction of more nuclear power plants slipped from 69 percent in 1977 to 46 percent after Three Mile Island.[24]

Relying on statistics like this the snake charmers at the head of the anti-nuke movement could enchant government bureaucrats and learned judges into believing almost any anti-nuke complaint. Soon the industry was being strangled by red tape. The movement had triumphed! Or had it? Had the American people accepted the anti-nukers' "era of limits" claptrap? Were they now in accord with Ralph Nader's prophecy? "We are going to rediscover smallness," he had sung. "If people get back to the earth, they can grow their own gardens, they can listen to the birds, they can feel the wind across their cheeks and they can watch the sun come up."[25] Is there anyone in the Republic who can actually imagine this incorrigible busybody listening to the birds and languorously feeling the wind across his cheeks? Yet out in the Golden State one of the New Age's model pols responded to such ludicrous poetry and even composed some himself. In 1980 he read the polls and was stirred to action. Using opposition to nuclear energy as the centerpiece of his campaign the Hon. Jerry Brown set out to topple the Wonderboy and to become the New Age's most perfect specimen of a presidential candidate. Unfortunately for him opposition to nuclear energy was not a sufficient issue even after the Three Mile Horror, and soon Jerry was a corpse. Nonetheless, he and his campaign deserve scrutiny. Along with the Wonderboy, Jerry was the exemplary

New Age pol, and of the two he may actually have believed some of its arcane dicta.

The Mullah Brown entered the 1980 presidential race with an aura of mystery and glamour. His late entry into the 1976 presidential race had become legendary. In five of the last six Western primaries, he had actually flattened the political genius of 1976! Had those primaries come at the beginning of the race rather than at its end there is no telling what heights he might have scaled. For the next four years pundits smitten by New Age rumble-bumble sensed that the boy governor was destiny's child. Hence when he declared his 1980 candidacy by denouncing nuclear energy and intoning his mysterious message about "a benign energy path" as yet untrodden, the legend grew and shimmered. Even *The Wall Street Journal* was fetched, and on the eve of his entry into the race the *Journal* wrote reverently of his whole goofball song and dance, especially his opposition to nuclear energy: "the governor's strongest political position."[26] Four years before, even *The Village Voice* would have been incapable of such a howler. Characteristic of the era, opposition to nuclear energy had suddenly become an obsession with an influential elite. During the 1970s practically every timorous, goody-goody, bred-on-the-left enthusiasm gained a swift and profound purchase on America's elites. Its journalistic elite was particularly gullible. Four years later the "nuclear freeze" and the "gender gap" would wow the popinjays. Now their catnip was opposition to nuclear energy. In their resolve to doubt everything the journalists became suckers for anything as long as it had the left's cachet.

The average American, however, was not such a pushover, and his anti-nuclear fever remained low-grade. In 1980 the Mullah was soon being snubbed and bruised in every primary. In New Hampshire, home of the clam, he was soundly thrashed. In Connecticut he was even beaten by Lyndon H. LaRouche. By the Wisconsin primary he was gasping. Then he was a corpse—his casket soon to be flown back to California profaned by snickers and abandoned by the mobs of fawning journalists and New Age college kids who had composed his constant entourage during the late struggle. The electorate again had turned its *gluteus maximus* on an anti-nuke prophet, despite the fact that this prophet was one of God's true Barnums.

No dictum from the vaults of American thought more wondrously illuminates the character and achievement of Jerry Brown than Gertrude Stein's pithy appraisal of Oakland, California. As Miss Stein observed, her eyes full of the sheer concrete of the place, "There's no there there." So it was with Mullah Brown, and for that matter his fellow New Age pol Jimmy Carter. Oh, there was, perhaps, something there. There were energy and guile, and in the Mullah's case there were those enormous rough-hewn benches placed in the gubernatorial reception room to symbolize New Age innocence. As a novel solution to one or another of the Mullah's novel problems there was the Governor's Office of Appropriate Technology, which awakened all Californians to the environmental menace of the flush toilet. There was the rock star he squired about even on fact-finding safaris into the Third World, and there were the dirty shirts he would wear to symbolize some vague anti-bourgeois desideratum. So there was theater, but there was little else.

His oratory was the vaporing of a nincompoop, and a paraverbal nincompoop at that. His statesmanship was the conjuring of a facile con man. The oratory went through two phases. In the first phase his subject matter was of a personal nature presented in weirdo stanzas, at once ominous and esoteric. Consider: "I see the world in very fluid, contradictory, emerging, interconnected terms, and with that kind of circuitry I just don't feel the need to say what is going to happen or will not happen . . . It's the circuitry of semiconductors and computers and electronic interconnections, that's what's happening today."[27] Pour yourself a drink, and consider another of his observations: "I go from Whale Day to Space Day, from one issue to another. Life is a mosaic. Life is many themes. Life is many seasons. So is governorship. So is culture. So is history."[28] Before meeting Hitler, Mussolini sounded a little like this, but such oratorical rhapsodies are relatively new to our political discourse. Was there any intelligence being communicated here? In moral and philosophical heft are these statements any more substantial than the red-white-and-blue solemnities of the late Harding or of a Chicago alderman weeping over a renamed street? I am doubtful.

In his second phase he attempted to show that he had leaped from the Renaissance to the post-industrial society, and he grew even more tedious, sounding now like an autistic sociologist steeped in quack science: "There are technological fixes and then there are changes in the culture and in the way of life. . . . We're going to have to do both. . . . The present imperative is to maximize material consumption resources and resource-depletion and ecological disaster," he informed Alexander Cockburn and James Ridgeway during an interview.[29] In an earlier day friends of the English language would have assassinated an editor for publishing such cackelocutions. Relatives, concerned for the honor of the Brown family name, might have had the boy governor declared *non compos mentis*. Yet in the glorious 1970s Mr. and Mrs. Brown Senior were actually proud of their brat.

The God-fearing tell us that either you yearn for goodness or you come to hate it. Whatever the merits of this view, I have no doubt that there is a kind of mind that either yearns for intelligence or comes to loathe it. The oratory and the antics of the Mullah Brown suggest that he was the possessor of such a mind. He was not merely indifferent to intelligence, he was downright hostile to it, to culture, and to ideas. In fact he was hostile to all that rises from the mind and spirit of a superior man, and so in the New Age he was a wow.

American journalists of a certain cheap type find his kind of gibbering entrancing, and the Mullah could always count on a madly scribbling mob of journalists trailing him on his journeys. The mob found his behavior endlessly fascinating. Here was a bachelor governor, living in a rented flat rather than the governor's mansion, sleeping on floors, cooking vegetables macrobiotically, and traveling hither and yon not in the gubernatorial limousine but in a 1974 Plymouth Satellite. Surely it is one of the ironies of political history that in the last stages of his disastrous 1980 campaign a dazed and daunted Jerry began grousing that it was the media that were doing him in.

They called him Snowflake and Governor Moonbeam. He had expected better of them, and now he was deeply hurt. Can we adduce any more compelling evidence that Jerry was mostly empty space? No politician with any dignity or serious principle would ever have made such a buffoon of himself, not even for headlines, not even for votes. He was a mountebank hustler and nothing more.[30] As with most mountebank hustlers he was eventually chloroformed by his own performance. He actually came to believe his esoteric blah.

Study the record for yourself. The Mullah was all restless ambition. Every time one of his pet projects incurred hostile fire from the California legislature he dropped it and went on to some other trendy enthusiasm. When Liberal collectivism fell out of favor he became vaguely "neoconservative," and he did not object to the term. When hypochondria came into favor he became a friend of the earth, a defender of the consumers, an intrepid reader of patent-medicine labels.

In the late 1970s he promised voters he would move to the left and right "simultaneously."[31] To some degree he was successful, but only because he was without principle. Philosophically he was an empty chamber; but it is important to note that when he moved left and right he embraced the most misanthropic traits of both camps. He became a skinflint, thus soothing the right. He abused some middle-class pieties; thus the left was comforted. One of the ineluctable lessons of the 1960s and 1970s was that once one had opened the public schools to meetings of the Huey Newton–Eldridge Cleaver Defense Committee (as he did), or lowered state flags for the Kent State Four (as he did), the left's passion for "fundamental change" was pretty much spent. Such outrages of middle-class dignity quenched leftist demands for reform just as thoroughly as a threat against welfare spending quieted the right's rhetoric about personal liberty. These things the Mullah understood, much as the neighborhood cat knows how to deal with a chipmunk.

In many ways the Mullah was at one with Ralph Nader, the human handkerchief who for decades went about collecting bacteria, viruses, and other human miseries, all of which he attributed to the turpitude of his neighbors. Like Nader,

Brown was another of those weird 1960s Puritans, a misanthrope surrounded by political fanatics of one magnitude or another, a man with no roots, no strong affections, few fixed ideas, yet a man given to ceaselessly lecturing productive middle-class society on its deficiencies. Endlessly wandering into idiot spectacles like Whale Day, endlessly issuing cryptic and imbecilic epigrams like one of the fat swamis he apparently admired, the Mullah wore a perpetual scowl. He scowled at the tobacco industry, the automobile industry, the medical profession, to cite but three taxpaying cabals that roused his wrath. So sour was he on the docs that in January 1980 he put ten chiropractors on California's regional medical-review committees, committees charged with overseeing the professional conduct of physicians. It is but another example of the era's decadence that such misanthropes as Brown and Nader could be accepted as humanitarians and progressives.

As with Nader, Brown was all rigorism and bile. In all the hagiographic books written about him never is there a suggestion of a genial moment, a convivial lapse. He was intense, abrasive, remote, and sullen. He missed appointments, forced himself upon others, and abused employees. Yet no Bible-pounding evangelical was a more sempiternal preacher. A forty-two-year-old bachelor whose adult life was mostly spent deep in the public trough, he spent his time lecturing the taxpaying, productive public, whose lives were as remote from his own as they were from the life of Pope Julian the Unspeakable. He was a *philosophe* whose philosophizing was always crackpot and primitive. How to account for his electoral triumphs in California and in the 1976 primaries? All I can come up with is that a large number of voters must have tired of civics and yearned for dramaturgy. As governor the Mullah sponsored prayer breakfasts featuring meditations on peyote, snakes, and pregnant goats. He was always easy copy for the press and a wild show for the electorate.

On the 1980 campaign trail, while denouncing an energy source that had already proved itself useful and indeed necessary, he prattled on about the need to establish space platforms for exploring the universe. On some days he exhaled sonorities about how "We are a vibrant, yeasty society that still wishes to explore different ways of living, different ways of producing food, different technologies, and to expand our awareness that we are all interdependent on a planet that is part of this almost unimaginable universe."[32] On other days he was leading a mob of modern-day Luddites devoted to banning one of the world's most advanced branches of science. What T. D. Lysenko did to Soviet biology the Mullah Brown would do to nuclear physics, only Brown would be more thorough. He would bring in the quacks to shut nuclear physics down.

"Protect the people, preserve the planet, explore the universe"[33] was his bizarre campaign whoop; and—*mirabile dictu*—no longer did he wear dirty shirts and rumpled suits. Now he was attired in pin stripes and a fashionable Burberry trench coat. The press was fascinated. In the words of one of his top lieutenants—a man named Jacques—"he dressed conservatively . . . spoke conservatively . . . he's personally conservative,"[34] whereupon the Mullah slipped away from the campaign to drop in on the fifth annual International Trans-Personal Psychology Conference in historic Danvers, Massachusetts. There he shmoozed with some exotic called Swami Mukhtananda, explaining afterward that the Hon. Swami "is an important religious figure in his country. . . . People meet with Billy Graham, the Pope, the Archbishop of a Greek Orthodox Church. It's rather ethnocentric to say one religious grouping is more important than another. . . . This planet is very small."[35] *In fine*: through all his dramatics there was always the damp plop-plop of cattle droppings hitting the barn floor. The New Age abounded in these cheap acts.

In 1980, however, theater and plop-plop were not enough. Things had changed since 1976 or even 1978. Well-born snots like the Mullah might be intrigued by a candidate's discourses on the righteousness of scarcity and on visionary journeys through space and time, but the ordinary voters were experiencing scarcity at first hand. Inflation was burning into their savings; plants were closing. The ordinary fellow now worried about how to heat his home, and at the polls the dreamer from Sacramento was slaughtered. Once it became apparent that the voters were not intrigued, the members of the press corps who were always being shocked by 1980's election news departed too. Jerry Brown went home to the loneliness of the San Francisco Zen Center, and only reporters from *The Village Voice* still followed.

The anti-nukers had piously lectured the citizenry that the Great Republic was standing in the vestibule of an "era of limits." They issued strenuous admonitions that Americans must cut back drastically on consumption, take note of changed circumstances, and put an end to their prodigal ways.

Ironically, Americans had altered their prodigal ways. Oil had become increasingly expensive and subject to Arab temper tantrums. On the basis of current growth rates, it appeared that the earth's oil pools would be depleted within a half century. Americans effected significant economies. Under the pressure of the market economy they conserved. In fact the public even grew more sensitive to nuclear energy's dangers. Meanwhile, the anti-nuke activists continued the same old rants against Babylonian America and in favor of enlightened puniness and pessimism. In view of the energy shortage, might the opponents of nuclear energy have adjusted their views? Would they agree to at least some nuclear power? Not at all; instead they boasted about the "innovative technologies" being developed by some ragtag New Age shaman hidden away in a commune full of morons.

Finally in 1980 the public went to the polls and voted for the most dramatic political change of the century—a sea change that the press once again failed to notice. Rather than continue with Jimmy Carter's timorous agitations the electorate opted for the same political principles that the American majority had thumpingly defeated in 1964. Not even the election of Franklin Roosevelt in 1932 represents so vast a break with the past as the election of Ronald Reagan. Roosevelt ran as a moderate, professing alarm over every species of heterodoxy. Reagan ran as a staunch conservative, his speeches reiterating themes held up as abominable in 1964. One would have to be far to the right and doltish to argue that America had gone Goldwaterite, but by election day it had assayed two grades of "limits of growth" bosh—Jerry's high-grade, Jimmy's low-grade. America voted for growth.

Typical of the fanatics of the Age, the anti-nukers disrelished sensible reforms in favor of quack remedies—or "innovative technology" as their insufferable cant put it. Of all such "technologies" none brought more joy to their otherwise gloomy hearts than "solar power": a Coppertoned genie eager to serve all mankind! Once put to work, its shafts of energy would free us from the giant utilities, the Wall Street bankers, the victims of "our collective nuclear psychosis."

The list of innovative technologies was long and riotous. Along with the heliomaniacs' there were the devotees of giant windmills, decomposing cow dung, huge nets to trap ocean tides, and synthetic fuels. Eventually the anti-nukers prevailed upon Congress to create the Synthetic Fuels Corporation, giving it an $88 billion mandate to produce 2 million barrels of synfuels per day by 1992. More than three years later, syndicated columnist Donald Lambro reported that the Corporation "plagued by mismanagement and scandals" had "squandered more than $70 million—mostly for administrative expenses—hired nearly 200 employees at big salaries and ensconced itself in expensive offices. Yet it has not produced a thimbleful of fuel."[36]

Behind all these dreams were squirrelly profs and crank inventors of the most preposterous sort, amateurs at best and also rogues, whose "technologies" put the intelligent observer in mind of nothing so much as Jonathan Swift's eighteenth-century Academy of Lagado where one old dreamer had turned his talents to "extracting Sun-Beams out of Cucumbers"; and where, enveloped in a "horrible stink," "the most ancient Student of the Academy," covered with excrement, labored to reduce stools to their original potency "by separating the several Parts"—with his hands! Doubtless in the late 1970s our Department of Energy would have handsome checks awaiting these experts, and surely they would command laudations from Miss Mayo in *The Village Voice*. Is it worth noting that all the experiments described by Swift in his fictional Academy were actually being proposed or undertaken by his contemporaries in the Royal Society three centuries ago? To a certain kind of mind sunshine and feces are apparently timeless inspirations to scientific inquiry; but does our government have to subsidize such idiot labor?

Though claiming to be a friend of the atom and indeed somewhat of an amateur nuclear physicist, President Carter turned out to be an easy mark for "innovative technology." The sheer meretriciousness of it sozzled him, and his Department of Energy readily encouraged the quacks with lush grants for further experimentation. Every once in a while there would appear hilarious news stories about some greenhorn mechanic in a remote corner of the Republic operating on a grant of a few hundred thousand dollars to develop some imbecilic contraption for harnessing the sun or the tides or the flush toilet. Always there were the obligatory comparison with the Wright brothers, the optimism of the idiot child, the suggestion that there in a jerkwater garage made ludicrous and probably dangerous with gimcrack gadgetry and a jungle of pipes, a modern David was preparing his slingshot and Exxon's doom. Millions in boodle were squeezed from the taxpayers for these schemes and always with the approbation of the anti-nuke movement as long as the grants did not go to actual corporations competent in the area of energy production. When that happened the protests would go up, complete with admonitions against tampering in the free market and suggestions of conspiracies in high places.

Next to innovative technology the anti-nukers favored conservation, and here Jimmy Carter was with them wholeheartedly. Throughout his administration the Wonderboy had an almost mystical affinity for the futile: for negotiations with murderous mullahs, for wage and price controls that would be *voluntary*, for preaching human rights to the Soviets. When he heard conservation was an energy alternative he found it irresistible. Conservation stimulated the mean little Puritan within him. Deny yourself those sensuous hours under the blow dryers. Silence those hot tubs and massagers. Resist supererogatory heat in the winter, the air conditioner in the summer. Sweat! Freeze! Be righteous! Jimmy and the prohibitionists stood shoulder to shoulder scowling at us. Yet amid all the sanctimonious testimonials to conservation it must have occurred to many that conservation produces nothing. It is the timorous policy of fated dopes. Surely, at some point all doomed people conserve. When did the sixteenth-century settlers of Roanoke Island hear their first sermons on the wonders of conservation? As the provisions ran out, they must have become more frequent. How many more happy days did conservation bring the settlers? No one knows. We know only that the Roanoke settlement came to be remembered as "the Lost Colony." Jimmy's was the Lost Country.

In the 1970s futile policy alternatives never daunted a protest movement as long as it could summon sufficient volts of moral intensity and general fanaticism. Through their superior fanaticism the anti-nuke activists managed the coup that every 1970s protest movement needed for success. It got reasonable men to ponder its unreasonable propositions, and in time the extremist propositions took on a mantle of legitimacy owing simply to the attention reasonable men had accorded them. Anon, the movement's hysterical charges had the pro-nuclear forces sweating. They found themselves in the idiotic position of having to answer every charge. Helen Caldicott, Dr. Ehrlich, Amory Lovins, the whole gang became respected participants in a debate that resounded with the tintinnabulations of nonsense. Catastrophic visions, no matter how improbable, are always more arresting—especially in televisionland—than the cool refutations of thoughtful scientists.

Looking back on the debate over nuclear energy one is staggered by the vast nonsensicality of the thing: Beethoven's *Missa Solemnis* performed by a chorus and orchestra of chimpanzees; Einstein interpreted by schoolchildren. Here you had a society whose very existence depended on cheap power. Its major source of that power, oil, was at best uncertain. Yet that society's technicians were being forced to build power plants in such a way that they would not have a major accident for thousands of years. More to the point, many of the worries thrown up against nuclear power were sheer fantasy.

To a large extent the anti-nuke movement relied on the environmentalists' prophecies of fictitious catastrophes, though their prophecies had a slightly different twist. As with the prophecies that were to be adopted by the anti-defense movement these were prophecies of hypothetical disasters, disasters somewhat reminiscent of horror movies or of the ludicrous disaster movies that were so popular in the 1970s. Posit a world whose energy source is nuclear fission and the anti-nuke mind envisages Boeing 747s suddenly falling from the sky, crashing into the most tender spots of nuclear power plants and causing virulent clouds of radiation to head straight for Boys Town, the Rose Bowl during halftime, Midtown Manhattan at the penultimate hour of Christmas shopping. There would be earthquakes under nuclear plants. There would be Hiroshimas in every state.

Radio and television shows concerned with the nuclear debate were interlarded with these prophecies. Watching them and reading about them brought to mind the catastrophic prophecies of white racists warning of the genetic horror certain to befall the Caucasian race if blacks were ever admitted to white-only toilets and other cultural centers in their domain. Yet the racists' propaganda was written to dupe hill-ape morons. The anti-nuke propaganda was prepared for the college-educated.

Comparing the nuclear debate with other national hullabaloos one came away with the suspicion that the anti-nuke movement's arguments were no less spurious than the diatribes of American Nativists, know-nothings, anti-Masons, and teetotalers. Imagine scientists and government officials putting themselves to the task of calculating precisely the mathematical probabilities of various nuclear accidents that had never before taken place. Once they had calculated the probable incidence of these accidents they were to design plants so that the fanciful accidents would be less likely—apt to occur, say, once in 1,000 years rather than once in 500 years. Then the opponents of nuclear energy who had set off the whole farce would thunder against the new nuclear plants' added costs.

As Fred and Geoffrey Hoyle wrote in *Commonsense in Nuclear Energy*: "For events that have never happened in human experience, it is impossible to assign probabilities in a meaningful way. . . . The correct way to assess the probability of future accidents is on the experience of past accidents for similar circumstances. For the civil nuclear industry there has been no clear-cut evidence of any accident leading to death or injury, which means that according to every extrapolation formula known to mathematicians the best estimate for the future number of injuries and fatalities is zero. . . . Attempting to guess what has never been shown to happen is not merely logically unsound. It is a sure recipe for the dissemination of alarmist propaganda."[37] And alarmist propaganda is precisely what most of the complaints against nuclear energy amounted to. The thing astonished even me.

After all the horror stories and all the prophecies of hypothetical catastrophe, what was the anti-nuker shouting about? Cooled and decocted of all its anti-capitalist, pro-socialist claptrap, the complaint was that nuclear energy was dangerous for the environment, unhealthful for the citizenry, and certain to spread nuclear weaponry. It was, then, an artful exploitation of the narcissism, hypochondria, and pessimism that the American left had done so much to create. All these complaints were overwrought and can be expeditiously and unceremoniously deflated.

The members of the Sierra Club, the Friends of the Earth, and all the other adepts of the land-of-milk-and-honey hallucination were easily snookered into believing that nuclear energy was an ecological peril. Radiation was the culprit. Yet, as anyone conversant with the literature on radiation knows, our environment already teems with radiation from natural sources, and its plenitude varies widely from one geographic setting to another.

Truth be known, nuclear energy plants leak very little radiation. Many coal-fired energy plants leak more. In fact, so does Grand Central Station. As Petr Beckmann, an advocate of nuclear energy, points out, the granite in Grand Central Station emits so much radiation that the Nuclear Regulatory Commission would be duty-bound to board it up were it a nuclear energy plant.[38] Actually our exposure would increase scarcely at all even if all the world's electricity were produced by nuclear energy plants.

The International Commission of Radiological Protection's

standard for annual exposure to radiation is set at 500 milli-rems (mrem). By this standard even Miss Mayo can relax. Background radiation exposure in the United States ranges from 50 mrem to 175 mrem. There is an additional exposure of approximately 120 mrem of man-made radiation, most of which comes from medical sources. Radiation can be found in amazing places. Color television accounts for about 1 mrem. All nuclear plants in service at the end of the 1970s accounted for about .003 mrem annually. The average American is ex-posed to about 250.003 mrem of radiation annually. If the opponents of nuclear energy succeed in shutting down these plants they will save us from about .003 mrem.[39] On the other hand we might freeze to death.

Radiation's threat to health is not all that clear. Survivors of Nagasaki and Hiroshima were exposed to doses of radiation of approximately 80,000 mrem, yet there is still no detectable increase in genetic damage among their progeny. In fact, ac-cording to studies done by Jablon and Kato life expectancy in those cities is higher than for a normal Japanese control group.[40] It seems to be true that massive doses of radiation increase one's risk of leukemia, but even then the risk is no greater than the cancer risk incurred by a heavy smoker.

The prohibitionists' radiation fear is simply another link of their overstuffed bologna. Even under an exceptional circum-stance such as the Three Mile Island accident the emission of radiation is hardly worrisome to a normal mind, adequately informed. According to the findings of the US National Acad-emy of Engineering, the average exposure suffered by people living within 50 miles of that power plant was only about 1 mrem, which is "about the amount normally received from natural sources in 3 days of living, or perhaps ⅓ of that re-ceived on a jet flight across country."[41]

Practically all the charges made by environmentalists against nuclear energy could be made with equal weight against non-nuclear energy sources. Take the charge that nuclear power plants cause "thermal pollution." The thing is overdone. All thermal power plants cause "thermal pollu-tion," and if one happens to be a lobster, thermal pollution can be very congenial. Thermal pollution is, after all, only warm water. Warm water might discomfort a few species of cold-water fish, bereft of the acuity to move on to cooler neighborhoods, but is this a sound reason for refusing to build more thermal power plants? Some marine life will thrive in warm water, and as for the casualties, no thermal power plant ever heard of was as murderous to local fish as a normal family of hungry gray seals or—as my researches have shown—killer whales. Is there an environmentalist on this orb who bears hostility toward the noble gray seal?

The environmentalists' arguments against nuclear energy are difficult to take seriously. Samuel McCracken's scabrous observation is probably sound: "Far from being our most dangerous source of energy, nuclear energy is our safest."[42] It is safer than coal, gas, or oil. Even hydroelectric power has filled more cemeteries than nuclear energy.

Coal's danger is a matter of record. McCracken estimates that one large coal-fired plant leads to between 31 and 111 yearly fatalities from mining accidents, black lung disease, pollution, and fatalities incurred while hauling coal. "In contrast, when we calculate all the deaths caused by a 1000 mwh light-water reactor—including all those killed by the fuel cycle, by the operation of the reactor, and by the waste disposal," McCracken avers, "we arrive at a total of one-half a death a year. This half-death, by the way, is still largely hypothetical, since it includes amortized figures for a number of accidents that have not yet happened."[43]

Every energy source is dangerous. Liquid gas kills thousands of people around the world every year. In the summer of 1977 at the Spanish resort of San Carlos de la Rápita a tanker truck rolled off a road sending a wave of fire over a densely populated campsite, instantly incinerating 100 people. Another 150 were injured grotesquely. Months earlier burning gas was responsible for an even more appalling death toll when two jumbo jets collided while taxiing on a runway on the Canary Island of Tenerife. Five hundred and eighty-two died.

Even such a wholesome source of energy as hydroelectric power is dangerous. Hydroelectric power means dams, and dams collapse, sending killer floods down on nearby inhabitants. This is what happened in 1889 when the dam above

Johnstown, Pennsylvania, suddenly gave way and more than 2,200 people were swept to their deaths. In 1977 at least 2,000 people suffered a similar fate when a dam gave way in Gujarat, India.[44]

As for the claim that the peaceful use of nuclear energy is going to aid in the spread of nuclear arms, well, here we have a kind of isolationism that not even America's original isolationists attempted. It assumes that America can isolate itself from the passage of time. Typical of the New Age's infantile solipsism, this isolationism calls upon us to be truants from history's march. Yet the mere fact that the United States might shut down its nuclear science does not mean that the rest of the world would follow. Did the other countries of the world become more peaceful in the late 1970s when the foreign policy of the United States became more irenic? At the end of Jimmy Carter's administration more nations were at each other's throats than when he arrived in Washington. The peaceful use of nuclear energy has nothing to do in fact or in logic with international hostilities or with the spread of nuclear weapons. Moreover, it is futile and pigheaded to advocate an end to scientific research. Contrary to the wisdom of the New Age, neither a citizen nor a nation can withdraw from the procession of time and history. There is no secure withdrawal except into the grave.

5

The Suffering Situation

The Exaltation of the Bleak

AT the heart of American Liberalism there has always been sobbing: profuse, inconsolable sobbing. Yet the Liberal heart is a sizable organ and so there is room for much more—for instance: shouting, brave and indignant shouting. Then too there are manifestos, full-page ads in the *Times*, in-depth studies from the institutes, and all sorts of scientific analyses. Shouts and sobs, research and analysis, manifestos and laments —Liberalism is a very noisy philosophy. In fact it is the public philosophy that will not shut up, its very clamorousness having come to be a revered element in the Legend: "When all others were silent we dared to speak up." This timeworn boast has often been quite true, but could we not have been spared all the maudlin hooey? As the Legend of American Liberalism swelled and developed its smirk did the public discourse have to take aboard all the gasps and blubberings? There are those of us who would have preferred something bold and fast-paced, like the storming of the Bastille. Why all these whimperings and recriminations?

Well, let us be humane. We are talking about New Age revolutionaries in an American era of affluence. Try as they may to share the concerns of worldwide *gauchisme* they are as akin to their Continental antecedents as *l'eau* is to *l'eau de vie*. Few could rouse themselves from bed before noon even for a storming; and for those who could I can foresee only disaster: the pothead trampled to death en route; the health nuts disabled by asthma as a cigarette is lit. We are not talking about would-be Robespierres. We are talking about Pecksniffs from the League of Women Voters, Common Cause, the combined faculties from the Afro-Affairs Department and the Women's Studies Program, plus their credulous students—people who do not eat meat, people who flaunt bumper stickers proclaiming their intention to "brake for small animals," low-level psychopaths!

By the 1970s American Liberalism had become distinctive for petulance, moral preciousness, and an amplitude of exigent causes, most of which have been comic when not downright pernicious. In a review of New Age Liberal writing the English political philosopher Maurice Cranston notes that American Liberalism has transformed itself into a kind of girlish socialism fraught with a multitude of contradictions. However we may judge it, all civilized observers will agree that Liberalism lacks coherence and no longer follows such maxims as David Spitz laid down for it in *The Real World of Liberalism*: "Esteem liberty above all other values," he wrote in the late 1970s, "even over equality and justice."[1] Then he died. Had Spitz lived he would have grimly joined the cause to "desex" English or some such New Age fanaticism, or he would have been marked down as a Black Shirt. Now Liberalism was juddering along the path foreseen for it long ago by Kenneth Minogue in that wise and eloquent book, *The Liberal Mind*. New Age Liberalism was by the 1970s obsessed with searching out what Minogue called "suffering situations" —that is to say the aggrieved: aggrieved classes, aggrieved sexes, and the aggrieved in such idiotic categories as flora (rights for trees!) and fauna (farm animals! laboratory animals! the Hollywood Ten!).

In a free and affluent land where people were living longer, healthier lives than ever before and with more physical comforts, the New Age Liberals had developed a morbid preoccupation with suffering, disease, and grievance. In this new atmosphere conviviality constituted suspicious behavior. Joviality was the mark of the heathen. America's New Age Liberals became stupefyingly earnest and besotted in adolescent sentimentality. In the universities, the bureaucracies, large corporations, wherever they and their allies in the judiciary could slam down their petty humorless tyrannies, hobgoblins were ushered in, and with them an ineffable morbidity somewhat suggestive of Berlin in the waning days of Weimar. Large public areas of American society had fallen under a foreign regime. All was not as it appeared to the untutored eye. There were secrets and lies that could not be opposed or even acknowledged.

Life could be gruesome. Less than two decades after McCarthyism a new habit of mind put a frown on the faces of millions of Americans. Disloyalty was no longer the point. Rather it was righteousness *vis-à-vis* dozens of issues that had scarcely been issues before, and the righteous were apt to accost their innocent victims anywhere, in public or private, and always with odious slogans and idiot harangues. Witch-hunts were begun over some poor slob's unguarded remark apropos of the environment, nuclear energy, fur coats, women. The French during the Second World War called the occupying Germans "the gray lice." This is precisely how I have come to view the agents of righteousness of the 1970s. Some of their exigent causes were creditable at the outset. Some were discreditable from the start. All were taken to absurd and deleterious extremes that disparaged and abominated normal life, and by the end of the 1970s the gray lice were everywhere.

6

The Feminist Enthusiasm

The Grievance, Cheap Thought, the Women of the Fevered Brow

THE gray lice made sex a major theater of operations. The righteous are always alarmed by the amatory arts, and with the rise of feminism every normal sexual act came under scrutiny. Ultimately, Americans spent more time talking about sex than pursuing it. In itself that is not very unusual and could have been very agreeable, sex being the protean pleasure that it is. Unfortunately, the sex acts most often discussed were the sex acts least frequently practiced throughout history, even by animals.

No topic became more gruesome than heterosexual sex. A grim sodality of females had stepped forward in the 1960s to curl their lips at the erotic world. They brought the sexual revolution to an ignominious halt. All over the Republic the wine stopped flowing. Moonlit nights were left unused. The New Age was to see the revival of a decidedly adamant strain of Puritanism, particularly toward heterosexual passion.

A handful of anaphrodisiac women had observed the rise of Eros and they were, as they so delicately phrased it, "pissed off." Life in the suburbs made them "pissed off." The kids and the idiot who snored and coughed when they were trying to get some sleep made them "pissed off." Plato and Shakespeare; Euclid and Newton; all history's goddamn generals and dictators; its veterans, peasants, and hard-hats; even mothers and girlfriends left these ladies "pissed off." Needless to say the Liberals came across these pissed-off women and began to blubber.

Here was the classic suffering situation, and the Liberals set out to do something about it. With the utmost diligence they applied themselves to the bureaucracy and the judiciary until they had banned such infamies as all boys' choirs, father-and-son dinners, and girl-less Boy Scout troops. Then the Liberals passed on, in search of still more suffering situations. The thing had become a compulsion with them. Soon they were wailing over the victims of 1950s anti-Communism. Then they were gasping for the homosexuals, the consumers, the handicapped, the aging, the carriers of *Herpes simplex* #2, the vanquished of the Mexican War. Yet the Liberals were in for an unpleasant discovery. After a dozen or so of their suffering situations had come and gone these women of fevered brow were still pulling at their sleeves, and now they were really "pissed off." They had established themselves in that one secure and influential realm where in concert with so many other "pissed-off" persons it is easy and indeed profitable to cultivate resentment and crackpot ideas. The women of the fevered brow had set themselves up in academe!

Their rancorous ascension there was the Liberals' own fault. The Liberals had always been successful at keeping these lovely places very much to themselves. There were never many divisive Republicans on campus or even many vocal moderate Democrats. It was simply not deemed part of the natural order of things to offer a representative sampling of American political opinion or even social opinion in academe. The way the Liberals viewed it, campuses were to be untroubled incubators for the Liberal gripe. Very rigorously they had kept troublemakers out. Yet *hubris* overcame them. Thinking they could still maintain tranquillity and homogeneous thought, they made the mistake of applying one of their social-engineering schemes, affirmative action, to their own domain. Were they wrong! Affirmative action opened the halls of ivy to hundreds of thousands of disagreeable fanatics, none of whom had a deep commitment to learning and many of whom seethed with contempt for the university and for Liberalism itself. The campuses became centers for fanaticism with the women of fevered brow becoming the campuses' ascendant fanatics.

Occasionally I would speak at universities during these days just to measure the extent of the damage. The morbidity was everywhere, even in the athletic departments, where rancorous female coaches, usually lacking any genuine athletic achievement or even experience, would sit cheek-and-jowl with male coaches, many of whom had spent glorious youths on the playing fields and now were striving to become Vince Lombardis. Well, were they surprised.

Signs touting consciousness-raising stood out in abundance. Wife-beating was the topic of seminars, as was incest, which apparently had become a "real American problem"—not in Appalachia but in white, middle-class suburbia! Curiously, I can recall no seminars on sodomy or child molestation, but I did hear of many lectures on women's theretofore unacknowledged breakthroughs in science and the arts. There were even lectures on witchcraft. I recall chilling notices on how to avoid the campus rapist and where to report a prof's salacious smiles.

The most instructive encounters were with the lady profs. As with so many junior faculty in the 1970s they were usually rather stupid and as uncouth as a Russian airline stewardess. More to the point, most loathed intelligence, especially if it had been exhibited before 1963 and by the villainous male of the species. Mention any aspect of intelligent thought dating from before the feminist prof had arrived on campus, and her eyes would narrow into slits suggestive of machine-gun slits on armored personnel carriers. It was time to change the subject, but to what? Intelligent ideas were increasingly taboo. The feminists' imbecilic agitations were rapidly rendering the universities irrelevant to modern life and inimical to intellect.

Feminist enthusiasms were more disruptive to the university than the quack enthusiasms of any other minority group, so-called. They threatened every field of learning except for some areas of science, and they completely overwhelmed the humanities. Without any intellectual support whatsoever, they had become the new certitudes, irrefutable and sacred. From Marx the feminists had lifted the idea of false consciousness, and every time a male prof begged to differ he was put down as a mindless robot of "the white male power structure" in need of a consciousness-raising from these ruffians. The male profs could not even "establish dialogue," their favorite 1960s technique for soothing dyspeptic youth. By the late 1970s the male profs were whipped and confused. Sometimes the feminist profs would insist on all the rights and privileges of ladies. Other times they would insist on being treated like he-men. Always they demanded to be the center of attention. In their frustration many of the male profs became pathetic figures, whining unconvincingly that they too were now feminists. This merely pissed the feminists off all the more.

By the end of the 1970s feminism had burned through most of American society and begun to cool. On the campuses, however, it became well established along with all the other quaint manifestations of radicalized Liberalism so that universities were in danger of becoming little more than museums wherein were displayed the thoughts of the 1960s for curious tourists. There on campus feminism has thrived, inflaming the innocents with its key insight that civilization has been a male conspiracy—"the misogyny upon which Western civilization is based,"[1] as Professor Anne Barton called it. From this ignorant yawp all the nut arcanum of the movement has issued, and so in that august province where literacy and the liberal arts were once explicated, genital metaphysics and bathroom lore have gained a huge and revered prominence, leading to such ludicrous scenes as the following reported in the venerable *Cornell Daily Sun*:

> Rape gives man control of his vulnerable sexual self, feminist poet and writer Susan Griffin told her audience in Hollis E. Cornell auditorium Saturday.
> Speaking on "Rape and the Rape of Culture," she told the 100 people present, "This culture is profoundly ambivalent about sex." Ashamed of the body and nature, we try to control them with our culture, she said.
> But "sexuality is the moment of truth," since "the sexual act makes everyone feel vulnerable," she said. . . .
> "The fact that rape exists, changes our whole experience

of life. . . . It is a devastation whose dimensions we haven't begun to understand," Griffin said. . . .

Any system which treats women as separate beings contributes to rape, Griffin said. "Not having women in positions of equal power causes rape, not having women in tenured positions at this university causes rape," she said.[2]

Or consider this from Miss Suzanne Donovan, who took time out from her studies at the University of California at Berkeley and, via *The Berkeley Graduate* (now defunct), apprised the university community of a promising new direction in the women's movement:

Robin Kuhn is a dancer, works in a San Francisco cafe for financial support and acts out sadomasochistic (S/M) fantasies with her lover. She is also treasurer for Samois, a social and political club for lesbians exploring their S/M fantasies. . . .

Lesbian sadomasochism has been debated in lesbian and feminist circles since about 1975. Many women believe that lesbians and sadomasochists are antithetical to one another, that lesbian S/M is a violent manifestation of men's social domination and power over women. But Robin feels that by acting out these oppressive social and political relationships, they become less painful and burdensome.

S/M sex is highly ritualistic with partners choosing dominant or submissive roles. Robin said her most erotic fantasies are those that are closest to reality. She calls S/M sex "play," and said Samois women have a real sense of humor about themselves and their sexuality. She and her lover perform demonstrations for Samois women just beginning to experiment. "We're both exhibitionists," Robin said. "There's a lot of joking and everyone just laughs at the demonstrations."

. . . "Lesbians are still mommies and social workers, doing things for the rest of the world. One of the reasons we're so hated is that we're doing things just for ourselves."

The group first met in June, 1978, when the anti-pornography movement in San Francisco was gaining strength and lesbian S/M women felt pressure from other women objecting to S/M violence. . . .

At their meetings, one of the things Samois women talk about is how to enjoy S/M sex safely. Robin said she discourages women from taking too many drugs while playing and encourages them to tell their partners when it hurts and if it hurts them too much. "Our bodies can take a lot," Robin said. "Slapping, scratching, biting. If you have cysts, you don't use tit clamps, but you can take more than you think."

Robin said lesbians, as others in society, make too many assumptions and judgments about sadomasochists' lifestyles; "we're not some weird cult. . . ."[3]

It is my considered opinion that the Liberals of the New Age should have given a wide berth to these unhappy women. The facts are indisputable. Behavioral studies demonstrate that women have a peculiar proneness for what is called the persecution complex. They also have a peculiar emotional tenacity, a subtle strength that has allowed them to influence our lives profoundly, for instance, as Alexis de Tocqueville tells us, to shape mores.[4] By encouraging the complaint that womanhood was oppressed by "the white male power structure" the New Age Liberals ignited dangerous fires that will be burning for a long time. "I have spent too many years of my life," Leah Fritz shouted in *Thinking Like a Woman*, "too much of my energy, supporting the male ego. I have quietly tolerated macho in men while it sickened me to the point of vomiting. I no longer tolerate it in men. I puke openly. I have learned to puke at the government, at the police, at the FBI; later to puke at the Black Panthers and the Symbionese Liberation Army. Why should I tolerate a new form of macho in women? Eventually it will be directed at me. . . it always is."[5] White-hot women like Miss Fritz are not going to be easy to cool, and wherever they go they are going to leave a hell of a mess.

One of the unfortunate achievements of the New Age Liberals in the 1970s was the destruction of the American melting pot. In their compulsive hunt for suffering situations they fragmented American society, aggravating established ethnic and racial resentment and encouraging new, heretofore unimagined enmities. It took Europe centuries of civil and religious wars, class conflicts, and nationalistic struggles to arrive at its present arabesque of resentment. America did it in but a few prosperous years, and not by war or tyranny but by a mere act of bilious imagination. Now, Americans seethed against each other because of gender. Here was *casus belli* unknown even in the most remote reaches of the Balkans.

This is not to say that all Americans have lived harmoniously in the Great Republic. Certainly blacks have not, and they have had reason to resent particular groups and governments. But New Age Liberalism has magnified every complaint and inflamed every complainant, allowing the grousers a free hand to transform their hallucinations into burning national issues and to destroy America's sense of community.

In point of fact there never was a "white male power structure." The fabulous male-chauvinist pigs never took the field against the feminists anywhere. The women of the fevered brow marched forth, battle standards snapping in the breeze, TV cameramen in tow; but they warred against shadows. In New York City they trampled bouncers who for more than a hundred years had maintained the sex barrier at McSorley's Old Ale House. Soon hundreds of similarly august enclaves of male privilege fell. Laws that regulated female labor, the residue mainly of the Progressive Era, were overthrown, as the women of the fevered brow saw to it that their sisters be allowed to sweat and to grunt in heavy industry—the coal mines! the docks! garbage trucks! Ultimately, police and fire departments were ordered to drop strength and stamina requirements so that female cops could walk the beat and female firefighters could dangle from the hook-and-ladder truck.* The feminists tyrannized language and fashion—changing

---

* The citizens of Seattle, Washington, had to fork up $10,000 a head to strengthen each female fire-department candidate in preparation for her attempt at the fire department's physical test. When the women continued to fail, requirements were lowered. The State of Washington was probably paying less to turn out a college graduate than Seattle was paying to turn out inferior firefighters![6]

manholes into person holes, exiling the masculine pronoun, and so forth. They hid their legs with trousers only to expose their steatopygic rumps. They bravely unhitched their hellish bras. Still the fabled chauvinists would not take the field against them.

Truth be known, the chauvinists never existed, at least not in politically significant numbers. Professor Barton's findings were in error. There never was a masculine equivalent to the fierce National Organization for Women with its clever acronym. Nor were there many male chauvinists trumpeting male superiority, at least not beyond the walls of the loony bin. And just as it was inaccurate to speak of a "white male power structure," it was also inaccurate to speak of a "women's liberation movement." America is not a dictatorship. It has not been in need of a "liberation movement," and angry feminists have not been the friends of freedom anyway. Rather they have been intolerant authoritarians. One can argue for occasional reforms, especially if one is young and pious, but "liberation" goes too far.

The term that came into usage in the 1970s, "women's movement," was an even crasser misnomer. Better it would have been to call it "some women's movement." Most American women were not in sympathy with it; and anyway many had been banned from its precincts for fraternizing with the enemy and suffering the grim consequences: babies. Bearing children was particularly loathsome to the women of the fevered brow. They derided mothers and hated practically every manifestation of heterosexual affection. *Amour* with them is as improbable as a moment of silence. These unhappy women longed to be a certain kind of man, the kind that runs beauty parlors and, in San Francisco, dresses up for Halloween.

All these misnomers the Liberals indulged, because generally they sided with the feminist fervors. The "movement" had rapidly metamorphosed from a reasonable plea for equality of opportunity into a far-ranging critique of American life and government. It was, then, as profoundly radical as the anti-nuke movement.

Moreover, it was incoherent and garrulously irrational. In sum and *in fine*, the so-called women's liberationists were another of the New Age's misnomers. They furiously belabored a past that has never existed with arguments shaped more like bludgeons than like syllogisms. They were pests countenanced only by Liberals of the New Age who shared their hallucinatory visions of the future. Everyone else with any sense scrambled to get out of their way.

Contrary to feminist rants, the customs and laws that enraged them had not been handed down by an all-male dictatorship. They had been established and acquiesced to over generations not only by men but also by their wives, mothers, sisters, and lady friends. The democratic character of American law was not belied merely because the feminists had disinterred the complaints of a few ancient public nuisances. True, contemporary customs and laws had begun to pinch, but not because they had been passed by a misogynist elite or because of the feminists' agitations. Developments in the economy, in technology, and in birth control were allowing and occasionally forcing women into the work force. By the 1960s millions were leaving their homes to enter what had theretofore and usually of necessity been all-male preserves. Naturally there were not going to be enough women's washrooms. There was also going to be some prejudice; but there is often prejudice against newcomers. This was not misogyny but reality. Feminism misconstrued and exploited the anxiety of both sexes during a historic shift in American work habits. It spread myth and ignorance, leaving men and women more in the dark about their natures than at any time since the reign of Queen Victoria. The love life of the Republic was brought to flummox. Less amusing, America's children were denied important rights and amenities. Women's liberationists spread the notion that men and women must by nature haggle; the only peaceful family is one in which either the wife is enslaved or the husband is androgynous. As the haggling caught on the kids were abandoned, but in school they were indoctrinated into unisex. Reformers and revolutionaries alike are always quick to use their chisels and hammers on the brains of schoolchildren, and in the 1970s American schoolchildren were exposed to more quack indoctrination than at any other period in our history. No wonder by the 1980s vast areas of American life seemed to have experienced a massive loss of intelligence.

The ancient Greeks believed that the good society is the society that fosters the virtues. New Age Liberals and the feminists believe that the good society fosters equality. They abhor distinctions and yearn for sameness. It is illustrative of how low our intellectual life has sunk that the New Age Liberals and feminists imposed upon us the question "Are men and women equal?" by which they mean "Are men and women the same?" Through the ages intelligent people have raised the question only in sport. Only a humorless mind of the bleakest prosaism would take it seriously. Yet the third-rate minds infesting our public discourse have pondered it grimly.

In brief, the answer is obvious. All laboratory experiments on animals and humans demonstrate that male and female are not: they are not equal and they are not the same. They are different. Anyone with a few watts of common sense or but two of the five senses can distinguish male from female and rejoice in the findings. But in our age neither the findings of science nor those of common sense constitute admissible evidence where ideology holds sway, and so both science and common sense have been delicately circumvented by feminists busily adducing more and more preposterous arguments to sustain their claims of sexual sameness. Women, they insist, can endure more pain. They are emotionally stronger. They live longer. During Jimmy's reign feminists in the Pentagon argued that female soldiers, though lacking in "upper-body" strength, are superior in "lower-body" strength—presumably making them what? Sex symbols? More comely in retreat? Fine targets for bayonet charges? Any review of this credo of poppycock will leave the discerning mind convinced that the feminist adjudges all truly feminine women inferior to he-man males or—more appalling still—he-man females. The feminist always tries to argue that women should be men, rarely that men should be women.

The question of male and female sameness and all the slippery arguments that go with it would never have found a place in the public discourse were it not for the inescapable fact that New Age Liberalism has become obsessed with materialism and power, two of history's most reliable sources of corruption. Where the ancient Greek contemplated the virtues the New Age Liberal contemplates median income or the distribution of appliances; plus the race, creed, and "sexual orientation" of every elected or appointed official, every corporate officer, every plumber, coal miner, and operator of heavy-duty equipment. These are the concerns of our contemporary *philosophes*. To our Liberals the virtues are passé. The real question is how much bellowing and spending power does one have. Though the New Age Liberal still scowls at materialism, material terms are all he has for measuring the good society. He has fallen into the absurd condition of frothing alternately over America's high consumption of the earth's resources and over the inadequate number of color television sets in Bedford-Stuyvesant.

The Liberal of the New Age is incompetent to judge human worth. He lacks the tools and the wit. Because most women have not been quantifiable sources of wealth the Liberal must credulously accept the feminists' complaint that women are slaves and, when in the maternity ward, animals. Adrienne Rich pithily bespoke the feminist position in her great work *Of Women Born*: "The patriarchal institution of motherhood is not the 'human condition' any more than rape, prostitution, and slavery."[7] By the late 1970s all the lugubrious New Age faithful concurred.

Of course, in a better age better questions would interest the intelligentsia. Lively men and women might ask, *"How are men and women different?"* or "Are they equal in terms of virtue?" In a stupid age we ask stupid questions.

American women's estate has, as a matter of fact, been declining for decades—always they have been the victims of the reformers and of those heralding ideological revelation. The decline began in the 1920s when women's traditional source of power, the family, began to be subverted and held up to derision. The decline quickened in the post-war period, owing to the Republic's increasing absorption with materialism and power. Now only the traditional activities of men were adjudged worthwhile. Yet not until the rise of feminism was American womanhood confronted by an overtly hostile force. When feminism won acceptance as American womanhood's sole authoritative voice things had reached a critical stage. Not since the Rape of the Sabines had a country's women been placed in such mortal peril. The voices of American womanhood were suddenly drowned out by such howlers as Jane O'Reilly notifying *The Washington Star*, "Frankly, women are tired of being cast as madonnas or whores."[8] Viragoes like this could turn April in Paris into February in Siberia, which was pretty much what the typical feminist had in mind.

The vast majority of feminists were disagreeable misanthropes, horrible to behold, uncouth and unlovely. They were inferior women, contemptuous of the superior women, who through their charm and intellect have so often been able to establish such enviable lives for themselves: home, family, friends, ample leisure, *amour*, and so on. By contrast, the feminists have lived their whole lives in canvas underwear, burdened by a splitting headache, halitosis, body odor, and other ailments too terrible and obscure to mention. The gay and relatively unfettered lives of their more spirited and successful sisters have enraged them for decades, magnifying all their petty jealousies. In the 1960s and 1970s they sought with specious arguments to convince the Republic that life in a coal mine or contiguous to a desk was actually liberation. Very few traditional women were fooled, but their lives soon lost much of their gaiety. Aided by other preoccupations afflicting the intelligentsia, the feminists quickly imposed their obsessions upon our intellectual elites, especially judges, bureaucrats, and educators. Soon the full power of the state was bent to the task of knocking off the superior woman and getting her into the nine-to-five grind where she would have to sweat alongside her pissed-off inferiors.

Historically speaking, women have no reason to be ashamed of their record. Down through the ages they have borne several billion babies, of whom many have turned out decent and useful. They are responsible for millions of blissful morns and congenial evenings spent by the fire. True, they set off a few fabulous wars, but they are responsible for many more armistices signed by woebegone generals and diplomats, anxious to get the hell home. Though weaker and less savage than the male of the species, the female has endured handsomely. Far fewer women than men have gone down as casualties of brutality, stupidity, or even natural disaster. Far from being the pathetic slave that feminism has made her out to be, the female has actually been the slave driver, snaring an unsuspecting male, yoking him to a small army of indigents, and then appearing at the poor soul's deathbed to bid him adieu and see that all the insurance papers have been duly signed.* The true enemies of American womanhood in this century have been the Liberals and the reformers who have denied the superior woman her unique character and all the rights and privileges derived therefrom, preeminent among which is the right and privilege to maintain a slave.

The feminists' attempt to turn romance into a series of grim crimes is the final assault upon the superior woman's way of life, attempting as it does to end forever the amatory chase by which females since the earliest ages have controlled males and their own destinies. ("Control of our bodies," bah. That feminist demand is a horselaugh. The average American woman has actually controlled two bodies and sometimes more, usually by employing only one or two parts of her own.) What the feminist wanted was to bring down her better: to make it impossible for the charmer to charm; to render all women plain and disagreeable, all men impotent and afraid to tip their hats, open doors, send a dozen roses. In the New Age all women would be hags; this was the logical imperative of the feminist revolution. Long ago, that great humanist, H. L. Mencken, saw it all coming. Pursuant to their feminist goals, Mencken predicted that the 1920s feminists would have "to shave the heads of all the pretty girls in the world, and pluck out their eyebrows, and pull their teeth and put them in khaki, and forbid them to wriggle on dance floors, or to wear scents, or to use lip-sticks, or to roll their eyes. Reform, as usual, mistakes the fish for the fly."[9] During the 1970s most of these measures were minor desiderata on the feminist agenda along with some even more violent items. Only slowly did the

---

* By the late 1970s wives were outliving their husbands by nearly eight years, and sitting sumptuously on most of their accumulated wealth!

Republic's superior women become aroused, and then it was almost too late.

In America there has always been a market for a certain kind of cheap thought. It came with the inheritance bequeathed us from Northern European Protestantism, the Protestantism of the dissenting churches that idealized individual effort, believing in man's limitless capacity for self-improvement. Cheap thought glows through the work of Henry David Thoreau, who loitered around Walden Pond recording spasmodic thoughts that were as likely the product of his ague as of his intelligence. He produced vast quantities of cheap thought for Americans of the Liberal persuasion, but the capitalists too have had their oracles. The go-to-it philosophizing of Dale Carnegie is cheap thought and nothing more. Always cheap thought promises self-improvement, or personal growth, as the 1970s phrase had it. All that is necessary is to awaken the marvels reposing within. In past decades the awakening was usually provided by a bolt from the Gospels. More recently secular, scientific, and occult sources of prodigious variety have supplied the requisite cock-a-doodle-doo. Borrowing from the most advanced marketing techniques, and from the arcanum of sociologists, psychologists, and other such public nuisances, a huge herd of pontificators has prospered, lecturing us on how to refurbish and at times apotheosize ourselves: "There is a technique. It is a wisdom. I shall impart it to you. It will improve your marriage, your brats, your sense of well-being. It will make you slim, amorous, close to God."

In the post-war period dozens of varieties of trained therapists and counselors appeared to minister to our problems— family therapists, sex therapists, marriage counselors, job counselors, "life-skills" counselors. Millions of Americans, many of whom seem decidedly short on wisdom, make their livings by solving the problems or alleged problems of others. They are components of a growing service economy abundant in quacks. All have paved the way for the profusion of pontificators who appeared in the 1970s. Blending homespun advice with the jargon of pseudoscience and pop philosophy, the pontificators promised to counsel Americans on such discoveries as "the hyperactive child," "the burnt-out worker," "women's fear of success"—the list is capacious. They offered ontological refurbishment through diet, exercise, intoning gibberish, the smile, the stretch, the *word*. Some still favored the old-time religion. Others favored cults. Still others were content to merchant curious and readable analyses of the dreadful mess we are in. All packed a powerful jolt for the credulous and the scared. All to one degree or another have been gnostics like the late Dr. Freud—that is to say quacks who believe in the existence of a technique that will reveal a heretofore hidden system of knowledge capable of wondrous enlightenment.

By the 1970s these advocates of ontological refurbishment were everywhere, influencing the eminent, even influencing the Credo of Wholesome Progress. Tom Wolfe touched upon the phenomenon in his seminal work "The Me Decade and the Third Great Awakening," but he could have undertaken a twelve-volume study and still not have exhausted the available material. An institute could be established in Cambridge, Massachusetts, to monitor the condition with funds provided by the National Science Foundation. In fact, let me recommend it. Bearers of cheap thought are everywhere, even on American campuses. They are a legitimate object of intellectual curiosity. Let the scholars fall on them. They lecture to the Rotary and on campus. Some serve as adjunct professors and occasionally even hold some sort of bogus chair: Hiram H. Seagrams, Professor of Social Growth and Phantoms, Xerox Professor of Technology and Infrastructure; Phyllis R. Smelly, Professor of Well-Being. They publish books, many of which appear on the nonfiction best-seller lists for months and even years.

Once its leftist politics and simple human malice have been fumigated, feminism is in essence part of this colossal outburst of personal-growth philosophizing. This is not surprising: many of the leftists of the 1960s and 1970s were very congenial with cheap thought. In fact, the New Leftists' vulgar version of Marxism was shot through with it, and once their Marxist cheers lost their glamour many an ambitious leftist turned up as a sucker or an entrepreneur in the self-improvement industry: Rennie Davis of the Chicago Seven announcing "There's a practical method to end poverty, racism, sexism, imperialism" and becoming a follower of the Rev. Maharaj Ji, Spiritual Master of the Divine Light Mission;[10] Jerry Rubin going through Esalen and yoga; Eldridge Cleaver, after many new editions, a Moonie; Tom Hayden launching fat-removal manuals with his wife, Jane, and evangelizing for wholesome foods —"It is a way of life," Jane declaims. Even the Marxism of the Rev. Jim Jones was overwhelmed by cheap thought, which influenced his rants far more profoundly than did the Gospels. Practically all the New Left's molls eventually transformed themselves into feminists, assertiveness training having replaced prior instruction in small-arms training and the proper construction of Molotov cocktails.

There they all were, back in the belly of Amerika. Were they fetched there by the dark force of the profit motive or by the eternal American lure to mumble gibberish from the lectern? I give up. At any rate, there they were: New Leftists, women's libbers, side by side with Maharishi Mahesh Yogi, Werner Erhard from est, Guru Maharaj Ji, the Bible-pounding reborn, the vegetarians, the yogaists, the desperate joggers —and forget not Dr. Leo Buscaglia, indefatigable propounder of the hug. Dr. Buscaglia's career is emblematic of a relatively benign species of cheap thought, far removed from that of the evil Rev. Jones but still in the great tradition of pontification and personal renewal.

Beginning, not surprisingly, as an assistant professor of special education at the University of Southern California, Dr. Buscaglia rose to become an enormous draw on the lecture circuit with his message that "the psychological benefits of hugging are just now being discovered. It changes your chemistry toward positive things."[11] He was a natural for the best-seller list, for his prose style was hypnotic. In a decade, more than 1.5 million copies of his first best-seller, *Love*, went to his questing, clutching followers. By 1982 he had written eight more masterpieces including *The Fall of Freddie the Leaf*, which when it began its rise up the *New York Times* best-seller list was described thus: "The seasons of life as experienced by a leaf and its companions: a parable."[12] The women's liberation movement had no Rev. Joneses that we know of; but it had a lot of Dr. Buscaglias, its most enduring and illustrious being Betty Friedan.

Friedan had two great gifts that distinguished her from her fellowesses, as a foundation garment is distinguished from a foundation. She was not insane; doltish perhaps, but not insane. In addition to that rare asset, she knew how to adjust her spiel to change—George Washington Plunkitt's saying could have been her saying: "I seen my opportunities and I took 'em."[13] Plunkitt's opportunities were vouchsafed by the corporations, the trusts, and government. Friedan's, despite all the decades separating them, were from about the same sources plus the Ford Foundation and a few trendy university faculties. So astute was Friedan in squeezing opportunities during the 1960s and 1970s that the historically minded can almost plot the changing fortunes of feminism by her utterances alone right down to her 1982 bombshell, a bull in favor of pregnancy. Abounding in unreadable jargon, Friedan prospered on the feminist tide.

What she really thought about it I am not sure. She was dead set against the giant corporations, the villainous Republicans, Kiwanis, Rotary, every manifestation of America's Junker class. However, apart from this ritualistic leftishness the true Friedan remains hidden beneath a mound of protean pontification. She was a founder and first president of NOW. She had a hoof in the establishment of the First Women's Bank, which was shaky from the start, plus the National Women's Political Caucus, the International Feminist Congress, the Economic Think Tank for Women, and a dozen or so other bizarre operations.[14] Always, throughout the New Age, this daughter of Mr. and Mrs. Harry Goldstein of Peoria, Illinois, advanced. Though certified solely with a B.A. from Smith College, she became a visiting professor in sociology at Temple University. Subsequently she held forth at the New School for Social Research, Queens College, and venerable Yale. Even the United States Military Academy invited her to discourse; she admonished the assembled warriors to be "sensitive and yearning and vulnerable."[15] Friedan was also a

Senior Research Associate at the Center for the Social Sciences at Columbia, and the Ford Foundation too recompensed her outbursts.

Hers is not the record of a lunatic, and let us here declare and render evidence for what has thus far been only suggested, to wit: except for those who were swindling the credulous, most of Friedan's associates were quite mad. In more than two centuries of political high jinks the Great Republic has witnessed no other movement so consistently dominated by nuts. In comparison the Know-Nothing party was dignified and benign; so were the Prohibitionists, and even the hill-jack Methodists. A catalogue of the loud ideas rising and falling during the years of feministmania will make the most amusing and outlandish reading since Rabelais. Rabelais's work was fiction. The feminists, however, desired to be taken as women of ideas, adepts of social science or political philosophy. The sobering fact is that many were. Their core lunacy—that women and men are the same—is now propagandized in the schools and etched into the laws of the land.

Friedan's tolerance for her sisters has been amazing. My guess is that she found some of their hallucinations very plausible. Did she believe with Susan Brownmiller that rape is fundamental to all male–female contact? Some of the ladies judged their petite dimensions a consequence of the "white male power structure." What did Friedan think, and where did she stand on her private parts? Many feminists believed that theirs would have been convex where now they were concave, and pilose where now hairless, were it not for the countless oppressions they had suffered from you know who.

The lunacy of American feminism is a matter curiously ignored by the pundits. Many feminists believed that twelve thousand years ago women ruled the earth, that war exists because men head governments, that witchcraft is the true religion of all enlightened gals. Every month such hysteria was proudly published in *Ms.* magazine, the feminist magazine launched to overthrow *Ladies' Home Journal* and all the other traditional women's magazines catering to women's domestic tastes. *Ms.* ignored these tastes, published feminist tracts, and contained almost none of the kind of advertisements seen in traditional women's magazines. What ads *Ms.* did run were curious, coming mainly from cigarette companies, automobile companies, and every booze merchant ever heard of. Now, there is a coincidence for you: *Ms.*'s advertisement revenue has come mostly from the same sources that have always been the mainstay of *Playboy* and other male porn magazines. But *Ms.* hated *Playboy.* What gives? Is the coincidence sheer chance or significant of some primeval lusts common to both audiences? I urge further scholarly investigations.

Unfortunately, there were never enough booze-swilling, nicotine-stained harridans to support *Ms.* and eventually it hoisted the white flag, retreating from the competitive wars of the free market and declaring itself a tax-exempt foundation.[16] The evidence of feminism's limited appeal was mounting.

Ms. has, however, served a useful purpose. In its pages almost all the insanity of feminism was proudly displayed. Most of the aforementioned feminists appeared there along with many others. Inspect the evidence further.

The July 1972 issue published this piece of social analysis: "Body Hair: The Last Frontier" by Harriet Lyons and Rebecca W. Rosenblatt, wherein the gals divulged that "The implication that a woman's underarm and leg hair are superfluous, and therefore unwanted, is but one embodiment of our culture's preoccupation with keeping women in a kind of state of innocence, and denying their visceral selves. . . . While our puritanical attitude makes the hairless female body the quintessence of femininity, our obsession with cleanliness works to modify the acceptance of hairiness even in men. Long hair and beards are for dirty hippies. The clean-shaven and the crew cuts satisfy the American ideal."[17]

Here is what a reviewer said of Andrea Dworkin's *Our Blood: Prophecies and Discourses on Sexual Politics* in February 1977: "She scrutinizes historical and psychological issues, including female masochism, rape, the slavery of women in 'Amerika,' and the burning of nine million witches during the

Middle Ages. Then she calls for—insists upon, really—a complete cultural transformation, the rooting out of sex roles from our society."[18] And here is the authentic sound of Miss Dworkin herself in December 1976: "In fucking and in reproduction, sex and economics cannot be separated. The man takes a body that is not his, claims it, sows his so-called seed, reaps a harvest—he colonializes a female body, robs it of its natural resources, controls it, denies it freedom and self-determination so that he can continue to plunder it, moves on at will to conquer other land which appears more verdant and alluring. Radical feminists call this exclusively male behavior 'phallic imperialism' and see in it the origin of all other forms of imperialism."[19]

Nor was the insanity limited to *Ms.* writers. A sizable number of *Ms.* readers were even madder, as a perusal of its correspondence columns indicates. Many of their letters were collector's items. In August 1976 a virago from Toronto writes: "Ahhh! The joys of womanhood in a sexist society! To have the power to turn men to mush by virtue of our 36DD breasts. Now that's strength! How elevating it was to read, in a feminist publication, such insightful and comforting affirmations. Yes, men do judge a woman's attractiveness by the amount of fatty tissue that is piled up on her chest. . . . Yes, big 'tits' can be a woman's most valuable possession, and should be exploited to their fullest extent. Yes, there is some discomfort involved: the inconvenience of wearing 'disguises,' the painful bursting of your illusion when you discover your leg man really wanted 'knockers' all the time. 'Sex objects,' you say, 'depersonalization,' 'degradation'? Why with all the attention our big tits attract, who has the time to notice?"[20]

In November 1976 another of the sisters theorizes: "No woman is truly free to be anything until she is also free to be a lesbian."[21] Lesbianism had become an important feminist lifestyle. Feminist logician Martha Shelly writes that "If hostility to men causes Lesbianism then it seems to me that in a male-dominated society, Lesbianism is a sign of mental health."[22] It is also the sign of a woman who wants to keep her private parts especially private. Scortatory lesbians are almost as rare as scortatory octogenarians, and the typical lesbian is the New Age equivalent of the old maid. But let us return to the correspondence section. In August 1977 a feminist philologist asserts: "Why is it important for women to use 'dirty words'? . . . to *defuse* them. . . . And it's fun, after all these years of proper servitude to a restrictive language code, to bounce them all over the walls and hear not only their echoes but the shockwaves . . . take the power to hurt from the particular vocabulary list. In fact, fuck it!"[23]

Weighing one howl with another, however, I believe history was made in December 1982 when the movement's first militant bed wetter appeared: "As a woman who only recently began to have 'heavy spurting emissions during intercourse,' I am grateful for the research being done. First, I'm not a freak, and second, no uninformed doctor will be able to talk me into surgery to correct 'urinary incontinence'—as they've done to ejaculatory women for years. There is nothing wrong with our enjoying sex more, and I, for one, am glad I found my spot. Having this additional way to experience orgasm has enhanced my sexuality 1,000 percent. Although some men are turned off by messy gushes (where do they get off anyway?), I wouldn't go back to dry orgasms for anyone.—Name withheld."[24]

Feminism by the late 1970s had become an *omnium gatherum* of dementedness, abhorring all men who were not androgynous and all women who were not feminist and preferably nulliparous. The key to understanding the women of the fevered brow is that the movement abhorred nature. Werner Dannhauser saw it whole when he asserted in the early 1980s that "The resentment of nature is the key to the women's movement. It explains its alliance with the Left, which cannot be due to the way women are treated in countries calling themselves Marxist. It explains the movement's grim mood, the absence in it of humor, and of gratitude for the world we inhabit. It also explains why the women's movement may begin by promoting sexual equality, but forever bends in the direction of assaulting sexuality as such. It is as forthrightly sexual beings that we are most natural."[25] Ultimately, feminism was a doomed movement. It was touched with madness, and it was futile. Nature cannot be obliterated by rhetoric. It cannot even be obliterated by storm troopers and holocaust. Nature endures.

Feminism could influence wide areas of American law and custom, but it could not claim finally to have triumphed, for it never reached agreement on precisely what it wanted. It was, alas, incoherent. It claimed that men and women were the same but acted as though women—feminist women!—were superior. Alternately it would demand equality, then privilege. It claimed to be democratic but lost on the democratic front and had to rely on every undemocratic expedient short of *coup d'état*. Having failed to shove the Equal Rights Amendment through the more representative state legislatures by 1978, the feminists returned to the less democratic Congress to devise a four-year extension. Once again the ERA failed to gain the three additional states needed, and now it began to lose states. Despite all the votes across America required to defeat the ERA, somehow the feminists convinced the media that the ERA was the victim of a conspiracy. During all its palmy days, the movement had resorted to pressure tactics on friendly government bureaucrats and the judiciary to becloud the truth and to deny elementary freedoms, for instance: freedom of association, and in such harmless activities as Little League, no less.

Bully tactics were its forte, and by the late 1970s it had settled into that one citadel where bullying is so frequently seen and admired, the university. Having failed to win the hearts and minds of the superior women it would now propagandize them from tenured positions. Already the movement had intimidated the publishers of dictionaries and reference books, who now fell in with an authoritarian cabal to "desex" the English language, turning it into an Orwellian instrument for further indoctrination.

How authoritarian had the movement become? Authoritarian enough to hold ceremonies such as the following, without shame or memory of the spectacle's antecedents: "Baltimore's First Unitarian Church had a symbolic book-burning yesterday," the Baltimore *Sun* reported on October 5, 1981,

". . . in which centuries of Jewish, Christian, Islamic and Hindu writings were 'expurgated' because of sections described as 'sexist.' . . . Nine women—some in dressy gowns, others wearing pants—filed to the altar from the congregation and read 11 'sexist' passages aloud in turn, adding their commentary."[26]

Surely Friedan noticed the feminists' collapsing fortunes at the polls, for by the end of the 1970s her pontifications had changed markedly. Having begun her reign as bogus sage in 1963 with a book condemning the idealized concubinage of womanhood in suburbia (*The Feminine Mystique*), she ended with a new bugaboo, "the feminist mystique" whose aversion to the family had played right into the hands of Ronald Reagan and "the far right." The solution, Friedan wrote in 1981, was a "second stage." Her 1980s tome *The Second Stage* was vintage cheap thought: execrable prose, pop sociology, pontifications, and endless nostrums for personal growth. Friedan was now for "the choice to have babies." She had discerned "that core of women's personhood that is fulfilled through love, nurture, home." The family "is the nutrient matrix of our personhood." Thus the second stage must be "generative" and observant of "the grounding . . . realities of daily life." The male chauvinists, however, were not going to be allowed a counterrevolution, for the second stage would be lived in strict accordance with what she called the "Beta mode." That is the feminist mode, characterized by prodigious "synthesizing, into intuitive, qualitative thinking" that comprehends the "relational."[27] There you have her findings. After almost two decades Friedan remained a master of cheap thought.

Since the 1960s this dreadful gasbag and her lunatic sisters had harangued an entire generation of young women and left millions of them miserable. Housewives were harried by doubts and embarrassments about their way of life. Would-be mothers and housewives were now scrimmaging for their daily grub, some in tony professional careers, but most in far less prestigious jobs. It was a spectacle to fortify every misogynist in the Republic, for though the working gals had multiplied in numbers they had not multiplied in any achievements not directly tied to politics and to government coercion. What is more, in some areas of endeavor—for instance, international athletic competition—American women had lost their edge to the women of the least liberated lands of all. Now they began complaining that their Eastern-bloc counterparts, owing to huge injections of hormones and steroids, were almost indistinguishable from male athletes. Taking into account the whole feminist position, this complaint was particularly senseless. What the Eastern-bloc gals had achieved via endocrinology was precisely what the feminists had wanted and what hard-pressed American Liberals had tried to accomplish through the courts and the bureaucracies. One would have expected the feminists to be cheering Marxist-Leninist progress, but no—they were "pissed off" as always.

For the 1980s Friedan prescribed having babies.* Of course, those of her customers who since the early 1960s had been burning their bridges to the other half of the baby-making mystery might be a little impatient with this new departure. One's time for making a family comes and goes, and if a woman fouled things up properly with the opposite sex during Friedan's first stage, she might not be in any condition to participate in the second. Asking people to throw their lives into the pursuit of a quack abstraction was characteristic of 1960s and 1970s charlatans, and by the 1980s the casualties of this sort of pontification were mounting.

In July 1982, after the ERA expired, I expressed such skeptical thoughts in my syndicated column then carried in many of the Republic's major metropolises including Boston, Los Angeles, New York City, San Francisco, and Washington, D.C. With heavy heart I returned to my atelier to think of Mother and to await the hysterical fulminations in the correspondence columns. Surprisingly, the response was feeble—a few peeps signifying despondence and hurt feelings but none of the bloodcurdling yells so often heard in the 1970s. Frankly, *entre nous*, I was disappointed. Had all the women of the fevered brow finally turned themselves in to the mental-health

---

* So did another early feminist, the vastly more intelligent Germaine Greer. In her 1984 book, *Sex and Destiny*, she thumped for motherhood, babies, the extended family, and many more of civilization's necessities; but she remained pissed off to the point that it was still very difficult to say exactly what she really meant.

authorities? Had they vamoosed for the Isle of Lesbos, or the bedrooms prescribed by La Friedan—the latter can be fun! Whatever the cause, feminism in the early 1980s was not the ravening cause it had once been. Rather it became but one more of the accumulating mounds of weird false pieties observed in America by the disingenuous and the stupid.*

Weird false pieties? Yes; and as with all other aspects of feminism's rise and fall, ERA's expiry was reported weirdly in the media. Following the commentary one got the impression that the ERA had fallen victim to some dark immensity, inscrutable and implacable, albeit very Amerikan. No one in the media was able to describe its triumphant opponent in any detail whatsoever. The ERA's defeat is one of the few political losses in modern history covered almost exclusively from the campaign headquarters of the loser. Most news stories featured interviews with Mrs. Eleanor Smeal, NOW's chief potentate.

Smeal did identify her opponents. The forces against equality are large, she advised, and she named the Republican Party and "special corporate interests." There you have it: ERA was unhorsed by that corporate mafia that "profits massively from sex discrimination particularly on the local level."[29] Born of the lie that generations of American males had been perpetrating a conspiracy against females, the ERA was buried with the lie that the ghastly monstrosity called ERA had finally been destroyed in an ambuscade led by the Fortune 500. The truth was that through artifice and fury the feminists had succeeded in bringing down on "the corporate interests" and everyone else harsh policies such as quotas and reverse discrimination, moving the Great Republic from a land of opportunity to an ascriptive society where all honors, privileges, and jobs would be distributed according to physical characteristics rather than personal performance.

The facts were plain. With millions of dollars pouring into the pro-ERA coffers, with most of our elites supporting it,

---

* As false pieties go, those created by feminism probably did more violence to truth than most, a particularly flagrant example being a 1983 column begun by George Will with this preposterosity: "The ongoing emancipation of women is this country's finest social achievement."[28] Perhaps George forgot those millions of blacks who not long before could not even vote.

the pro-ERA forces were stymied for four long years, during which several states actually tried to rescind their earlier acceptance. What had happened? A truly grass-roots movement, abhorred in the media so strongly that it was almost never mentioned even in its hour of victory, had organized and won. Its members recognized the feminists for the mad radicals that they usually were. The movement was composed of mainstream Americans led by traditional women left cold by the feminists' vague utopia of endless litigations and bawlings. This anti-ERA movement was not the work of American males. For the most part, and much to their discredit, they ducked the pissed-off harridans. The anti-ERA movement was led by America's mothers. They knew the value of their kids, and did not share La Smeal's vision of the good life populated by female garbage-truck drivers, gung-ho gals sweating out the nine-to-five, and abandoned kids.

Those of us who know that life in America is best lived after 8 P.M. and in the company of a superior woman owe our mothers a lot. So do America's kids, the real casualties of feminism. Left behind in broken homes or in day-care centers by their careerist moms, they were the suffering situations of the 1970s for whom no one stood up until the very end. Throughout the 1970s, as adults elaborated ever more frivolous rights, the rights of America's children to decent homes and decent educations were ignored. Indeed the feminists seemed to equate kids with house pets, and so imbecilic had the Liberals become in their conception of family life that they were allowing lesbian couples to claim the right to possess a child as though it were a piece of property. In California the country's first feminist clinic talked of lesbians' giving birth after artificial insemination, as though any adult had a right to a cute little human being, the care of which was no more demanding than caring for a potted plant. Now a new breed of human could be raised. Feminism could be passed on through the ages. But what kind of kids would these be? Was the traditional family of mothers and fathers really unnecessary or, as many utopians thought, the cause of our unjust society? The growing incidence of social problems associated with the kids of fatherless homes suggested the opposite.

7

The Enthusiasm for the Faraway

*From Uniworld to the Third World:
The Resentment, The Confusion,
and The Derangement*

IN those magistral realms where the great work of transforming the world into Uniworld was initially excogitated and is
now monitored, is Dr. Gunnar Myrdal often thought of as one
honey of a cheerleader? I think not. Sociologist, anthropolo-
gist, professor of economic development, and Swede, Dr.
Myrdal has long been esteemed as a visionary. He was an early
proponent of Uniworld; thus did he become a proponent of its
by-product that amazing New Age exemplar of virtue, the
Third World.

Yet ponder this: Sometime around 1960 someone slipped
Dr. Myrdal a manuscript entitled *Blossoms in the Dust* and
suggested that he compose its foreword. The book is a chronicle of Kasum Nair's yearlong trek through the Podunks of the
Indian subcontinent. Nair had undertaken her fact-finding
tour during the 1950s when hope swelled for turning primitive
environs into modern Western societies and thereby achieving
Uniworld: an entire globe inhabited by pleasant souls, all
looking and acting precisely like Dr. Myrdal and his wholesome peers. Well, when given a book like this people like Dr.
Myrdal used to hold little festivals in their hearts, but did
they read the books? Had they visited the Podunks?

Nair had interviewed Indians from all walks of life so that
she might "assess the impact of development upon the indi-

viduals and communities involved."[1] She was an honest woman. She chronicled an appalling scene, peopled by a congeries of dim souls not one of whom really shared Dr. Myrdal's faith in Uniworld. Some opposed it violently. Others were no more capable of envisaging it than of mastering ancient Greek or performing the rumba. India, as *Blossoms in the Dust* made clear, would not become a land of instant Swedes. So tight was the hold of India's holy men, castes, and ignoramuses that it would be decades before India could even become a land of Arkansans. Nonetheless, when the time came for Dr. Myrdal to compose the book's foreword, the cheerleader in him leaped to life:

> As the Prime Minister of India, Jawaharlal Nehru, never ceases to stress, the problem facing the country . . . is how to bring about a social and economic revolution by peaceful means. India . . . moulding all her public life . . . national down to . . . local level. . . . framework of democracy . . . universal suffrage. The hope . . . reform . . . total remaking of social and economic relations . . . carried out by the people themselves . . . a minimum of direction . . . without resort to compulsion. . . . reforms need to be planned. . . . the planning should be democratic. . . . the welfare of the masses . . . its supreme goal. . . . done by the people . . . expresses their desires, ambitions, and needs. . . . compulsion is excluded. . . . Indian democratic planning . . . initiating a social process. . . . the masses . . . become increasingly motivated . . . improving their lot as individuals. . . . improving society by co-operative endeavor.[2]

Blah, blah, blah. The very book put the lie to the blah. Twenty more years of painful experiences in primitive lands were to emblazon the lie on the blah. Yet the blah endured. It gained adepts. Year after year at UNESCO, at the United Nations, at other such hot-air factories the blah was to grow more meretricious, prehensile, and brutal. Mankind, however, never outgrows its need for lies.

I cite the Swede Myrdal because his preachments were spermatic, and because his bubbly foreword to the depressing tale chronicled in *Blossoms in the Dust* superbly illustrates how oblivious the early proponents of Uniworld and the Third World have been to reality. In the West there has steadily grown an enthusiasm for lands faraway, but have any of the enthusiasts ever visited these lands? If so, were they squiffed?

In the main, of course, it was not Old World dreamers like Myrdal but dreamers from America who have been responsible for the balmy idea of a Third World. Heady with the fumes of idiot idealism, and unembarrassed by a colonial past, Americans at the end of World War II threw their enormous prestige behind the notion that there were developed and undeveloped worlds. The developed world included North America, Western Europe, Japan, and South Africa. Practically every other land was heaved into the Third World, though the USSR and its principalities were given a somewhat hazy classification—sometimes they were of the Third, sometimes not.

Eventually the proponents and adepts of Uniworld categorized about two-thirds of the human race as "undeveloped" and awaiting their ministrations. What lay ahead was the challenge of turning these peoples into sleek Westerners, then fusing all worlds into Uniworld. By the 1970s the adepts of Uniworld believed that the great work was well along, for a "world culture" was rapidly developing, coaxed into being by what a smiling Columbia University sociologist once described to me as "the imperative of the gonad." Yahoo! The mind lights up with visions of Kurdish herders experiencing the delights of Smith College's finest and most volupt. French industrialists leap into the arms of Andean milkmaids. A Cambridge scientist walks arm-in-arm with a gal from the suburbs of Ouagadougou. There you have it: progress through coitus heterogeneous. "ONE WORLD THROUGH WORLDWIDE ORGY"; what a bumper sticker that would make!

Uniworld and the Third World are concepts rooted deeply in the most fertile balderdash. There could never be a Uniworld, for nations would never voluntarily yield the required sovereignty and no Uniworld visionary could ever impose his dream militarily. The concept of a Third World is an even grosser delusion. In time it became hopelessly confused as the West's original condescension toward the primitives clashed with Western egotists' growing contempt for the West. By the 1970s Uniworld's proponents were steadily losing their confidence in Western values, yet they were ambivalent toward the primitives' traditional values; and so they pothered purposelessly atop hundreds of international do-good organizations, servicing the schemes of international con men and achieving little else.

Was life in the Zambian bush superior to life in Scarsdale? The aging proponent of Uniworld could not say. He seemed to thump for material improvement around the world, but without materialists. He wanted America without Americans. His enduring confusion is to be seen in the ceaseless changes he has made in his nomenclature. At first there was the undeveloped world, which became the underdeveloped world, then the developing world, then the lesser-developed world, then the South. No one really knew what to call it, probably because it had never really existed. All that really existed was the blah, but as the blah spread, ill-assorted leaders throughout the non-Western world were persuaded that they were the great potentates of the "Third World," and they lined up to claim from the West their just deserts, namely bundles of gold Rolex watches, gold pen-and-pencil sets—and huge quantities of military hardware with which to butcher each other.

By the late 1970s the potentates of Podunk were frequently at war. Most could hardly feed their citizens but they eagerly equipped their armies with the most modern weaponry so that they might wage war more ferociously than ever before. Terrorists supplied by them were even bringing violence to the West. If the terrorists or one of the more violent non-Western powers could ever lay hands on nuclear weaponry they might even be able to blow up the planet. These were the great days for the clients of Uniworld; and, goaded and dazzled by the blah, they soon overcame their diversity to form at least a kind of Third World, a mass of nations characterized by a hankering for the West's foreign aid and by two evolving habits of mind: The Confusion and The Resentment.

The Resentment was resentment of the erstwhile colonial

powers that had wiped out cholera and cannibalism; that had introduced pants and shoes; that, *in fine*, had brought modernity to peoples who apparently wanted to wait and see what their own indigenous Bronze Ages might one day be like. Would Tonga ever develop an Athens or a Rome? What might the Zambian Aristotle say, and when would an Aeschylus pop up in Burundi? All these long-awaited dis-coveries were obviated when the colonial powers barged in with their quacks and their pettifoggers. Admittedly, some of the Third World *enragés* lived in the ruins of what had once been high cultures, but these civilizations went to seed long ago, and despite all the boodle extracted from the West there were no signs of a Hindu Renaissance or of cultural rebirth anywhere else in the so-called Third World except perhaps in Islam, where cultural vigor did stir anew as the galoots began slaughtering their fellows with an avidity reminiscent of the glory days of Suleiman the Magnificent.

Eventually The Resentment focused on one colonial power beyond all others: the United States of America, oppressor of Puerto Rico and irrepressible matrix of foreign aid, technical assistance, health services, the Peace Corps, and uppity women whose professional ministrations you can be sure raised a few eyebrows among the yokels of every Third World backwater. The Union of Soviet Socialist Republics never sent out a Peace Corps. It sent out tanks and chemical and biological weapons, nipping in the bud any possible resentment. The United States sent foreign aid; and against Uncle Sam The Resentment grew incandescent, receiving its most eloquent articulation at the United Nations, where the Third World governments expressed their pain and frustration by voting against the United States as often as possible, abominating Israel, and amassing colossal accumulations of parking tickets.

The last-cited phenomenon is a political manifestation that has received scant consideration in the scholarly journals of Western Liberals. Yet here are some portentous facts. In 1980 alone, Cuba accumulated the prodigious total of 5,888 unpaid parking violations, with one diplomatically immune Cuban personally accounting for an amazing 651. Not even Nigeria, with 4,016, surpassed the Cubans, though 4,016 is an eloquent statement. Nonetheless, on the basis of the number of cars in their respective missions Angola was probably the preeminent delegation of scofflaws, with 227 tickets per car, followed by the Cubans (190) and Senegal (163).[3] The thing cries out for further analysis.

As for The Confusion, it is something altogether more subtle and exceptional. V. S. Naipaul and his brother Shiva have become its most authoritative chroniclers. The Confusion is that uneasiness that hits every yahoo in jerkwater once word of America spreads to his dusty burg. Let him hear of the folkways and mores observed in Hollywood, California, and the grim sonorities of the Prophet will never curl his hair quite so tightly again. Once a Coca-Cola vending machine or the golden arches of McDonald's have been raised above the bush, neither grubs nor caterpillars will taste so savory; immerse them in the choicest grease—it will do no good. Once the wireless has been installed and the TVs are in place, news from godless and gorgeous America will unsettle every swarthy mullah, every fuliginous patriot, and all the *caudillos* of Patagonia. Whether a village eminence is blessed with a wife as strong as a water buffalo or a dozen nubile and marketable daughters, there will still be days when he secretly sighs beneath the burning sun and dreams of discoing like mad in nocturnal Manhattan. The Confusion afflicting the regions of the Third World, then, is that uneasiness which comes when modernity whirls toward lands that are not yet modern and in some cases not even medieval.

Throughout the Third World almost everyone takes pride in his ancient ghosts and goblins. All extol the timeless rhythms of their antique cultures and disdain the corruptions of the foul West. Nevertheless, word of Uncle Sam's fleshpots still diverts. People on every rung of the Third World ladder want to know more, and this creates problems. Fundamentally, the source of The Confusion resides in that searching question so presciently raised by Sam Lewis and Joe Young in the title of their 1919 cantata "How You Gonna Keep 'Em Down on the Farm After They've Seen Paree?"

The Confusion can be observed right here in America, where it scrambles the brains of all the mediocre graduate students sent by Third World governments to make off with the American magic. Watching them brood pays double dividends, instructing us at first hand in the dementia brought on by The Confusion and occasionally introducing us to the future eminences of far-off lands. After all, these dolts cannot remain on American campuses forever. Once they have spent a quarter of a century or so pursuing their degrees in tele-communications they grow restless. By then they have clipped as many lingerie ads from the newspapers as can possibly be smuggled home to their agape and unshaven countrymen. They have admired the work of Thomas Crapper. They have chased and enraptured herds of ugly coeds with tales of the family Taj Mahal back home. They chew gum and suffer no side effects. There was a time when they were always swallow-ing the stuff or getting it in their hair. Now they chew smoothly and rarely even bite their tongues. The galoots are now educated and can return home to take up responsible positions . . . or, as luck might have it, be beaten to death in one of Utopia's dungeons or in a bongo drum. After all, the proverbial rat race is run in the Third World too, and fre-quently it is won by real rats.

Let me not be misperceived. Certainly not all Third Worlders are mediocrities. Some obviously are people of sound character and high intelligence. An astounding number, how-ever, are third-rate, and whether they attend Harvard or Slip-pery Rock they are amazingly vulnerable to The Resentment and The Confusion.

Actually matriculation at an American university often worsens these third-raters' afflictions. The foreign grad student immures himself in his dormitory room, meditates on TV's melodrama and on radio's simian blare, visits Disneyland and Atlantic City. The brummagem sentiments that emanate from these sources bring on hallucinations and daft reveries. Soon the yokel is identifying with every celebrity and every vulgar enthusiasm. He returns to jerkwater confirmed in the belief that he has mastered the culture of Einstein and of Beethoven. No wonder his awe of the West is mixed with hatred. I am an American, true-blue; but I am also a scholar committed to the highest standards of objectivity. After carefully weighing the evidence I have arrived at the unhappy conclusion that one of the main sources of the Third World's miseries is us!

Upon seeing how a forthcoming trip to America transformed the gruff Leonid Brezhnev into a bundle of nerves, Henry Kissinger, in *Years of Upheaval*, notes: "It is one of the glories of our country that it seems endowed with a special, almost magical quality even to its adversaries."[4] The quality is not magical at all; it is unnerving. America staggers the world by its stupendous energy, its enormous material achievements, its orgies of self-love and self-hate, its combinations of grandeur and sheer awfulness. All this overwhelms and lends to us the trappings of legend. Moreover, through the wizardry of electronics and the genius of marketing our culture has spread to the ends of the earth, tempting and subverting. An Iranian holy man excoriating American imperialism relies on canards picked up from our own naive press. A UN scofflaw threatening us with international law and the brotherhood of man reiterates the bromides of a deceased American idealist. A herder in a remote Southwest Asian valley about to blow a week's yogurt money probably will acquire among other treasures some artifact of American pop culture, perhaps a record; possibly he blows a year's yogurt money and buys a record player.

The Third World lives off the West. It would not exist were the West not out there to shout at and to swindle. After a journey through Islam, V. S. Naipaul offers his perception of The Confusion: "All the rejection of the West is contained within the assumption that there will always exist out there a living, creative civilization, oddly neutral, open to all to appeal to."[5] Naipaul illuminates this ambivalent parasitism with amusing cameos. In Teheran the Rev. Khomeini's dirty-necked galoots are seen peddling Western-made cassettes that carry the master's anti-Western tirades. Khomeini himself sends forth Islamic warriors in American F-15s somewhat in need of a tune-up. And then there are the last days of Maulana Maudoodi, the patron saint of Pakistani fundamentalism. The maulana had preached rejection of the West. Yet when he heard God's final call, he booked the first flight to

Boston, and in a spotless hospital, surrounded by the most advanced instruments of Western science, he reluctantly became a ghost. Naipaul solemnly marks his passing: "Of the maulana it might be said that he had gone to his well-deserved place in heaven by way of Boston; and that he went at least part of the way by Boeing."[6]

The ambivalent parasitism of Islam pervades all of the Third World. Wherever The Resentment and The Confusion fester one finds this parasitism, and it is not only Western technology that is fed upon. In the Third World the West's higher values are the warp and woof of oratory; but the West's coarser tastes, manifested so garishly in American pop culture, are the subject of lewd reverie. The West's higher values duly parroted can bring excellent returns to Third World leaders working the foreign-aid angle. Every Third World panjandrum is in agreement on this. Yet the benefits of American pop are less widely agreed upon. While the flotsam and jetsam adore it, some leaders have come to loathe it.

I stand with them. Their mullahs and witch doctors are right on the money. American pop culture is mischievous. It ought not to be admitted into their pristine realms. For that matter it ought not to be admitted into any of the Great Republic's fifty states. But what can we Americans do? There is the First Amendment, and so we have to suffer the inroads of the Hollywood intelligentsia, the New York promoter, and the cheap publishing conglomerates.

Hollywood, American broadcast media, and most of the giant publishing houses have all converged to turn out popular arts and fashions that are almost barbaric. Reinforcing one another's crassest impulses, they market a lurid fantasy composed of their foulest creations—a book based on a movie, a movie based on a murder, T-shirts and calendars and posters based on all the above—America's interlocking media have created a kind of dope that sets its customers apart and nearly moronic, hallucinating on the Gringo Fantasy. No wonder Third Worlders love the stuff. No wonder their leaders are alarmed. But the dispiriting fact is that many of these giants are themselves addicted to our media dope. Truth be known, there is hardly a George Washington in the Third World who would not like to take a few weeks off and go on a clandestine mission to the haunts of Dr. Hunter Thompson.

Think of it! The global village is here! Over thousands of godforsaken miles American media dope is borne thanks to the horrible devices of mass communications. It is beamed into the most remote jungle hamlets. State radio and television broadcast American songs and TV reruns. Vendors sell posters of movie stars, rock-star T-shirts, memorabilia from every trashy pop event imaginable. "Sock It to Me," "Tell It like It Is"—all the inscrutable patois of American pop culture eventually is carried to the farthest reaches of the Third World. In an African river community Joan Baez wails through the night turning a hard-bitten Indian merchant into a melancholy lump. Old copies of *Newsweek* and *Vogue* are treasured. Even behind the Iron Curtain, where American hedonism is damned by virtuous comrades, the picture of a callipygian beauty encased in Levi's is a treasure and the Levi's salesman a god. American soap operas, ancient prime-time masterpieces, the works of 100-percent-plastic Yankee memorabilia, penetrate where no CIA agent would dare to go. Just as in America, the dope plays upon the acedia of the locals. It subverts some, causing them to snicker at old myths. It stirs up others, leaving them snarling with bellicose illusions. Whether in America or in the Third World, American popular culture leaves in its wake herds of vicarious movie stars, rock singers, professional athletes, all from the Gringo Fantasy.

America has never won the hearts and the minds of the villagers with its technical experts or even its social workers, yet one species of Yank triumphs wherever standards are low and life is dull: the disc jockey! His world-view is admired where America is reviled. He is the mentor for every would-be wisenheimer. Bombastic, juvenile, hysterical, sentimental, sleazy—he is emulated and adored. Here is a piece of cultural imperialism unforeseen even by V. I. Lenin.

V. S. Naipaul, the inveterate traveler, has had countless encounters with the addicts of American media dope. In faraway Rawalpindi, he meets Syed, the self-absorbed son of a devout Moslem, who speaks sententiously about his vast knowledge of the declining West. Syed once spent a year in England, and there he became an avid reader. Harold Robbins, Pearl Buck, Ian Fleming all were devoured. *Time*'s bestseller list was gospel. He watched Perry Mason studiously, and read twenty books from the Perry Mason canon. He read thirty sex books, "to become stable," and he confides to Naipaul that people unfamiliar with such monographs become "overexcited" when they suddenly come across one. Next they reach for *Playboy*. Not the learned Syed; those thirty books cured him. "I also read sex books of the academic sort. *Married Happiness*. That kind of thing."

Syed also applies himself to the tone art. "In between all these books I got into pop songs and Western music. . . . Not the rock-and-roll noisy types. But the ones that really carried a message. . . . I liked very much the Carpenters. . . . They sing about basic innocence." Syed ponders the songs about "beliefs," by which he means "Like doing something because you really believe in it. Like love. Basics." "Basics," to Syed, meant "Relating to people. The innocence. People are always trying to trick people. The victims and the hypocrites. Everywhere you see the big-fish–small-fish thing. Big countries trying to dictate to the small countries. . . . They tried to do it in Iran."

Naturally such a sap writes poetry:

> *The hypocrite sounds like a lark*
> *the bite is worse than the bark*
> *A hypocrite may appear fearless and bold*
> *all that glitters is not gold.*

How many of these gibbers poor Naipaul had to endure I do not know, but before he could vamoose or slit his wrists this dunderhead imparted his masterpiece, "The Big Black Man" [Muhammad Ali, naturally]:

> *. . . who wouldn't break a twig*
> *but at one blow can fell a tree. Do you dig?*[7]

Shiva Naipaul, having read "the broken grammar, the fractured, nebulous prose" of revolutionary Guyana's political tracts, and having seen the decaying facade of its Third World

"Showcase" projects—so costly in development dollars but so valuable to the local grafter—laments that it all seems "to hint at a kind of universal mental retardation."[8] In his despair he has come very close to a summation of The Confusion and The Resentment. He would, however, have done better had he used the term universal mental derangement. What he observes in the violence and incoherence of Third World radicalism is possibly a deficiency but more likely an insanity. What is unassailable, however, is the universality of the phenomenon, for the Third World revolutionary twaddle of the 1970s had adherents even in the West.

The Third Worlder and the New Age Liberal ultimately came to agree. Both had wearied of the harum-scarum of Western progress. Both would settle for mediocrity. The noble savage had his champions whether in Zaïre or in Cambridge, Massachusetts. It is illustrative of the universality of this derangement that, as the Carter administration reached to embrace Third World revolutionaries and the revolutionaries scowled back, both were immersed in the works of pinheads such as E. F. Schumacher, Alvin Toffler, and Ivan Illich.

Many of the third-rate minds that left American graduate schools for their homes in Podunk and many of the third-rate Americans who thrilled to the election of Jimmy Carter found the poppycock of *Small Is Beautiful, Future Shock, Deschooling Society*, and other such works of pidgin thought very soothing. They were bewildered by Western science and technology, and they longed for a respite from change. Then too, the Third Worlders were in need of an alibi for their apparent backwardness. By dwelling upon the portentous bromides of these infantile thinkers both groups could take leave from the appalling realities rising up in the Third World, where unimaginable brutality was increasing, apace with pervasive corruption. Theretofore prosperous European colonies were sinking into abysmal poverty.

After the 1980 election Theodore White asked a detumescent Jimmy Carter what he viewed as his lasting presidential achievements. His answer exemplified the meaninglessness into which Liberalism had sunk. "Emphasis on human rights" was the Wonderboy's staggering reply. "[I] printed that commitment on worldwide consciousness."⁹ Alas and egad! While he was orating like a schoolmarm, horrors of a kind not experienced in Africa and Southeast Asia in more than a century were becoming commonplace. Chemical and biological warfare was being practiced by the Soviet Union and its clients. Genocide was again a reality. Meanwhile Jimmy lectured to the Chileans, the South Koreans, and the Argentines; and he came to be viewed as a pest by the Soviets.

Jimmy was managing the amazing feat of rendering human rights dubious and absurd before the world. His secretary of state was Cyrus Vance, a statesman as prepossessing as a hamster. His representative to the Third World was Andrew Young, a periphrastic maniac, who knew every Third World canard and had a grand old time hurling them all back at America's White Anglo-Saxon tyranny. "I don't believe that Cuba is in Africa because it was ordered there by the Russians. I believe that Cuba is in Africa because it really has shared in a sense of colonial oppression and domination," Andy asseverated when informed that Cuban troops were patrolling the Dark Continent and shooting any African trying to unhorse a Marxist regime. The Cubans, he insisted, were "basically doing technical assistance."¹⁰ Rather than apply Carter's human-rights standards to the corrupt and vicious regimes of the Third World, Andy questioned the human-rights record of Great Britain and Sweden and the United States, where, he insisted, there were "hundreds, perhaps even thousands" of political prisoners.¹¹ He actively alibied for left-wing revolutionary gangs and even entered into clandestine negotiations with the Palestine Liberation Organization, the only political organization on earth that as a matter of policy eschews battle with its enemies' soldiers and attacks its enemies' civilians. Having Andy as a human-rights ambassador to the Third World was like having a state dinner catered by professional clowns. When the Rev. Khomeini took over Iran, and the bones began to be broken, Andy pronounced him "some kind of saint" who would be so recognized "when we get over the panic of what is happening."¹² "Of all the people I have known in public service," Jimmy Carter declared, "Andy Young is the best."¹³

Possibly this was true. After all, when Jimmy was elected there were so very many people he just did not know. It was not wise, however, to raise to a position of such wide international visibility a human noisemaker devoted merely to the parochial pursuit of putting on Whitey. I mean, the rest of the world was a bit startled. Surely, despite Jimmy's narrow range of acquaintances, he could have come up with a better choice for the United Nations. How about the aforementioned Vance? He knew him well enough to make him secretary of state, and given Vance's state of mind surely he would have been a more felicitous choice for the UN than for the State Department. Vance was one of the many old-line Democratic foreign-policy practitioners who had been unnerved by the Vietnam War. Every time a foreign government growled at the United States Cy winced; better it would have been to have such a mild fellow at the UN, where no American can do much good, than at the State Department, where a mediocrity can do so much harm.

Vance from his earliest days in government suffered the historic failing of America's foreign-policy establishment—to wit: the inability or refusal to recognize that America does indeed have enemies in this world and that there are people on this earth who hate each other, now and forever. This failure to recognize the world's immunity to goodwill has stultified our diplomacy wherever conditions have been intractable and the need was for resolute policy and the exercise of power. Whether it was the rise of Castro or the invasion of Vietnam, our foreign-policy elites have been forever trying to sweet-talk the brutes. Affluence and isolation have always allowed our foreign-policy establishment to believe in happy endings; and so Jimmy Carter left office believing that he and his State Department had "printed" a commitment to human rights "on worldwide consciousness."

Balderdash. In Cambodia during the Carter administration huge numbers of people were murdered. In the rest of Southeast Asia chemical and biological warfare were brought down on those whom the Soviets' clients could not "reeducate." There were the boat people, and throughout the Middle East brutality and treachery spread. Then there was Africa, where vicious tyrants like Idi Amin, Sékou Touré, and Jean Bedel Bokassa snuffed out life and returned much of the continent to the bush, while one-party regimes sent democracy packing. Whole populations were deported from various African nations or simply starved on racial or tribal grounds. These were years of horror, and the violence kept spreading. American diplomats and civilians were harassed, kidnapped, and murdered. While Vance presided so meekly from the seventh floor of the State Department dutifully carrying out Jimmy's human-rights charade more people in diverse places died violently than during the peacetime tenure of any other secretary of state with the possible exception of Cordell Hull.

Yet the Carter administration continued to issue sonorities about human rights, and the Liberals of the New Age continued to romanticize the Third World, including such despotic lands as North Vietnam, China, and Cuba. During much of his bloodthirsty rule even Idi Amin received benign coverage. As late as 1977 the New York feminist and lawyer Florynce Kennedy lauded him at a Yale Law School conference for being an "outstanding figure" unjustly maligned by fuddy-duddies given to thinking that "if a black man is in charge of a country, he isn't really supposed to be in charge."[14] Incidentally this gambit of charging bigotry against anyone who criticized a particular black was a familiar tactic in the 1970s used by blacks and by white Liberals in defense of almost any rascal. Why they were so eager to defend rascals is a very good question, but to defend an emulator of Hitler and at the Yale Law School is rather too much—suggesting, however, how far the mental derangement of the era had spread. By the end of the 1970s praise of North Vietnam began to recede as the evidence of its brutal hypocrisy began drifting in open boats across the China Sea, but Cuba remained a New Age heart-warmer, attracting an absurd reverence even as such favorites as Hanoi and Peking dimmed.

Typical of those infatuated with Cuba was George McGovern, home from a 1975 visit with Dr. Castro, which actually included a joyride across the island paradise. Reminiscing about how he had sat there beside the cigar-chomping dictator in a humble jeep, the 1972 presidential candidate said he had found his companion "soft-spoken, shy, sensitive, sometimes witty. . . . I, frankly, liked him."[15] Anon, the exuberance grew. Miss Sally Quinn found that "An attitude of sexuality is as pervasive in Cuba as the presence of Fidel Castro. You can feel sex in the atmosphere. . . ."[16] And Dr. Doug Hostetter, having assayed conditions on La Quinn's Isle of Eros, returned to headquarters—namely, the United Methodist Office for the United Nations—and reported that Cuba vibrated with a "combination of spontaneity and bureaucratic rationality," making it "one of the most exciting countries" in which he had ever disported.[17] My favorite romantic rendering of the Third World prison camp came from Senator Lowell Weicker, the Braggart of the Senate, who returned from Cuba extolling Fidel's "enormous intellect and idealism." "Castro's been known to snow people, but he didn't snow me," the jackass hollered, and he wanted to know why the hell the United States was not down in Cuba pitching in. "We can gain the affection of the Cuban people by working side by side"[18]— perhaps in building small arms with which to harass the anti-Communist army of Jonas Savimbi and those other Africans then fighting to remove Cubans from their countries.

No matter how barbaric a Third World regime might have been in the 1970s it could usually find a gaseous American apologist if only it was sufficiently anti-American: "The entourage around Khomeini," Princeton's Professor Richard Falk wrote in 1979, "has had considerable involvement in human rights activities and is committed to a struggle against all forms of oppression. The constitution he proposes has been drafted by political moderates with a strong belief in minority rights. Contrary to the superficial reports in the American press about his attitude toward Jews, women, and others, Khomeini's Islamic republic can be expected to have a doctrine of social justice at its core . . ."[19]

Next to these declarations the high-minded blah of Dr. Myrdal is sobriety itself. In the 1970s the Liberals of the New Age returned from Third World hellholes in the same condition as 1930s intellectuals returning from Stalin's Russia. That is to say they returned soused with poesy and lies. The most comprehensive lie was that there resided in the Third World

the answers to all the problems facing the West, from alienation to nuclear war to spastic colitis. The lie appealed to all
the constituents of the New Age: the hypochondriacs, the
prophets of doom, the nature lovers, the enemies of the throwaway bottle. All wanted to believe in the superiority of some
far-off, wretched non-Western land.

Popinjays like the Rev. Young and the Rev. Jesse Jackson
propounded the lie tirelessly and at a profit, for it had now
become a matter of dogma to the adepts of Uniworld. "I believe we should look to the Third World for an answer," the
Rev. Jackson sermonized in April 1976. "The message from
there is clear: Through the proper use of money and a positive
attitude, we can stimulate self-development and give the people a vision. It has been fascinating for me to observe what has
happened in South Vietnam in the past year. The new Saigon
leaders have spent little time talking about the Americans
who carpet-bombed and defoliated their country. Instead they
have concentrated on rebuilding, putting people to work, in-
culcating new values and attitudes. They did it with military
authority and a liberated attitude."[20] What is this? "Military
authority" and "a liberated attitude"? And he found this
marvel in conquered and yoked South Vietnam a full year
after the North Vietnamese takeover? Is such a thing plausible? Are any of the above propositions and observations from
this wizard plausible? Such was the universal derangement of
the 1970s that the Rev. Jackson was viewed as a savant. By
1983 he was presidential material.

Here was another of the weird transformations that so often
crept upon the Liberal credenda in the New Age. The great
goal of enlightened opinion was no longer to turn the primitives into instant Westerners; rather it was to turn Westerners
into instant primitives, their lives led according to the dreamy
counsels of Schumacher, Illich, and their ilk, their bodies sus-
tained by whole grains and organic nutrients. In Stockholm
and Los Angeles there would be oneness with nature. There
would be serenity and smiles. The true citizen of Uniworld
would live modestly and eat wholesomely. He would forsake
the gadgetry and the pace of modernity. No more acid indiges-
tion or irregular colonic contractions for him. Like his en-

lightened brother the pastoral Masai of Kenya's Great Rift Valley, he would be a grain consumer and a producer of prodigious and well-formed stools. There, beneath him, would rest the evidence of Western man's final escape from the modern harum-scarum!

The key to all this was resource transfer. As the eminent P. V. Narashima Rao, foreign minister of India, asserted at a 1980 special session of the United Nations General Assembly, there must needs be a "massive transfer of resources on a predictable, long-term and assured basis."[21] I guess we all know whose resources were to be transferred. Actually the transfer was already well under way. Wherever the orators of Third World poverty would gather, one would inevitably see an abundance of Swiss watches, Mont Blanc pens, Italian silks, Saville Row tailoring, and Mercedes-Benzes; but by 1980 Third World leaders wanted more and "Third World" was no longer a nebulous term. It was now a full-fledged swindle led by countries that had mastered the Marxist analysis, implemented its policy prescriptions, and, of course, gone broke and indignant. Facts are facts: Dr. Marx was a swell rabble-rouser but an economic moron.

Dr. Kwame Nkrumah, the late prime minister and president of Ghana (formerly the Gold Coast), stated the Third World's flimflam eloquently in his epic tome *Africa Must Unite*:

> Thus all the imperialists, without exception, evolved the means, their colonial policies, to satisfy the ends, the exploitation of the subject territories, for the aggrandizement of the metropolitan countries. They were all rapacious; they all subserved the needs of the subject lands to their own demands; they all circumscribed human rights and human liberties; they all repressed and despoiled, degraded and oppressed. They took our lands, our lives, our resources, and our dignity. Without exception, they left us nothing but our resentment [That word again!]. It was when they had gone and we were faced with the stark realities, as in Ghana on the morrow of our independence, that the destitution of the land after long years of colonial rule was brought sharply home to us.[22]

Dr. Nkrumah was one of the Third World's most venerated gasbags until cancer finished him off in 1972. Fittingly enough he expired in Bucharest, for in Ghana he had socialized everything from the cocoa-marketing board to commercial laundries, and soon his economy was as alluded to in his above cackelocution. The more he harangued for transfers of wealth from the West the more impoverished his country became. Owing to gold mining and cocoa exports, it had been a prosperous country at the time of independence, with an educated elite and $481 million in reserves. Then Dr. Nkrumah took over; and soon, as *The Wall Street Journal* lamented, Ghana was "as close to the brink as any country in Africa."[23] Corrupt and slipping into a dark age, it was ruled by someone by the name of Flight Lieutenant Jerry J. Rawlings, age thirty-four.

The Third World's charge that the West is responsible for its poverty and therefore must pay up fares very badly under the scrutiny of intelligent minds. "Far from the West having caused the poverty in the Third World," P. T. Bauer writes in *Equality, the Third World and Economic Delusion,* "contact with the West has been the principal agent of material progress there. The materially more advanced societies and regions of the Third World are those with which the West established the most numerous, diversified, and extensive contacts. . . . The level of material achievement usually diminishes as one moves away from the foci of Western impact. The poorest and most backward people have few or no external contacts; witness the aborigines, pygmies and desert peoples."[24]

Moreover it is rather hard to swallow Dr. Nkrumah's implication that "human rights and liberties" existed in his happy land before the arrival of Western man. Certainly I have not heard of an African Magna Charta or anything like it. Surely if some pithy statement of man's dignity could be exhumed from any Third World paradise it would have been plastered all over the United Nations building and waved from flagpoles. Returning to Bauer: "As late as the second half of the nineteenth century Black Africa was without even the simplest, most basic ingredients of modern social and economic life. These were brought there by Westerners over the last hundred years or so. This is true of such fundamentals as public security and law and order; wheeled traffic (Black Africa never invented the wheel) and mechanical transport. . . . roads, railways, and man-made ports; the application of science and technology to economic activity; towns with substantial buildings, clean water and sewerage facilities; public health care, hospitals and the control of endemic and epidemic diseases; formal education."[25] Contact with the West has brought prosperity not only to former colonies in Africa but also to other lands of the Third World, and some of the most benighted and poverty-ridden lands never fell under the colonial yoke—for instance Afghanistan, Tibet, Nepal, Liberia, and Ethiopia. Some prosperous lands are colonies still— for instance, Hong Kong. And others doubtless would be infinitely better off were they returned to the Queen, the Kaiser, or whichever Western potentate would have them.

The notion that the Third World's poverty exists because the West snatched up Third World resources is nonsense, reflecting the widely held myth that the prosperity of the few stems from the exploitation of the many. Some of the richest and most advanced countries of the world never had any Third World colonies to exploit: for instance Switzerland and the Scandinavian countries. Other rich and advanced countries were themselves colonies: for instance those of North America and Australasia. Moreover, most of the resources of such Third World nations as Zaïre and the oil countries would never have been of any value at all were it not for Western discoveries and Western enterprise.

In some of the countries of the Third World there would be far fewer resources had the West not actually brought them. The rubber trees of Malaysia did not originate anywhere in Asia—as the trees' botanical name suggests: *Hevea brasiliensis.* Nor did tea originate in India (*Camilla sinensis*). Both were introduced by the diabolical British.

Before colonial rule in Ghana there were no cocoa trees. When Dr. Nkrumah sent the imperialists packing, cocoa exports amounted to hundreds of thousands of tons, all produced from African-owned-and-operated farms. Soon these farms were nationalized by Dr. Nkrumah's socialist wand, and now they are ruins. One hundred years ago there was no cocoa production in what is now Nigeria. There was no export of peanuts or cotton. Only small amounts of palm oil and palm kernels were produced. At the time of independence Nigeria exported all this to a world market. Two decades later Nigeria is a net importer of all these products save cocoa.[26] Other post-colonial countries have fared as badly.

Blaming the West for the brisk slide back into primitivism that characterizes much of the Third World is a futile business made plausible only by the receptiveness such canards have among New Age Liberals. Economic achievement is usually dependent on individual capacity, drive, social arrangements, and institutions. Nations far poorer in resources than Zaïre have advanced and prospered: for instance, Japan. Japan's wealth has nothing to do with the Third World. For that matter the United States' wealth is also completely unbeholden to the Third World. The United States prospered as a collection of colonies, and grew even faster thereafter. During those decades hardly any American ever ventured into any Third World kingdom or tribal realm for plunder or for pleasure. The fact remains: those in the Third World today who have some wealth are generally those who have realized that wealth from contact with the West.

Finally, it is doubtful that income transfers will do anything but maintain Third World backwardness. The nations of the West all developed without foreign aid, in times when development was far more difficult owing to the paucity of markets, capital, and technologies. Transfers of wealth to poor nations may temporarily lift them from poverty. Yet some of the most gluttonous recipients of foreign aid—Zaïre, for instance—have actually experienced a drop in the per capita income of their poorest citizens while corrupt leaders have grown immensely rich.[27] Zaïre's President, Sese Seko Mobutu, is one of the world's richest men. Transfer payments cannot be a tool in developing primitive economies unless social and political arrangements and attitudes become conducive to modern economic growth.

Considering the cast of preposterous characters who make up the leadership of the Third World it is doubtful that they really want economic development at all. Possibly some want to turn their cities into booming modern metropolises; but do the petty tyrants, the religious fanatics, and the simple reactionaries? How would an imam or a colonel rule if his lowly subjects really had some jingle in their pockets and a sinful Ford in the garage? Is the easy secularism and social mobility of an affluent society what the Rev. Khomeini wants? How could he thwart the allures of *Playboy* magazine? And even if the Third World's leaders do want development it is increasingly obvious that foreign aid is not the way to achieve it. The problem was summed up poignantly in a *New York Times* story about the wretched lives lived by the Karamojong nomads of famine-stricken northern Uganda. There foreign aid has been generous, but its benefits have been fleeting. "While the aid is saving lives," the *Times* reports, "it also is doing some harm. The people are being made dependent on it. A proposed work-for-food program, building roads for instance, is regarded in some circles as removing the Karamojong another step from self-sufficient farming"—a kind of farming they have yet to develop.[28]

As Bauer is fond of saying, incomes are not extracted but earned. The myth that wealth is extracted by exploiters from the West is the con of the Third World swindler. No one with any economic sense believes such tosh. The claim works only because many New Age Liberals believe this myth too. They do not know how property is accumulated and how it gains in value. What is more, they relish objurgations against their countrymen. Bauer's analysis of all this is sound and enlightening. Yet when he explains the motive of the New Age Liberal, I mutiny. He lays the blame to Liberal guilt. Here he is in error, as are so many others who speak of Liberal guilt and self-hate. They look for complexity where there is only celebration.

8

Liberal Guilt

The Ego, the Tube, and Fantasyland

DANIEL arap Moi, President of Kenya, is by all odds one of the nicest men ever to put in an appearance at the United Nations. He is also one of the simplest. President Moi's artlessness is legendary. Whatever ambles through his mind he is apt to eject instantaneously onto the public record: his intention to irrigate arid lands, his love of blue skies, his yearning for his dinner companion's puce tie, his urgent need to slip into a dry pair of socks. Reticence is as alien to him as the poetry of Sigfried Weisberger. He hides nothing. He tells all. Fears and velleities burst out of his mouth at their moment of birth.

It is the autumn of 1981, and because Mr. Moi is chairman of the moribund Organization of African Unity, a Lucullan luncheon is held to honor him in the diplomats' dining room of the United Nations. Secretary General Waldheim has spared no expense; he never does. The china is out; so are the silver and the fresh flowers. Fully one hundred and twenty ambassadors are here for the debauch. Some have brought their antacid pills lest these luscious viands disturb the delicate ecology of an ambassadorial gut. At the UN cacophonous tummy is a frequent curse.

There are cocktails. There are five courses, including lobster hors d'oeuvre, vichyssoise, and layer cake, accompanied by ice cream and cherry sauce. The *pièce de résistance* is a slab of roast beef the size of a manhole cover. Three wines flow in exuberance. Then come liqueurs and cigars, and the joy subsides. The oratory has begun. Eyelids grow heavy. Snores are heard, then those cacophonous tummies.

First to rise is Secretary General Kurt Waldheim. Now he is the world's top diplomat. Later he will be shipped back to his native Vienna, a has-been; shortly after returning, he was nearly flattened by a Viennese bus, but the world cared not, and some of the bus's passengers actually had a good laugh. For the nonce, however, he is the *primus inter pares* of this august body and so he toasts President Moi in the stirring cant that is the UN's *lingua franca*. Mellifluously he declaims: *the brotherhood of man! end the arms race! stop pollution! North–South dialogue! self-determination! world hunger!* and, finally, *President Daniel arap Moi!!!—innovative and brilliant leader of the dynamic and auspicious Organization of African Unity!!!*

President Moi arises, peers down at his notes, and responds: *the brotherhood of man! end the arms race! stop pollution! the roast beef!!!* What? Yes, *the roast beef!!!* President Moi has jerked his head up from his notes. His eyes widen. He commends the secretary general on a lovely repast. He notes the wines, the layer cake, the fresh flowers. But President Moi would have liked another helping of roast beef. He had looked around for a waiter, but, alas, none had responded to his frantic winks and whistles. A sigh is heard through the great hall, and the President of Kenya resumes: *North–South dialogue! self-determination! world hunger! leadership!*

The next day America's deputy ambassador, a man who knows his fish, accosts Secretary General Waldheim. Our man, Kenneth Adelman, is a merry fellow, and in complimenting his host on yesterday's luncheon he assures him that he, at least, had had enough roast beef. "Yes," an earnest Waldheim replies, "wasn't it beautiful?" "Yes, a beautiful meal," Adelman nods. "No, the toast." "The toast?" "Yes, the toast. President Moi's point about the roast beef—using it as a symbol to remind us of the inequalities between the North and the

South." Adelman is a superb diplomat; he retreats behind a disciplined smile.

Dr. Waldheim reputedly suffers from what P. T. Bauer calls Western guilt. In America we call it Liberal guilt; even Liberals call it Liberal guilt. Supposedly it explains their blubbering for the poor and the low-down. Supposedly it explains their propensity to sniff at Western progress and to abhor the North American colossus. I doubt the diagnosis.

Consider Dr. Waldheim. His whole life has been absorbed by good works. This is true; I have scrutinized his record. His every utterance attests to a blameless career. He has embraced every noble cause, espoused every high-minded ideal. Liberal guilt? Dr. Waldheim admits to no personal misdeed whatsoever. In the entire Waldheimian canon there is no intimation that he is in any way personally complicitous in Western civilization's degradation of life on this planet. Others were the culprits. Dr. Waldheim has been what the Liberals call a decent man. In America this accolade is passed back and forth by such personages as Walter Mondale, Arthur Schlesinger, Irving Howe, John B. Anderson—all of whom reputedly suffer from Liberal guilt—ha! and ha ha!

These pert poseurs may speak of their private sorrow over Third World poverty, the American Indian, our disappearing marshlands, the ululation within lesbian poetry, and so on. None, however will reveal how exactly he has had a hand in any of these atrocities. The dirty deeds are laid to others: the rich, the powerful, General Custer, the Robber Barons, the Merchants of Death, members of men's clubs. Bad ideas spread faster than good ideas, and by the early 1980s Liberals and conservatives alike accepted the idea of Liberal guilt. If it exists so does Soviet goodwill.

For decades the Liberal metaphysicians have inched toward the advanced position that almost no one can be held guilty of anything. Their learned theologians preach that sin hardly exists; and it was far off in the long-ago that their social scientists believed in the notion of personal responsibility. In point of fact, evil is a word that the good Liberal is loath to employ, unless the topic of discussion is commerce or the corner cop or a new technology developed by a "giant corporation."

After decades spent skirmishing with mossbacks in criminology and jurisprudence the Liberals have made it just short of impossible to establish guilt in a court of law, and on those anguished occasions when the prosecution does win out the jailer is still frequently left empty-handed. For the Liberals often rush in a panel of shrinks and whisk the condemned off to their therapists, some of whom are obviously crooks themselves. Bearing all this in mind I respectfully take leave of those who attribute any of the Liberals' fevers to a tender sense of guilt. They know that Dr. Freud warned long ago that guilt can be profoundly injurious; and though many Liberals now find the Viennese quack stuffy, they still have a very hard time shaking him when he is warning of possible injury to their psyches.

Liberalism is institutionalized decency, a Liberal professor used to brag to me. What Liberal would disagree? By the late 1970s all saw themselves as morally superior or they saw themselves as nothing at all. Even the New Age pols had come to accept their moral superiority. When asked in 1976 to define his political position precisely, the populist from Plains, Georgia, tut-tutted, "How do you define liberalism? How do you define truth? How do you define honesty or love? How do you define compassion, understanding and compatibility?"[1] The New Age Liberal had it all. Liberal guilt can no more exist amid the Liberal vanities than the vow of chastity; or, more improbable still, the vow of silence. What proceeds under the name of Liberal guilt is—once the sackcloth and ashes have been removed—an almost unprecedented egotism. Behemoth, flatulent, unscotchable, it is megalomania *gazeuse*. The New Age Liberal swells with a vanity that exalts him above his civilization and above all the poor saps who acquiesce to it: those who plod along with the commonplace virtues, those who congratulate themselves on a day's work for a day's pay. All this banality the New Age Liberal transcends and sniffs at. Eschewing the workaday morality—its honesty, its frugality, its piety, and so on—he strikes the noble stance, admitting without blush that, yes, he is compassionate, sensitive, decent. In solitude he has pored over the immensities: Western iniquity, the treacheries of corporate giants, various apocalyptic treatises favored by the faithful. Come the dawn he ventures forth to solemnize once again to his mopish countrymen and to truncate further the Bill of Rights. This has been an amazing act. There have been few other groups of mortals in history so inflated by their own sanctimonious conceits, and there has been no other group in history that acquired these conceits without benefit of clergy or consultations with some derivation of Yahweh. Cromwell conferred with God; Galbraith conferred only with the ideological descendants of Eleanor Roosevelt.

When the Liberal of the New Age says that he is decent, he does not mean that he has just slipped on his trousers, so come on in. He means that he is the repository of all that is praiseworthy, so admire him. He means that he is good! When he says that he is compassionate he means that he is sublime! The sensitive New Age Liberal pops with numinous beatitudes and sizzles with self-righteous cant. He is a kind of esoteric Unitarian who in proceeding through the New Age picked up the mysteries of the Esalen Institute of California or some other such New Age holy order. Imagine such a braggart ever suffering from a sense of guilt? The thing is unthinkable.

Of all New Age Liberalism's highfalutin values compassion became its most vaunted. It was tailored by the gods for the vanities of the age. Compassion has been around a very long time, but as a political principle it is comparatively new. Its political uses were appreciated only after the evolution of representative government, but only after the pols' control of the mob had become tenuous did it become the revered principle that it is today. In earlier political epochs, when political power was a matter of pedigree and God's will, no leader with any dignity claimed to be compassionate. When representative democracy bumped aristocracy aside, however, leadership became a matter not of noble blood but of sweet talk and cheap dramatics. Since then the sweet talk and dramatics have grown ever cheaper: forcing the desperate pols to move from grand and gaudy oratory about such large items as patriotism to their present pathetic mewlings about how much sympathy they feel for the lowly voter—or more often, the lowly non-voter. "I know how you feel," the modern pol bawls; "I'm a redneck just like you. I've felt the same pains, been treated to the same rough stuff. If I ever lie to you don't vote for me." Then he raises taxes. It is a new low in yokel control. Those who believe patriotism to be the last refuge of the scoundrel have underestimated compassion. More hoaxes have been perpetrated in its name in recent years than in the name of Christian endeavor, economic education, or sexual therapy.

In the 1970s the adepts of compassion were not numbered only among the politicos, however. Compassion snagged disciples throughout American society—as probably should have been anticipated. Everyone who has ever studied its chemistry, including Rousseau, knows that compassion is particularly attractive to the vain, and the 1970s was a decade of ravening vanity. Did not Tom Wolfe call it the Me Decade? Well, compassion suited the prodigies of the Me Decade as the codpiece suited the gentlemen of sixteenth-century Florence. Of all moralities, compassion is the egotist's favorite. It never squeezes. It always inflates, visiting its smug adherents with visions of magnanimity and godliness. More than any other morality, compassion centers lovingly on the self, the me. "Let's talk about Me," Wolfe heard the prodigies urge.[2] "Let me tell you about compassion," the morally upright of the 1970s said. "Let me tell you about the big heart, *my* big heart." Compassion was his supreme virtue; and, as with all virtue, it was a greater menace to the virtuous than vice. In time it hastened an onrush of fantasy, transforming millions of goody-goodies into Quixotes.

When Wolfe spoke of the Me Decade he had it just right save for one detail: what had emerged was not a decade but a generation, strutting and sputtering a rude array of conceits and undignified self-revelations that would astonish the father confessors of almost any other era. The clowns of the Me Decade set the tone for an absurd era whose communications media were dominated by saps rumbling on about hollow immensities, empty celebrity, vanities based on puny achievements, and occasionally on what any other generation would identify as indignities. The ceaseless blah became reified in the fantasy world of television, a fantasy world that for millions of enthralled dolts preempts reality itself.

Consider a historic fact. Never before in the annals of the species *Homo sapiens* have music, voices, and entertaining images so suffused our lives. Mass communications constitute an electronic plague. Music, for instance, accosts us in airport terminals, hotel lobbies, medical reception rooms; along sidewalks, in parks, in our vehicles, in every room of our homes; even through many of our telephones while some saucy secretary places us on hold—new opportunities to spread the noise are visited upon us every day. Almost as pervasive, there is television. In the United States during no hour day or night are the airwaves void of the invisible cavortings of television's idiot images. Drifting above the landscape of the Republic there has now coalesced an imbecilic fantasy world revealed to us through the magical glow of our boob tubes.

Muggeridge's observation is wise and perspicacious; the camera is indeed a great falsifier of reality. What is more, it is a potent instrument for abetting the egotistical fantasies of the protagonists of the Me Generation. It renders the superficial gorgeous, whether the superficial is gorgeous or not, and it goes no deeper. In the 1970s television created and purveyed a false reality for millions of Americans high and low. The low came to think that human beings who are up-to-date behave as they do in television's fantasyland. The high came to think that they had better goddamn well behave that way if they were going to be taken seriously. Here is one of history's horse-laughs: when the giants of our time get together they act not in emulation of the giants of the past, as might have been the case in years gone by when a Roosevelt hoped to emulate a Lincoln, or a Dostoevski hoped to emulate a Gogol. Rather, today's giants emulate some empty-headed actor from prime-time televisionland. They smile and pose and say clever things, all aped from some vulgar, stupid prime-time masterpiece.

Furthermore our giants assume that their lives are the stuff of dramaturgy. They enter the lobby of the Waldorf with dramatic gestures, anticipating a strike from the paparazzi. At cocktail benefits they sculpt their witticisms to conform to the suavities that ingratiate on *Dallas*. Many of the giants of our time even invite camera crews along as they go on their idyllic adventures: the Kennedys go skiing; Jimmy Carter goes fishing and walks hand-in-hand with Rosalynn at Camp David; George Plimpton attempts yet another amateurish feat unexpected from the highborn and low-grade; the Hon. Mr. Bolling of Missouri goes through another of his Machiavellian days—he actually had eight hours of a day in his life taped in anticipation that millions would be edified.

Bring on the cameras. The Wonderboy had a camera crew taping every minute of his final White House hours. There he stands holding the telephone while the Iranian galoots keep him on hold. Who did he think would ever care? Celebrities invite camera crews along to record their parties for posterity, and their weekends in the country or aboard the family yacht. It tells us something about the special quality of 1970s egalitarianism that many of the decade's most egregious egalitarians thought their lives and their utterances were worthy of lights, camera, sound! In a world whose tastes and eminences are more ephemeral than ever before is it that the camera certifies, or does it sanctify? For the giants of the age, driven as they are by foolish issues and futile quests, it does both.

But there are those who will doubt the charge that in America television's fantasyland has preempted reality. They redden and argue that the camera captures life as it is. Well, myths have dominated in other ages too. It was widely held in times past that if one read a writer's personal letters, there one would find the artist's true personality shorn of all literary artifice. In the eighteenth century Samuel Richardson's novels depended on this stupid assumption. It took a Dr. Johnson to kill off this faith in the verisimilitude of letters. In point of fact, as Johnson demonstrated, no literary form is more artificial than letters written to a friend. Will it take a Dr. Johnson to stagger those who believe in the verisimilitude of the camera? Can we wait that long?

Televisionland has preempted reality in the minds of mil-

lions of Americans. When Laurence Olivier played Hamlet he
was never asked to testify before Parliament on domestic political conditions in Denmark. Today in America someone by
the name of Jack Klugman who portrays a medical examiner
in the series *Quincy* has been asked to testify on orphan drugs
before the House Subcommittee on Health and Environment.[3] Alan Alda, who played an army surgeon on *M*A*S*H*,
has lectured to medical schools.[4] An actress who portrays a
public defender on *Hill Street Blues* has addressed the American Bar Association,[5] and in February of 1983 Ed Asner, who
played a city editor on the *Lou Grant* series, lectured a meeting of journalists from the Inland Daily Press Association on
the exigencies of "investigative journalism."[6]

Consider the weird reverence accorded Walter Cronkite. Before his last reading of the *CBS Evening News* he was the object
of weeks of weepy farewells and encomiums. National magazines pictured him on their covers. He was awarded a Presidential Medal of Freedom. On March 6, 1981, when he read
his last headlines millions of historically minded television
viewers rushed to their television sets to catch a last glimpse of
the warm, oval-shaped vacuum that was Cronkite. Then he
was gone. How to explain it? Here was a man who in all his
public years never passed on more than a hint of intellectual
substance. He just sat there in front of that infernal micro-
phone! Yet he was esteemed as an authority on world politics
and a moral paragon. He left no substantial books, no essays,
no memorable epigrams. I cannot recall a heroic moment, not
even a romantic escapade, not even a scandal. He dwelt in the
land of bromides and wholesome attitudes. He was amiable,
but he was unexceptional too. His only candidate for *Bart-
lett's Familiar Quotations* is "And that's the way it was . . ." I
hope this oft-repeated line is accepted—in sheer fatuousness it
is so redolent of the man and his admirers. Moreover, that was
scarcely ever the way it really was. There were smells, doubts,
long periods of complete inactivity. Yet with dramatic camera-
work, sound, and superficial exegeses, Cronkite & Co. clipped
real events into two- and three-minute segments with phony
beginnings, middles, and ends.

Nonetheless, when he departed televisionland's *Evening*

News, Newsweek spoke of his "awesome stature as a national icon," his "almost mystical appeal," his "integrity, credibility, sagacity, geniality."[7] Well, far be it from me to snicker during such a solemn ceremony. I am sure that he was a good and kindly man. At least he was good and kindly enough to avoid a stretch in Ossining, New York's, public facilities. Still, beyond meeting the bare essentials for good citizenship I cannot see that he ever did anything all that transcendent, except appear night after night reading the evening news. When he retired he began touring the college campuses, identifying himself as one of the Republic's "international thinkers."[8] No one laughed. Students and profs alike lined up to hear him. The fantasies of the tube took precedence over the pathetic reality.

Television is the great engine aiding and abetting the vanities of the age. It has given us a false world populated with empty personages appealing to empty vanities. It hardly ever penetrates any deeper than the actors' makeup or the pols' pat answers. Its hollow truths flicker across the screen, and then they are gone. There is little to reflect on. There is only the gorgeous presence of some powdered persona uttering hopeless bromides, and then the fop is gone. Maybe he or she will be heard from again on tomorrow's broadcast and maybe not. Unlike print, television leaves none of that "mysterious and illuminating something that sheds its after-light in the reading consciousness and plays upon the mind's color-piano its silent yet suggestive tones."[9] The words are those of George Jean Nathan comparing prose and drama back in 1932. He was a modest figure in twentieth-century intellectual life, but his books are still around and his thoughts are still useful. When television's fantasy figures retire who will be able to cull their thoughts? And when the empty public men who have lived off this magic medium finally shut down where will we go to ponder their lives? True, some of their drivel is being collected in libraries, but is it read? Can a vacuum sustain life?

9

The Enthusiasm for Peace

More Misnomers, More Masked Politics, and Humanitarianism Without Costs

TWENTIETH-century Americans live their lives in blithe insularity. The condition stems in part from our geography, which has rendered us an island bordered by oceans east and west and by harmless nations north and south. Yet it is not merely that Americans live thousands of miles down the road. More than ocean reaches explains the mystery of American insularity. Its roots go back to our unusual history, our polity, our social structure, wealth, and individual sense of power. Even the thrust of technology contributes to it, detaching Americans from their fellows and allowing them to isolate themselves in audio and visual fantasy worlds outfitted to each person's individual tastes.

Americans arriving from the Old World filled an empty space. Without ancient ruins to daunt them or to chasten their dreams, without forbidding social barriers to restrain their pursuit of happiness, without even much congestion to slow them down, Americans have been free to attend to their own yearnings. Compared with older societies America is even relatively free of enduring enmities and bugaboos. The country has always supplied wide-open spaces into which its restless citizens could withdraw. Late-twentieth-century science has only enlarged those spaces, allowing us to live eremitic lives sealed away in a fastness of illusion and sound. Not surprisingly Americans have rarely looked abroad. When we travel we travel to Hiltons via TWA. Foreign ways do not much fetch us.

During the 1970s the world was coming to a broil. The enemies of Western democracy were becoming more ubiquitous and more furious than the Fascists of the 1930s or even the Nazis. Yet in America, all this terror, revolution, and war was compressed between ads on the evening news or lost to mind. Unfortunately, history does not respect America's right to privacy; and those same evening broadcasts that American technology had transformed into amusements were becoming political instruments for the world outside, instruments whose use encouraged ever more violence and instability. Not only were Machiavels bending the cameramen and the reporters of network news to their purposes; so were maniacs, and by the 1980s the maniacs' schemes were endangering everyone. Violent deeds staged for Western news producers made good theater in the beginning, but they encouraged more violence, and by the 1980s it was clearly in the cards that someday some maniac might stage a nuclear drama for the camera that could prove more calamitous than had the assassination of Archduke Francis Ferdinand in 1914. Nevertheless, most Americans remained deaf to the pothering.

Few of us have ever thought out a role for twentieth-century American diplomacy that would reconcile the youthful Republic to its burden as the giant of Western democracy. Americans are so chary of using power or of thinking in terms of affairs of state. They utter sonorous pronunciamentos. They vacillate. They send in the Marines. They feel remorse. In international relations Americans tend toward the sophomoric, and so naturally our country has been fecund with "peace" movements. In fact, for as long as there have been peace movements—which is to say only since the rise of mass communications—those astir in America have been among the world's most energetic and influential. This is not really inconsistent with our insularity. Peace movements are essentially a renunciation of the outside world and of traditional diplomatic practices. They are a denial of reality and of history, a sanctimonious retreat into an illusory realm.

The Enthusiasm for Peace

In the 1920s the American peace movement was more active and effective than its European counterparts. A wondrous variety of peace organizations championed the World Court, the League of Nations, disarmament, and the "outlawry" of war. With ample funds from high-minded men like Andrew Carnegie these organizations engaged in a wide range of activities, from establishing international-relations clubs to publishing journals and manifestos to investigating indigenous "militarism"—for instance, in the Boy Scouts. "If one word was repeated more often than any other," historian Robert Ferrell wrote of this period, "that word was 'peace.' Peace echoed through so many sermons, speeches and state papers that it drove itself into the consciousness of everyone."[1] Yet there was to be no peace. The Kellogg-Briand Pact to outlaw war failed. Disarmament failed. Years of isolation here and of appeasement in Europe culminated in world war. Only after the most expensive sort of military mobilization and a bloody struggle was peace secured. It was a tragically flawed peace at that.

After the war, Churchill, whose warnings against isolation and appeasement had won him the contempt of the ostriches of the hour, brooded over what he had been helpless to prevent: the incalculable carnage that followed the ostriches' futile solemnities, the peace that left half of Europe enslaved, the gray aftermath of a gigantic war with daggers still drawn. In his *History of the Second World War*, he elegized: "There never was a war more easy to stop than that which has just wrecked what was left of the world from the previous struggle. The human tragedy reaches its climax in the fact that after all the exertions and sacrifices of hundreds of millions of people and of the victories of the Righteous Cause, we have still not found Peace or Security, and that we lie in the grip of even worse perils than those we have surmounted."[2] Those perils were nuclear war and Soviet tyranny, a tyranny that had already accounted for as many casualties as Nazism and one that in its paranoid xenophobia would eventually reach out, inciting violence in every corner of the earth and cultivating hatred wherever there was dissatisfaction.

The cause for much of the tragedy and peril over which

Churchill brooded lay, in part, with the United States. We had, as the 1970s phrase was to have it, given peace a chance. Immediately after the war Washington was blossoming with good intentions. True to its nature, the Republic disarmed with naive swiftness. We had set out to make Franklin Roosevelt's Four Freedoms a reality, and simultaneously we reduced the most powerful military force on earth from the 12 million troops mustered by VE Day to 3 million fourteen months later and 1.6 million a year after that. While the Soviet Union was rebuilding its battered army into a huge force of more than 260 divisions, Washington reduced its defense budgets from $81.6 billion in the last year of the war to $44.7 billion in fiscal 1946 and $13.1 billion in fiscal 1947. There the figure stood until the invasion of South Korea. During these years the Soviets were rebuffing our high-minded attempt to put international controls on atomic-bomb production. They were gobbling up Eastern Europe, reaching for Germany, parts of Turkey, Greece, Iran, and even parts of Japan. Nevertheless, Washington loftily continued to try to remake the world into the international brotherhood envisaged by the United Nations charter.

Americans have such difficulty recognizing that other nations are different from ours. We even get confused about nations like the Soviet Union, with its record of genocidal purges in the 1930s, its complicity with Nazism in the 1939 partition of Poland, its brutal treatment of our diplomats during the war, its bloody policies of forced repatriation after the war—policies that made American and British soldiers accessories to mass murder and enslavement. President Roosevelt had prided himself on being able to "deal with" Uncle Joe Stalin. Even Harry Truman saw this historic butcher as a foreign version of a "big-city boss." Thus in the 1940s Washington remained amicable toward Moscow. Then, when events like the ham-fisted Communist *coup* in Czechoslovakia and the Berlin blockade fetched our concern, we adopted a policy of "patience and firmness"—but we remained disarmed. When in the 1970s the peace demonstrators sang the lugubrious chant "All We Are Saying, Is Give Peace a Chance," someone might have mentioned the immediate post-war period to them. Washington did give peace a chance, and it was only after the invasion of Korea that we mobilized, making the United States again militarily formidable and the Soviets less restless.[3]

Yet even while America has been militarily formidable the peace has been uneasy—the Russians make friends so poorly, and are so suspicious, so touchy; and of course they have to keep so many guns trained on their neighbors, their citizens, and their slaves. Hence, along with the growth of our vast military establishment, America has witnessed the growth of a very jumpy peace movement—peace movements being in this century a clear omen that the peace is in danger. As the danger waxes and wanes the peace movements grow and decline. With the growth of the Soviet thermonuclear force in the 1950s the movement waxed. It waxed again in the 1960s with the Berlin Wall and the Cuban Missile Crisis. During the war in Vietnam it expanded to heroic dimensions, and it appeared again in the 1970s after the breakdown of détente. Yet no peace movement has ever brought peace, except perhaps in Indochina, and there it brought the peace of the grave for millions and the peace of the cellblock for millions more. Peace movements never bring the peace desired. They are one of man's most futile and fatuous expressions. Looking back over the decades, reviewing their noble slogans and grandiose gestures, and then inspecting the ensuing calamities, one comes to the inescapable conclusion that peace movements are an irrational response to perilous conditions. What is more, they are another of our era's brazen misnomers. Taking into account their wretched performance record, the 82nd Airborne has been a more effective peace movement than any of history's so-called peace movements including such vehement outfits as the Riverside Church Disarmament Program, the Council for a Liveable World, and the American Friends Service Committee. It is their half-witted belief that the armies of the Western democracies imperil the peace, and not surprisingly they are always admired in Moscow.

Compared with the peace movements of the 1920s and the 1930s the so-called peace movement of the post-war period has been genuinely and increasingly radical. That is to say it has been strenuously leftist and, of necessity, deceitful. In truth, its members have no more warrant to portray themselves as advocates of peace than anyone else in America, possibly less. After all, their favorite panaceas—disarmament, appeasement, wanton negotiability—have invariably led to bloodshed and war. Their fundamental tenet is opposition to defense. Scholarly standards demand, then, that we redesignate this movement the anti-defense movement. What is more, by the 1970s the anti-defense movement had become pro-appeasement. It acted as though the democracies' 1930s encounter with aggressive totalitarianism had no lessons to teach.

As with other high-minded causes of recent history the postwar anti-defense movement's evolution from moderation to radicalism proceeded slowly and steadily until the late 1960s when it lurched toward rampancy. In the late 1940s the movement merely advocated banning the atomic bomb and kissing the Soviets on both cheeks, recommendations that could be marked down as naive, but understandable—the Russians had so recently been our "heroic Soviet allies," Americans were so tired of war, and nuclear disarmament seemed so simple. There were so very few bombs to ban. As the years ground on, however, experience shouted that the only way to tranquilize the Soviets was through resolute diplomacy and military preparedness. But the anti-defense movement was deaf to experience, and if it drew any conclusions from such dramas as the Berlin Blockade or the Cuban Missile Crisis, it drew the wrong ones. Rather than growing sober-minded and resolute it grew balmier. It advocated an increasingly passive American foreign policy. Always it prescribed negotiations, as though they were an aphrodisiac.

By the 1970s the movement insisted that American defense programs were mostly supererogatory and the justification for practically all Soviet bellicosity. Moreover, the movement laid almost any aggression against American interests to our own bad manners and admonished us to make things right with any champion of the earth's sullen masses no matter how barbaric. If an aggressor was especially volatile, the peace movement's demands on America grew especially importunate. If an aggressor was a former Western colony claiming

grievances against the United States, the anti-defense movement grew especially sympathetic. Here, the movement mixed
its fundamental futility with convenient lapses into stupidity.
Of all the great powers, the United States is the only one with
a clearly anti-colonial history. It almost takes an act of will to
avoid knowing that during the last world war the United
States steadfastly opposed Europe's colonial empires. Washington was more suspicious of British imperial designs than of
Soviet expansionism, and De Gaulle's historic distrust of us
was solidified by President Franklin Roosevelt's opposition to a
revival of France's empire. Yet by the 1970s the movement had
confected elaborate sophistries from the Marxist canon, all
presenting the United States as a bulwark of neo-colonialism.
Thirty years after America destroyed Fascism and Nazism we
were depicted as the chief source of international instability
and a huge impediment to Progress.

Now the so-called peace movement had in fact become
anti-defense and pro-appeasement. In so doing it accomplished
an absolutely amazing feat. Through all its disquisitions,
propositions, and slogans it managed to ignore most of the
growing evidence of Soviet truculence and all that this por-
tended. Consequently, the movement's members could perceive
the American military buildup as utterly irrational, and they
could diabolize Washington with the lusty shouts so fashionable with worldwide left-wingery.

The virulence of the movement's cant and the barbarism of
some of those regimes with which it sympathized ended forever
its claim to being a "peace movement." Too often, now, it
sided with aggression and cruelty. Even the reactionary barbarism of a lunatic like the Rev. Ayatollah Ruhollah Khomeini was sympathized with, its saving grace being, of course,
its violent hatred of the West.

Consider a sampling of the movement's harebrained cheers.
Late in March 1979, with the Holy Man's dirty-necked galoots
now in full rebellion against civilization, *The Nation* published a piece full of hope, envisaging thousands of indigenous
Gloria Steinems filling the streets of Teheran, bras waving
defiantly at the quavering mullahs: "There have been inci-
dents of execution for homosexual rape and flogging for theft

and alcohol consumption. . . . At the center, there has been a struggle mounted around the issue of the status of women. To Western liberals it has confirmed their worst fears about the fanatical character of the Khomeini movement. Yet the evidence is mixed. Demonstrations have been organized by women, their consciousnesses raised, their voices heard."[4]

And then there was Richard Falk, whom we have met before and who now must be quoted in full. With this one prosy sausage in *Foreign Policy* he interlarded most of the esoteric anti-Americanism of the era: America's benightedness, the complicated virtues of America's barbaric antagonists, the easy accessibility of such insights to adepts of the New Age and only to adepts of the New Age. Savor scholar Falk's performance:

> One of Washington's problems in formulating a position toward Khomeini's movement may be its relative ignorance of the ayatollah's philosophy and of Shi'ite Moslem doctrine generally. It is entirely different from the harsher Sunni variety that currently prevails in Saudi Arabia, Libya, and Pakistan, among other Moslem nations. The entourage around Khomeini, in fact, has had considerable involvement in human rights activities and is committed to a struggle against all forms of oppression. The constitution he proposes has been drafted by political moderates with a strong belief in minority rights. Contrary to the superficial reports in the American press about his attitude toward Jews, women, and others, Khomeini's Islamic republic can be expected to have a doctrine of social justice at its core; from all indications, it will be flexible in interpreting the Koran, keeping the "book of research" open to amendment and adaptation based on contemporary needs and aspirations.[5]

The anti-defense appeasers were given to explaining their own radicalization as owing to their visions of impending nuclear holocaust, the whole world incinerated upon the morrow! Yet how new are such fears? Did not the inhabitants of practically any town along the frontier of the late Roman Empire suffer precisely the same sense of danger? For them, living in times before mass communications made people aware of the outside world, their conception of the world was minuscule. Most likely it did not extend much beyond a nearby town or two. Moreover, their premonitions were evoked by visions of doom that were far from hypothetical. Living on the frontier of the Roman Empire, one heard of nearby settlements where the barbarians' sudden onslaught had reduced everything to ashes, leaving the townspeople's heads on pikes and their homes smoldering, never to be raised again. Such holocausts go on still in primitive regions. They are not new to human history. Modern war is admittedly horrifying but wars are usually horrifying. In fact, life itself has frequently been horrifying. The Old Testament with its tales of floods, fires, famines, and plagues makes that point. New weapons have been developed repeatedly in this century and many have duly terrified us—for instance: mustard gas in World War I and the heavy bomber in the 1930s. Nuclear war in the 1970s and 1980s is only marginally more frightening than in the 1950s and 1960s, and arguably less so. At least by later decades we had accumulated experience in deterring the catastrophe.

Yet in the late 1970s, out of all proportion to our peril and usually on balmy days, the anti-nuke hysteria erupted utterly unrestrained by other contemporary horrors that the truly responsible citizen had to ponder—namely: the horror of every Marxist triumph with its attendant extirpation of freedom and its frequent acts of genocide. All served to put nuclear war into a sobering perspective, but not for the anti-defense appeasers, who brandished such nihilistic slogans as "Nothing Is Worth Dying For." Albert Camus pithily refuted this bosh in "The Myth of Sisyphus" when he wrote ". . . a reason for living is also an excellent reason for dying."[6] Of course, when Camus wrote this essay the botches perpetrated by appeasers in the 1930s were impossible to ignore. Tanks were rumbling into action. Governments were hastily reshuffling. Now agitated and dismayed, the smug appeasers of the 1930s were calling in the Churchills and De Gaulles whom they had spent a decade reviling. Soon Europe would again lie in ruins; and the appeasers would be gone, at least temporarily.

It is not the growing horror of war that radicalized the anti-defense movement but the broad transformation of Liberalism into a riot of idiot enthusiasms. In other words, here we have another example of the general crack-up. Very few members of the peace movement were not numbered among Liberalism's faithful, and when the fevering began in Liberalism it afflicted the peace brethren too. Yet unlike Liberalism's other idiot enthusiasms this enthusiasm is not very amusing. There has not been a really funny war since the Serbo-Bulgarian burlesque of 1885; and it is always war that follows upon seasons of appeasement.

In the late 1970s the radicalized members of the anti-defense movement invariably professed to being nonpartisan or apolitical, but here is another of their deceits. Each peace activist was directed by a brain whose every nook and cranny had been fully stocked by the New Age *Zeitgeist*. Disarmament and appeasement might be his primary enthusiasms, but he was alive to every exigent cause fevering the brow of his fellow fanatics: infant formula in Ouagadougou, Upper Volta; throwaway bottles in Indian Orchard, Massachusetts; the plots of the Tobacco Growers Association of the United States; the hellish instruments of white-male dominance hawked in the lingerie departments of all capitalist department stores—all these infamies alarmed him and made him scowl. Nonetheless the peace activists specialized in flummoxing diplomacy rather than the energy industry, American medicine, the sociology of the American boudoir; and this was alarming. Sound diplomacy is fundamental to civilization's continuance. To flummox it in our time is dangerous business.

Yet consider some of the wild agitations of the movement's eminent minds. Consider Archbishop Raymond G. Hunthausen, Jesus Christ's personal representative to Seattle, Washington. In 1981 the Most Reverend Dr. Hunthausen harangued a group of Lutherans with such euphuisms as "Nuclear arms protect privilege and exploitation. Giving them up would mean having to give up economic power over other people. Peace and justice go together. On the path we now follow, our economic policies toward other countries require nuclear weapons. Giving up the weapons would mean giving up more than our means of global terror. It would mean giving up the reason for such terror—our privileged place in the world."[7]

"Privilege and exploitation"? "Economic power over other people"? All this is agglutinated into a discourse on nuclear weapons? This is not the work of a normal mind.

The peace was no more intensely imperiled in the late 1970s than in earlier post-war decades. Yet suddenly pontificators like the Most Reverend Dr. Hunthausen were swept by an ardor akin to mass hysteria, the kind that leaves teen-age girls suffering cramps and dizzy spells. "The next time you hear a politician talking about nuclear war," the critic Richard Ellmann sobbed on the February 15, 1980, broadcast of National Public Radio's *All Things Considered,* "why not vomit all over him? Or soon we'll be vomiting on each other."[8] These are minds trapped in the ardors of New Age ideology. Moreover they are shameless opportunists, practicing the masked politics of the New Age. The Archbishop exploits "nuclear horror" to unhorse the money changers and bring down upon Greater Seattle some sort of clericalism. Richard Ellmann's histrionics gain him a national audience for his quackeries, the esteem of his fellow fanatics, and the opportunity to advance the cause of the National Dry Cleaners Association.

The anti-defense movement was no "apolitical," "nonpartisan" movement. To the contrary it was politics of a particularly odious sort, that is to say the masked politics of the New Age, a politics that does not even admit its political essence, but with noble slogans sends off a mob of Don Quixotes, all "pissed off" and apocalyptic. Unfortunately if these Quixotes ever prevailed it would not just mean a spotless environment or the end of the white male establishment. It would mean havoc. That has been history's sad lesson.

The *modus operandi* of the anti-defense movement was the same as that adopted by the age's other puerile fanaticisms. Eschewing serious debate, intelligent analysis, and tolerance, the anti-defense appeasers created a Disneyland for zealots with gruesome displays, macabre parades, goofball theatrics, and that polemical device that the fanatical environmentalists used so well, prophecies of catastrophe. These prophecies smacked of science, however. Like those of the anti-nuke movement, these were prophecies of catastrophe based solely on balmy hypotheses. In place of reasonable debate, horrid forecasts were invented for every community in the Great Republic, and the indigenous hysterics would fasten upon them with the desperate literalness of a red-necked Christian rapt in the Book of Daniel or Revelations. "Suppose a one-megaton bomb were dropped near ground level over Cambridge City Hall," a typical scenario distributed by the city government of Cambridge, Massachusetts, prophesied. "Almost all Cambridge citizens would be killed. City Hall, the Central Square Post Office, and the YMCA and YWCA—all would disappear into a crater about 20 stories deep. A rim of deadly radioactive soil would be thrown up twice as far as where . . ."[9]

Enough! Note the punctilious attention to detail: "one-megaton bomb," "Cambridge City Hall," "the Central Square Post Office," both Y's! a crater "20 stories deep." When the polemic was not a maniacally detailed prophecy of doom it was often an infantile fantasy—the more infantile, the more persuasive to the radicalized members of the movement. The infantilism is no surprise. One of radicalism's cherished myths is that a child's innocent fantasies are often closer to truth than the certitudes of adulthood. Consider composer Leonard Bernstein's rubber-ducky vision of the aftermath of American unilateral disarmament; it was actually published on *The New York Times*'s op-ed page; my researchers double-checked!

What is your first thought? Naturally, that the Soviet Union would come plowing in and take us over. But would they really? What would they do with us? Why would they want to assume responsibility for, and administration of, so huge, complex and problematical a society as ours? And in English, yet! Besides, who is the Soviet Union—its leaders, its army, or its people? The only reason for the army to fight is that their leaders would have commanded them to do so, but how can they fight when there is no enemy? The hypothetical enemy has been magically whisked away, and replaced by 200-odd-million smiling, strong, peaceful Americans.

Now keep the fantasy going: the Russian *people* certainly don't want war, they have suffered far too much; and it is more likely that they would displace their warlike leaders, and transform their Union of Socialist Republics into a truly democratic union. And think of the example that would have been set for the whole world; think of the relief at no longer having to bluster and sabre-rattle and save face; think of the vast new wealth, now available to make life rich, beautiful, clean, sexy, thoughtful, inventive, healthful, fun![10]

As with so many other energumens of the New Age, a colossal, floodlit grandiosity had overcome each Bernstein of the anti-defense movement. Each saw himself a genius, often unsung, but nevertheless fully equipped to dispatch any problem no matter how complicated. Was foreign policy once the province of professional diplomats? Well, then, no wonder there was discord and war. Now was the hour to muster the no-nonsense anti-defense housewife, the pacifist cleric, the speech therapist with a lifelong interest in the works of Erich Fromm. That nuclear holocaust scheduled for the morrow could be postponed forever.

Though every gruesome scenario came purfled with facts and figures, some large facts passed almost completely unnoticed—for instance, our NATO allies' reliance on our deterrent capacity, and, of course, Soviet militarism. The whole question of nuclear disarmament, in point of fact, was addressed as though the rest of the world hardly existed—not our allies, not the increasingly volatile and brutal Third World, and certainly not Moscow with its chain of terrorism franchises. Whether this odd reticence was owing to traditional American insularity, the self-absorption of the Me Decade, or the anti-defense adepts' grandiosity and deceitfulness I cannot say. I can say that the omission ensured that the movement would go down as one of the most frivolous in American history.

How the movement frivoled with reality can be seen in its delusory portrayal of Soviet society on those rare occasions when it even acknowledged the Soviets' existence. Then the

USSR was depicted as a land just like America, populated by a congeries of inane yeomen awaiting a "growing peace movement" that would raise their consciousness and send them swarming all over the Kremlin bawling for nuclear disarmament. The anti-defense appeasers actually spoke of a "growing Soviet peace movement," echoing the American media's hackneyed references to a "growing American peace movement." Of course there was no growing Soviet peace movement, any more than there was a growing Soviet homosexual movement. On the same weekend in 1982 that 500,000 nuclear-freeze proponents demonstrated in Central Park, 11 members of a week-old independent Russian peace group were arrested in Moscow while attempting to meet in a private apartment. All were charged with "hooliganism," and their spokesman was confined to a "psychiatric hospital."[11]

Such sad realities were lost on the demonstrators in Central Park, who when they thought at all of life under Communism, thought much as the editors of *The Nation* did when they made one of their rare acknowledgments of the Soviet bloc's existence. They advised that members of the West's "peace movement" put pressure on "leaders of the undemocratic East" through a bold stroke: "Why not a letter-writing campaign?" The plan was elaborated upon: "This does not mean letters to their leaders—rather, millions of letters from ordinary people in the West to their counterparts in the Soviet bloc. Let us procure phone books and address lists from Moscow, Leningrad, East Berlin, Dresden, Warsaw, Krakow, Bucharest, Budapest, Prague. Let us distribute the lists of names at peace demonstrations in Western Europe and North America. . . ."[12] Halt! Halt! Moscow telephone directories indeed! Moscow is simply not abundant with telephone directories. Rather it is abundant with bugging devices, police, soldiers, and pols who dream of the perfect mushroom cloud.

Apparently America's popinjays for peace were incapable of conceiving the hoosegow nature of the Soviet regime, though herds of competent writers, such as Aleksandr Solzhenitsyn, have documented the drear. Moreover, they were incapable of facing up to the fact that throughout the years of détente the

Soviets had carried on the nuclear era's most extensive research, development, testing, and deployment program. Their unexpectedly rapid qualitative advances in missile accuracy, targeting, yield, and strategic defense, coupled with their unparalleled quantitative buildup in offensive nuclear weaponry, had arguably tipped the strategic balance in their favor for the first time in history. The Soviets' buildup in conventional weapons too had been enormous. From 1972 to 1982 they had outspent their American partners in détente by more than $700 billion* and were capable of wiping out at least two legs of the American strategic triad with a first-strike blow.[13]

Those were not the only disturbing Soviet realities that were ignored in the popinjays' slogans and diatribes. In Southwest Asia the Soviets had invaded harmless Afghanistan, where they used chemical and biological warfare against the country's ragtag tribesmen. Moscow was supplying the stuff to its henchmen in Southeast Asia for use against local tribes. All this was in blatant contravention of the 1925 Geneva Protocol, which forbids the use of chemical and biological weapons in war, and the 1972 Biological and Toxin Weapons Convention, which forbids the possession of toxin weapons. In point of fact that land of the "growing Soviet peace movement" was a giant police state, as much at war with its citizens and its neighbors as with the West. Oblivious to all this, the anti-defense movement urged still more treaties with the Soviets as though such treaties were something new and foolproof.

What we had here was another enormous act of denial. Rather than face up to troubling realities, the anti-defense appeasers simply denied reality. They denied that they were for the most part ritualistic leftists practicing their masked politics. They denied that the United States was following a perfectly defensible diplomatic approach to nuclear reductions. Finally, they denied the terrible nature of the Soviet

---

*It is interesting to note what we could have built and deployed had we spent the same amount of money over the same period of time: the entire B-1 program (244 bombers) originally planned, all MX missiles and shelters (200 MX) originally planned, all planned Trident subs and missiles, 7,000 M-1 tanks, a matching number of infantry fighting vehicles, plus all the F-14s, F-15s, F-16s, F-18s, and A-10s planned for Air Force and Navy tactical air modernization.[14]

system.* The whole thing amounted to an act of denial eerily reminiscent of the denials practiced in the 1930s by those who would not acknowledge the immensity of the Nazi evil, Nazism's steady remilitarization of Germany, or even its repeated acts of aggression. This act of denial, however, was harder to condone. After all, during the 1970s American popular entertainment abounded with Holocaust and World War II dramas. Surely our 1970s Quixotes were aware of the results of appeasing Hitler. They grew ever more eloquent on Nazism's barbarousness as World War II receded into history. It was modern-day Communist barbarousness that escaped them.

Consider the Ground Zero adventures. The deluded participants in these nonsensical pageants had persuaded themselves that the average American was wholly in the dark as to the destructiveness of nuclear warfare; if only the message could be conveyed to him nuclear war would become a menace of the past, as hookworm had become a menace of the past once the yokels were instructed to wear shoes. The leader of the Ground Zero movement was an odd fellow of suitably woeful countenance, Roger Molander, who would begin his tirades to the faithful with such grandiose salutations as "Welcome to the finest and noblest cause that mankind has ever known." In the spring of 1982 he and his followers orchestrated Ground Zero Week with a plenitude of infantile events some of which lasted into the summer—a very unusual occurrence, that, for most anti-defense demonstrations took place only in the gentle of spring and fall.

The Ground Zero events of the spring of 1982 included a "bicycle fallout marathon" in Marshall, Missouri, a "Run for Your Life" in Winston-Salem, North Carolina, a "puppets for peace" show in Albuquerque, New Mexico, and in Provincetown, Massachusetts, a historic "Swim for Peace." That event featured André the idealistic seal. André's owner and best

---

* They even denied President Ronald Reagan's charges of Soviet "involvement" in their movement, though clearly established Soviet agents such as Yuri S. Kapralov, *Counselor at the Soviet Embassy*, spoke to freeze groups. Kapralov actually sat on a panel at the March 1981 organizational meeting of the freeze movement![15]

friend, Mr. Harry Goodridge, sent André to sea on April 13 to swim for peace all the way to Rockport, Maine. Braving an unpleasant drizzle, the press turned out to record the departure. "The swim," one of Mr. Goodridge's friends explained to *The New York Times,* "reflects Harry's concern that even if a nuclear weapon exploded in the ocean . . . it would be all over for André and other ocean life. Nuclear war kills animals too."[16] It is possible that during this historic week the movement almost gained its first martyr. A Vanderbilt University Law School student fell through a bus window while trying to press his naked arse against it. Some moron had left the window open.

I once attended one of Molander's lectures on a major college campus, a campus with a renowned Soviet-studies program. He maundered on for two hours in front of a thousand or so of his mellow friends, speaking of nuclear weapons as "jelly beans" and insisting that the number of them that one had in one's arsenal was small beer. His recommendation was that ordinary Soviet and American citizens "get to know each other" and force their respective governments to disarm. No one objected. It was as though Orwell, Koestler, Solzhenitsyn, and all the others who have written so poignantly of the Soviet reality had never been born; or that there were no *gulag* swallowing up every brave Soviet citizen who, like Yuri Orlov or Anatoly Shcharansky, tries to suggest peace and liberality to the Soviet Union. Molander's lecture was a blatant denial of the strategic imbalance of the time, an imbalance that existed not only because of the number of Soviet "jelly beans"* but because of the Soviets' improved accuracy and defensibility. Here was propaganda for the self-absorbed. Molander claimed that his movement had been created "to inform and involve the American people on the issue of nuclear war," and, true to the movement's customary deviousness, this was the one thing it did not do. Rather, it was a carnival of moral exhibitionism abounding in grandiosity and futility.

That the peace movement survived as a credible political

---

* Our total number of nuclear weapons had actually decreased in the 1970s while the Soviets' had increased.

force into the 1980s is evidence of the political decadence of the late 1970s. As noted in Chapter 2, all the movement's prophecies about Southeast Asia had been proved thunderously wrong. All its truths had come a cropper. All its lies and perversions stood exposed. "If we know anything about the government founded by Ho Chi Minh," declared Shana Alexander, intoning the doves' current wisdom as Saigon fell, "it is that its social services are excellent: good health care, day care and educational programs abound, especially for the poor."[17] This was an imbecilic statement in 1975. Five years later such beliefs were imbecilic and unconscionable. North Vietnam's bloody and despotic conquest of Southeast Asia refuted every claim that the anti-war movement had made in the 1970s, and in 1983 just for good measure North Vietnam's General Vo Nguyen Giap obligingly told French television that the anti-war movement had been wrong on practically every point.[18] North Vietnam had been out to conquer and enslave the South from the start.

Yet the members of the movement had learned nothing by the 1980s; nor, sad to say, had many of Shana Alexander's associates in the media. With unsurpassed brazenness the movement continued to evade the truth and when possible to pervert it with sickening canards such as blaming Richard Nixon and Henry Kissinger for the outcome in Southeast Asia and blaming the American people for the mistreatment of our Vietnam veterans, men the movement had once taunted as "war criminals." The doves of the early 1970s now actually claimed to have been vindicated by the bloody aftermath of the fall of Southeast Asia, and they got away with it! There was no pandemic hoot. The lies stood unchallenged by media or by major political figures.

In the late 1970s truth had very little impact on the capital fellows and fellowesses of our society, and all their windily proclaimed ideals were quite hollow. It was an idealism that never required sacrifices from its idealists. Just as Jimmy Carter's Christianity was a Christianity without tears, the humanitarianism of the hour was a humanitarianism without costs. The peace movement baldly asserted that events had vindicated it. All evidence to the contrary was ignored. The few who objected were likewise ignored. Too many of the aforesaid fellows and fellowesses had drifted into complicity with Southeast Asia's grim fate for the subject to be faced. They would not acknowledge their errors, and so they buried the subject and solemnly turned to a new cause, human rights —not the human rights one fights for but the human rights one sermonizes upon. In the Me Decade here was the perfect way to forget one's own moral wretchedness, and it was cheap.

Thus the political decadence of the 1970s allowed the members of the peace movement to wriggle out of the consequences of their historic blunders, and soon they were all back dispensing their old moonshine. They would bring progressive government to Central America and prevail upon the superpowers to disarm. Bella Abzug, Jane Fonda, Robert Drinan, Daniel Ellsberg, the folksingers, the rock singers, the sanctimonious profs all were back representing what *The New York Times* in the spring of 1982 described as a "rainbow spectrum" of political groupings.[19] Even the chants were the same: "All We Are Saying Is Give Peace a Chance." Yet, once again, an American president had truly given peace a chance, and the futility of appeasement and disarmament had been verified anew.

According to the Wonderboy's speculations when he arrived in Washington, the opponents of the Vietnam War were the wave of the future. He staffed his White House with the disciples of McGovernism. He lectured Americans on their "inordinate fear of Communism."[20] He deemphasized military preparedness, stressed the omnipotence of negotiations, and fastened upon a foreign policy in perfect cadence with the self-absorption of the era—to wit: a policy of moral superiority and isolation from all the bloody consequences of each greenhorn miscalculation. Merely by displaying high-mindedness America would influence the world. "To me," the Wonderboy wrote in his memoirs, "the demonstration of American idealism was a practical and realistic approach to foreign affairs, and moral principles were the best foundation for the exertion of American power and influence."[21]

During the Carter administration the value of power in international relations was ignored. Its replacement was what the administration's assistant secretary of state for East Asian and Pacific affairs, Richard Holbrooke, had called "the basic moral force that exists in the principles of our system of government." And he went on, "we do not need to dominate the world in order to live safely in it. . . . we must retain our belief in the exceptional nature of our system of democracy. That is our ultimate strength."[22] For the next four years the Carter administration relied on this narcissistic blather, and the evening news crackled with the sound of small-arms fire. By the time Jimmy left office the world was for us and for others a more dangerous place.

Persuasion, moral exhibitionism, and offers of conciliation in response to any provocation were at the heart of the Carter foreign policy, and they proved useless. The administration was impotent in ending Hanoi's brutality toward the boat people or in ending Soviet occupation of Afghanistan; and when the Wonderboy attempted negotiations with the Ayatollah Ruhollah Khomeini, the old crank humiliated him for 444 days. Jimmy's foreign policy demonstrated the absolute futility of the peace movement's program, making its reemergence in the 1980s genuinely amazing. Jimmy had bought practically all its myths, and his foreign policy was not only a failure: it was downright dangerous. Conciliatory gestures in the face of brutality embolden the brutes, and sometimes enrage them. That is the lesson of the Wonderboy's misadventures in Iran.

But what is to be made of the fact that while the peace movement was bawling for disarmament negotiations Moscow was initiating warfare on two new fronts? In blatant contravention of international law it introduced chemical and biological warfare, and it supported worldwide terrorism. Both were without provocation in any way commensurate with the danger they brought to the world, and in the case of terrorism the danger of eventually setting off a chain of events that might lead to World War III grew steadily. The members of the peace movement were not the only fanatics involved here. The Soviets whose ghastly deeds the movement overlooked were fanatical too, which brings to mind a piece of wisdom uttered in the 1930s by an opponent of appeasement and disarmament who was soon summoned from obscurity to undo the disasters of frivolous statesmen. Charles de Gaulle revealed the delusions of the anti-defense appeasers of his day and of ours when he wrote, "If those who make use of the force of France lose heart, not only will our country be menaced, but the very harmony of the general order of things will be shattered. If wise men give up the use of power, what madmen will seize it, what fanatics?"[23]

10

The Enthusiasm for Spending

And the Mystery of Earning

SNICKER at the Liberal if you will, but when it comes to economics he has been right about affluence. It is gruesome. Going back to Biblical times, fastidious observers of humanity have been familiar with its morbid capacities, and today anyone of average intellect who has given the subject any thought or, say, been imprisoned *à table* with the pretty daughter of the twelfth Earl of Blavidshire comes to suspect affluence's meretricious facade. Making money is an adventure; but being surrounded with the stuff is a malaise, which must be treated with an appropriate remedy lest the patient be overcome by idiocy.

In practice affluence is second and third helpings of Beef Wellington when one would suffice. It is not one bottle of very good Bordeaux but several, and soon you are mistaking the waiter for the chef and then the washroom attendant for the newly promoted waiter. After the cognac you are boozily inviting the bewildered fellow home to admire your cheese vault. If he has his wits about him he will take you up on it; it is an easy way for a washroom attendant to lay hands on a nice stock of Port du Salut plus, perhaps, a silver setting or two. Riches cultivate their own ruin, leaving the fat cat crapulent and besotted. Let us give the Liberals their due: they have been aware of this for decades while the evangels of free enterprise have, to their discredit, usually ignored it.

Alas, in recent decades the Liberals have shown that they themselves are not free of the curse. These have been palmy times for them in and about the public sector, and many have become as unlovely as any bedizened rock-and-roll impresario. Clearly, Mammon fetched them. In fact Mammon sozzled them. In the 1970s they lost all sense of how economies work and how wealth is produced. Their tampering with the economy grew wild and extravagant. No industry was left unregulated, no group unsubsidized. To review a sampling of their economic pronunciamentos and reckless reforms is to witness the high jinks of a mob of happy drunks, all oblivious to the source of the riches in which they soaked. They seemed to think that wealth was the result of government distribution. They spoke of jobs as a matter of human rights and of work as an ignominy to be borne by no man. They harangued affluence as lustily as ever, but the affluence they harangued was always the affluence of others, particularly the affluence of the bourgeoisie.

The Liberals in their rush to vet affluence had dangerously underrated its toxicity. It is more horrible than these experts had estimated. It did the experts in.

Contrary to their welfarist notions, one cannot simply hand wealth over to the poor. To begin with, peremptorily grabbing it from the affluent imperils political liberty, discourages productivity, and destroys knowledge—to wit: the investment and entrepreneurial knowledge of those whose wealth is being grabbed; and bear in mind that this knowledge is at least one source of social progress. Then too, giving it to the poor is frequently as ruinous to them as a vast inheritance is to a prodigal youth. With depressing regularity the Liberals' welfare programs have actually enfeebled the poor and beguiled the working poor into indolence. Finally, doling out wealth even debauches the doler. It left the Liberals suffering advanced megalomania. From 1960 to 1980 the Liberals had increased transfer payments to the poor by $187.2 billion in 1980 dollars, yet their labors gave them no comfort; and their jeremiads on the poor's behalf grew nearly hysterical. By the early 1980s, having seen welfare's slice of the federal budget increase by nearly 100 percent,[1] they were bawling as though the poor were in worse condition than ever before. One could not argue them out of their gloom. As in so many other matters, the New Age Liberals had by this time become fanatics.

Affluence—only a handful of Medicis and Mellons, Rockefellers and Rothschilds have ever known how to handle the stuff. The Liberals of the New Age botched it totally, and by the late 1970s, as they uttered their last tantras to "small-is-beautiful" and "an era of limits," and as they heaved up their final reforms, it was apparent that they had changed radically. No longer were they mere critics of unfettered capitalism. Now they hated capitalism. Imagine a Medici loathing commerce or a Mellon hating banks. The Liberals hated both. In large numbers they became socialists by process of elimination. Socialism was the only economic system that did not set their blood to boiling.

In their fantasies they saw the poor as enduringly noble, competent, and—so one deduces from their twaddle—would-be millionaires were it not for the ceaseless oppressions of those brutes who had become millionaires first. The poor, in fact, became gods. Producers of wealth became society's enemies. In a fantasy that had grown for more than a decade, consumers became the human equivalent of baby seals.

In mild form the fantasy was simple consumerism: a sedate self-serving delusion portraying all who engage in commerce as suspected swindlers and poisoners; the rest of us are consumers, gullible and almost destitute; over us all presides the Liberal, the consumer*ist*, who warily patrols every act of commerce. It was a very public-spirited delusion.

Its more virulent form, however, was not so benign, for it left its victims nearly violent and given to diabolizing capitalism with an amazing passion, the kind that transforms the gentle features of a Jane Fonda into armament. Suddenly she is a shouter of the "Internationale," a champion of the down-and-out, an unremitting opponent of Little Lord Fauntleroy and all his goddamn fripperies. Not all New Age Liberals became out-and-out socialists. When Dr. John Kenneth Galbraith, Harvard's millionaire economics journalist, made his historic acknowledgment, he was in the bold minority. The rest were tacit socialists, allowing them to be at one with him in *vivre à droite et voter à gauche.*

New Age Liberals ceased to view capitalism as a medium for exchanging goods and services. Rather they saw it in terms of depravities, fiends, and innocent victims—that is to say, in terms comprehensible to small children or to believers of the Marxist sciences. The sensible remonstrances the Liberals of yesteryear had borne against capitalism's excesses gave way in the 1970s to frightening *pensées* such as Harvard's Dr. Stephen Marglin served up in *The Saturday Review*: "War and poverty; imperialism and subversion of the political system; racism and sexism; destruction of the community and environment. Each and every one of these social ills is used by capitalists to maintain their hegemony. Is the price too high? More and more people are coming to think so."[2]

Were more and more people truly coming to this position? Was it the end of the line for the Chamber of Commerce, Rotary, and the Giant Corporation? If so it was a curious way to end a dialectic, even a Marxist dialectic. About the time Dr. Marglin tapped out his grim judgment capitalists were beginning to swarm all over the Republic. By the early 1980s venture-capital funds were booming at an unprecedented rate, and business starts hit a record pace—nearly 600,000 per year for 1981 and 1982.[3]

Even before Dr. Marglin's announcement, America was in the midst of its most apolaustic swirl since the 1920s. Despite episodic recession and inflation, almost all Americans were conspicuous consumers, even the poor of Liberal legend. America's poor lived more prosperously than all the middle classes of the socialist Third World, or even the Communist world. In fact many of America's poor were quite fat.[4] Properly dressed and shaven many could pass for German bankers or Dutch clergymen, though they had more leisure time. The rotundity of many of America's poor is an embarrassing detail for our welfarists; and if they refer to it at all they cite it as evidence of improper nutrition, which to their minds is as much a concomitant of capitalism as pollution and sexism.

As for the nonpoor, millions of them were pothering exuberantly in shopping malls, department stores, and boutiques—wherever capitalism displayed its garish wares. If they shared Dr. Marglin's premonitions they betrayed no sign of it, and why should they? Even in times of economic unease they had an abundance of cash, which they willingly spent.

Americans were consuming rising percentages of their discretionary incomes on goods and services that in most societies would be considered luxuries and in some, miracles. Many Americans freely paid high prices for goods bearing esteemed logos. "Designers" put their marks on everything from automobiles to chocolates, and men and women from every walk of life paid top dollar to have the signature of one of these tenth-rate Michelangelos appear on their bedenimed rumps. Now, *there* was the mark of a happy commercial transaction! Yet the socialist dithyrambs of the New Age would not subside: "Capitalism kills. It is not just a matter of imperialistic wars or the treatment of human labor as expendable commodity. It is so vastly mistaken a way to organize human behavior that its cancerous costs are almost as great for the higher classes as for the lower," declared Dr. Hugh Drummond in another version of the hoary theme.[5] On the other hand, few who believed this tosh lived like stern Maoists or even like that abstemious old warhorse of American socialism, Norman Thomas. It is a mark of the corruption of the age—widely noted and never disputed—that most of capitalism's hostile forces would not turn their backs on Gucci or Pucci or a nice summer home on Martha's Vineyard, somewhere to get away from the pollution, sexism, and general tackiness of Capitalist America.

Though the anti-capitalist diatribes with their doomsday vaticinations were as incomprehensible to most Americans as the orphic gibbers of faith healers, they were hardly unfamiliar. Wherever the views of the New Age held sway denigratory images of capitalism and business became dominant. This was particularly true in Hollywood, California.

In an evaluation of prime-time television drama from the 1979–1980 season, the Media Institute, a private Washington, D.C., research group, found that "Two out of three businessmen are portrayed as criminal, evil, greedy, or foolish; almost one-half of all work activities performed by businessmen involve illegal acts; most big businessmen are portrayed as criminals; and television almost never portrays business as a socially or economically useful activity."[6] Now, here is a tantalizing irregularity for you. Increasingly it had become *de mauvais goût* to utter any irreverence whatsoever against one's fellow American no matter how absurd or unappealing he might be. America's high-minded pursuit of justice for all and prejudice toward none had swollen into a vast sentimentality, a phony scrupulosity against slighting the members of any group—neither the fat nor the deviant, the lazy nor the stupid. No one's vices or foibles were to be scoffed at or even noted. This scrupulosity was observed with particular intensity by the Liberals of the New Age, and naturally they were soon strangling on pent-up contempt. When they discovered that the money-makers and the moneyed were exempt from the sentimental niceties, they were greatly relieved, and they had at them with utmost fury. The idealists in the entertainment and intellectual industries were particularly effective, for they are very imaginative and arty. In fact they showed a flair for invidious stereotyping not seen on these shores since the Renaissance days of the Ku Kluxers.

The comparison is based on scholarly research. Benjamin J. Stein, whose pioneering anthropological studies of America's entertainment capital meet the highest standards of social science, has discovered in Hollywood a state of mind surprisingly reminiscent of the 1920s Ku Kluxian *intellectuel* cerebrating in a hill-jack metropolis hundreds of miles from Eastern bankers, Jews, Catholics, and other frightening caballers. Dr. Stein's *The View from Sunset Boulevard* has preserved dozens of Hollywood *philosophes'* thoughts on such dark mysteries as capitalism, banking, and general commerce. All are right out of jerkwater America. Among the writers, producers, and directors interviewed by Dr. Stein, many believe business is in cahoots with the Pentagon. Others see connections with the Mafia. Still others believe in possibilities so hellish that they cannot even be portrayed on film. Yet these yahoos gladly earn hundreds of thousands, often millions, of dollars annually, and with no pangs of conscience they spend them on all the joys the capitalists can produce—or does one think that they buy their goods and services from some socialist paradise? Come, come, these clowns are the most avid conspicuous consumers in the Republic. I was once trapped in an airplane with a pigsty of them en route to the Cannes film festival. The racket of junk jewelry banging against junk jewelry, the stench of horrid perfumes and colognes, the idiot yakking—all were enough to make a civilized traveler beg for a parachute; and, as Dr. Stein observes, practically every Hollywood genius believes that those who produce the luxuries that he adores are Fagins.

The denigration of the businessman takes on an aura of special absurdity when one recalls that in the 1970s the businessman, though hounded by a swelling crowd of government marplots, developed and marketed products that revolutionized our lives, adding immeasurably to our pleasure and productiveness. What is more, all major media were ravenous for heroes to celebrate. Why not whoop it up for a few score entrepreneurs to go along with all those actors, singers, athletes, models, human guinea pigs, and victims of disaster and disease? The burgeoning communications industry and the burgeoning public relations industry combined to serve our natural nosiness and make celebrity a national pastime. Magazines were founded to celebrate the celebrated. Newspapers reported their doings with high seriousness. Television and radio devoted a huge amount of time to talking with them and about them. Yet no one ever thought to celebrate the developers and marketers of the semiconductor, the microchip, the drugs such as antibiotics, painkillers, and promising antivirals.

We were living through the first stages of celebrity's golden age, yet the denigration of the businessman ran *pari passu* with the solemnizing of two-legged nihilities and occasionally of scoundrels. Unlike sports' golden age in the 1920s, when the accomplishments of the athletes were genuine, the accomplishments of 1970s celebrities were mostly in the realm of public relations. "Celebrity is now a substitute for fame," Michael Novak noted in the early 1980s. "The latter is earned by extraordinary achievement. The former is manufactured by freakiness."[7] Wit was lost in this world, as were all the higher forms of intelligence. In fact intelligence could be one's undoing, for it might bring agitation to the simpletons who composed the age of celebrity's hard-core audience.

In the golden age of celebrity vacuous mannequins like Bianca Jagger or Brooke Shields were photographed and quoted and asked to make special appearances merely because at some happy moment earlier on they had been photographed and quoted and asked to make a special appearance. How often was Robert Noyce photographed and quoted and asked to make special appearances? He was the major developer of the microchip, which was not so much held against him as the fact that he actually made a bundle on this little discovery. In the golden age of celebrity the only acceptable way to earn a fortune was through sports or entertainment or grotesquerie.

Now, one need hold no romantic illusions about the capitalists to reject this image of them as paradigmatic fiends. Doubtless there are businessmen who are rascals and worse. Surely many are dunces and philistines. I do not doubt for a minute that the average chief executive when he comes home at night removes his pants and spends the rest of the evening watching television in his undershorts; but certainly the average businessman is a better sort of fellow than the scoundrel portrayed on the tube, and probably he is a better sort than the Hollywood *philosophe* who believes that socialist hooey about capitalism but lives a life awash in Mammon's pleasures. Such hypocrites consider wealth evil but loll in it anyway. It is a rare businessman who takes his profits and scorns profit-taking. Those who do very likely work in the entertainment business. The industry has never been esteemed for its business ethics.

In the 1970s the socialist critique of capitalism gained a powerful purchase on the minds of many and for a perfectly understandable reason: capitalism is almost wholly absorbed with economics; socialism has hardly anything to do with economics. Its concern is drama.

Economics is, as they say, a dismal science. Economists and an alarming number of capitalists give themselves over to such tiresome stuff as interest rates, productivity rates, exchange rates, prices, and profits. Only these last two items divert the true-blue socialist. The other stuff puts him to sleep. He lives for action and inspiration, preferably religious inspiration. Socialism is one of the longest-playing religious soap operas in history, with bankers and bosses enslaving and impoverishing the rest of us, compassion and sweetness struggling against greed and brute force, good against evil. If socialism were merely an economic system, it would long ago have been heaved aside to be replaced by barter, hunting-and-gathering, or some other more advanced economic system not so given to socialism's shoddy merchandise, shortages, and economic stagnation. If it were only a political system it would have been dumped as a fossil on the order of feudalism, for its record of coercion, bellicosity, and brutal oligarchy is well known. But socialism is art, the art of self-delusion.

It is quite as misleading to speak of socialist economics as it is to speak of chiropractic science. The true socialist is not an economist but a storyteller, often a gifted storyteller but nothing more. Not one has ever been able to massage socialism into uttering anything that is true about economics or anything else. The most memorable of the socialist gogues remains Dr. Marx, and his contribution to knowledge is not in economics but in warfare. He provided men with a compelling new rationale for killing each other off, and since his passing more people have been slaughtered in his name than in the names of Allah or Jesus.

The socialist theory is a fable. The socialist reality is a very uncomfortable place to live: political tyrants having replaced the bosses of yore; coercion having vanquished liberty; shortages and want having replaced economic growth and self-reliance. Greed remains, but long ago it was surpassed in popularity and maliciousness by envy. Where there once was optimism there is now pessimism. The citizen who once hoped to be an entrepreneur now queues up like everyone else for a new pair of socks or a feast of moldy state-issued potatoes.

Wherever socialism has slithered into power there is either unspeakable cruelty or slow economic decomposition. Russia, the Socialist Motherland, offers its citizens both. The decrepitude of Britain, upon whose wealth the sun could not set four decades ago, is evidence of socialism's knack for despoiling an economy. More recently we have witnessed the amazing impoverishment of Germany under the Social Democrats and the almost instantaneous economic collapse of France's theretofore robust economy under François Mitterrand's Socialists.

By the late 1970s all the liberal welfare states of Europe were in a very dilapidated state. The most advanced of them, Sweden, had an average marginal tax rate of more than 60 percent and a deficit at 12 percent of GNP and rising. All the EEC nations combined exited the 1970s having created no more jobs than they had had at the beginning of the decade, and Germany under the Social Democrats ended 1980 with 2 percent less employment than in 1970.[8] Millions of immigrant laborers were now being booted from these progressive domains. Imagine if the United States treated its immigrants in this way! Imagine if we had the police power to search out and deport groups of people! In a socialist paradise, even a liberal socialist paradise, there is that kind of control.

The United States has suffered heavy bombardment from socialist critics for its economic problems, its low tax base, its rampant capitalism, and its renowned poverty class. Yet the United States, as *The Wall Street Journal* has delighted in informing us, has been able to establish a poverty line that is perhaps $1,000 above the median family income of the Soviet Union, and only approximately 6 percent of the American population was below that line in 1980.[9] During the 1970s the U.S. economy produced a net gain of 19 million jobs, increasing employment five times as fast as the French economy, and three times as fast as Japan's. As George Gilder points out, "While the U.S. economy absorbed a baby-boom population bulge that did not occur in Europe, and accommodated an estimated 12 million legal and illegal immigrants, the E.E.C. countries stopped the influx of overseas workers and payed hundreds of thousands to return to their homelands."[10]

So obvious are socialism's economic and political failures that at times even some of the faithful are moved to doubt, and when the dubiety steals in there can be eloquence. Such an instance came sometime in 1979 when one of Dr. Marx's most faithful Yank disciples, Sidney Lens, reviewed the good-government policies of the socialist camp and lamented: "How can one justify, for instance, the forced migrations in People's Kampuchea (Cambodia)? . . . Or consider the current conflict between Kampuchea and Vietnam: How is it possible for two *socialist* states to wage war against each other? . . . Worse still, how can *socialist* China regard *socialist* Russia as its chief enemy and insist, in its domestic and foreign propaganda, that war with the Soviet Union is 'inevitable'? . . . As for the Soviet Union, how can one explain its suppression of free speech, free press, and free trade unions years after the revolution? Perhaps a socialist regime must deny democratic prerogatives when it comes to power in order to forestall a counterrevolution—but for *sixty-one years?* . . . I wish I could resolve these contradictions for myself in simple, unambiguous terms." Yet the illumination is usually brief. "Like most people," Dr. Lens went on, "I would like to cherish the vision of a beautiful tomorrow. I would like to hold and share the conviction that there *is* a better alternative—for if socialism is not the alternative to the militarism, repression, instability, and injustice of capitalism, what is?"[11]

Militarism? Repression? Instability? Injustice? Is Dr. Lens talking about us? I fear that he is. We live in a world that has witnessed six decades of Soviet *gulags*, show trials, pogroms, despotism, and economic privation plus bellicosity on a worldwide scale. Every day enormities are committed against ordinary people in socialist and Third World lands that equal those reported in the Old Testament, yet in the New Age, capitalism's critics look across America and harangue ghosts ascertainable only through Marxist calculations. How does one account for it?

I return to affluence. It drove large numbers of capitalism's critics right around the bend. Much as the philanderer thinks of womanhood and envisages vaults full of luscious breasts and thighs and buttocks; trays of pert lips, intriguing noses, enchanting eyes; chambers echoing with hundreds of thousands of lovely laughs and sensuous sighs; boulevards shimmering with saucy walks, the Sidney Lenses of America think of capitalism and begin hallucinating, their vision blurred by wild dollar signs undulating and running amuck just beyond their grasp, ticky-tacky homes carpeting the land as far as the eye can see, mounds of cheap manufactured products glistening in the sunshine. It is a fevered vision and a positively demented way to view an economic system; but twenty years of having things pretty much their own way—every reform, every regulation—and still not seeing heaven on earth left the New Age Liberals in this sorry state. Reality repulsed them. Complexity and uncertainty daunted them. They yearned for the happy tales of socialism where after the last titanic battle against the captains of industry a tidy little world would be secured free of militarism, repression, instability, and injustice.

The difference between socialism and capitalism is the difference between fiction and history: the one is a story invented irrespective of truth; the other follows closely the way men and women live. Socialism is a way of life that has never been satisfactorily lived, outside a few choice monasteries and communes. Capitalism is a way of life that grew out of the actions of tens of thousands of ordinary people availing themselves of the exhilarating intellectual currents of the eighteenth century, and has been successfully lived for generations, much to our enrichment and happiness.

One is distracted from the capitalist reality when one fastens upon the legendary dollar sign, and one is diverted from the socialist reality when one fastens on socialism's ideals. The socialist ideals are alluring. Peace, prosperity, cooperation, equality, community, freedom—it is a honeyed vision. Yet is it a reality in any of those gray lands under Dr. Marx's suzerainty? Let us not belabor the subject, but let us be bold and forthright. Prolonged observation of the species *Homo sapiens* suggests that the only places on this orb where one will see even an approximation of these socialist ideals are those few voluptuous lands where there is capitalism. The thought does occur that if the socialist were really serious about his lovely vision, well, he would be a capitalist.

There is more peace, freedom, prosperity, dignity, and even equality in Dubuque, Iowa, than in Moscow or Peking or poor Mitterrand's Paris. Moreover, the early analysts of capitalism foresaw as much. Unlike the dyspeptic Dr. Marx, who retired from the hurly-burly to the reading room of the British Museum, there to dream up a world that never was, thinkers like Adam Smith reported on an emerging world. Two centuries later the expectations of capitalism's early analysts have proved infinitely more accurate than Dr. Marx's prophecies for the socialist fairy tale.

Montesquieu saw that commercial activity would ameliorate men's "destructive prejudices." From a continent recently torn by religious wars and the squabbles of pompous aristocrats, the French philosopher observed that commerce "polishes and softens barbaric morals." A long line of distinguished men of affairs followed, from James Madison to the twentieth-century secretary of state Cordell Hull, all sharing and championing Montesquieu's shrewd insight that "the spirit of commerce unites nations."[12] Doubtless the officers and customers of many modern-day multinational corporations would agree. Commerce was expected to usher in a more peaceful world because, as Thomas Paine could see, it "diminishes the spirit both of patriotism and military defense."[13] Beyond peace, commerce was seen as encouraging freedom, prosperity, and diversity not only for aristocrats but also for common folk. As Adam Smith noted, before the rise of capitalism men had "lived almost in a continual state of war with their neighbors, and of servile dependency upon their supervisors," but with the growth of capitalism men might experience "order and good government and, with them, the liberty and security of individuals."[14]

Capitalism was a new order brought into existence not by the clubs of thugs and the calculations of dreamers but by ordinary men aided by a growing sense of personal liberty. Always, economic freedom had to overcome the resistance of the state, save in the whelp Republic across the Atlantic. In no other country was the new order given more encouragement than in early America, where the founding fathers had eloquently argued the merits of freedom and commerce. Tocqueville was particularly mindful of capitalism's merits, and when he toured America in the 1830s he was stimulated by what he saw: free citizens "calculating and weighing and computing" as they shoved back a wilderness to transform the land into a civilization where even the meanest would someday live in unprecedented comfort and freedom.[15]

Today's haranguers for peace, freedom, prosperity, and equality, then, have chosen fantasy over reality. They exalt Dr. Marx over Adam Smith and the founding fathers. They venerate a crank, who dreamed of a world that never was and never was to be, over men who studied and celebrated a real world, a world progressing toward the very desiderata they claim to admire. Today's socialist is not greatly different, in truth, from the reactionary. The latter idealizes a past that never was. The former idealizes a future that never will be. Both have an unscotchable and irrational yearning to escape the present or to destroy it.

Capitalism has fulfilled its analysts' expectations. It has created a world with a higher percentage of self-reliant, competent individuals than history has ever seen before. It has encouraged the rule of law and the enlargement of personal freedom by putting limits on both the bully and the state. It has allowed an unparalleled growth in the world's wealth, a blurring of class distinctions, and ever more comfort and opportunity for the poor. Of all the systems in history only capitalism has allowed the ceaseless and relatively peaceful movement of huge numbers of people rising from poverty or falling from affluence. Capitalism is unsurpassed in allowing citizens to realize their potential. If some come out poor and others rich, at least the poor under capitalism are less poor than under other systems.

Liberating the competent to create wealth so that all benefit from the competent's industry was by the late 1970s so obviously a superior economic system that its New Age opponents could argue against it neither rationally nor on economic grounds. Thus they led jeers against it—*"trickle-down theory, trickle-down theory,"* they taunted. Did they believe that things trickle up? I believe they did. Many solemnly asserted that the proper prescription for economic vigor was to give wealth to the poor, thus increasing "purchasing power" and social justice. Yet where does wealth come from in the first place?

In the New Age the critics of capitalism never could explain how wealth is created. Most simply avoided the matter, taking the prosperity of America for granted. Others believed that wealth was stolen goods taken from the noble poor—else how did the poor become poor? Neither group confronted the hard little truth that wealth is created by work and faith, and that without work life is not only penurious but also tedious and barbaric. Any diligent observer of our species knows the truth of this. How many times have you encountered men and women who live intellectually, morally, and culturally at the level of animals? Only when one comes to the topic of their occupations does one begin to see a human being. It is by selling paint or by bringing the kids to basketball practice that these people begin to experience humanity. Here they learn about others and they learn the important things about themselves. Moreover, they avoid mischief. Dr. Freud understood that work is the best therapy. How he discovered this I cannot say, but he did and it put him a step ahead of the economic wisdom of the New Age.

Ignorant of the value of work and of the source of wealth, the New Age critic of capitalism employed flamboyant rhetorical flourishes to lay practically all society's shortcomings to capitalism. "The efficient rapacity of our raider-rulers," Professor Garry Wills wrote in *The New York Review of Books*, "has made consumption expand at a dizzying rate, equaled only by the rate at which resources diminish—air, earth, fuel, and water."[16] Close textual analysis suggests that Dr. Wills is one of those New Age adepts who believe that capitalism is theft and presumably that a comfortable middle-class life is the natural condition for all if only the greed of the Business Roundtable could be thwarted. A research expedition through this nation's hoosegows, however, establishes clearly that a very high percentage of our prison population is composed of those who have never committed their first capitalist act. In fact many prison inmates have performed no productive work whatsoever that is not *malum prohibitum*. Most of our nation's jailbirds share the socialists' delusions about how wealth is amassed, and I for one find it vastly reassuring to know that you can still be sentenced to ten-to-twenty for taking the socialists seriously. No wonder so many believers in the New Age have had a special solicitude for those behind bars. But all would have been better off had they realized that the surest path to riches is steady work and law-abidingness.

There is no doubt that beyond the prison bars, out in America where men sweat after dollars and perquisites, there is mischief and mayhem, but the fault lies not with the economic system that as aforementioned has encouraged law-abiding behavior and peaceful commerce. There is only so much an economic system can do for a society. Neither capitalism nor socialism is a substitute for higher cultural and moral commitments. As Michael Novak has asserted, "The commercial virtues are not . . . sufficient to their own defense. A commercial system needs taming and correction by a moral-cultural system independent of commerce. At critical points, it also requires taming and correction by the political system and the state. The founding fathers did not imagine that the institutions of religion, humanism, and the arts would ever lose their indispensable role. They did not imagine that the state would wither away. Each of the three systems needs the other. Yet they did understand that an economic system without profit is merely spinning its wheels, providing neither for the unmet needs of the poor nor for progress."[17] George Gilder goes further.

In the 1980s Gilder arrived as capitalism's most subtle champion and possibly its most ardent. He endorsed what Walter Lippmann had written during the Great Depression in *The Good Society*: "for the first time in human history" there was a system that gave men "a way of producing wealth in which the good fortune of others multiplied their own," and in which "for the first time men could conceive a social order in which the ancient moral aspiration of liberty, fraternity, and equality was consistent with the abolition of poverty and the increase of wealth." Sounding as Gilder would fifty years later, Lippmann went on: "Until the division of labor had begun to make men dependent on the free collaboration of other men, the worldly policy was to be predatory. The claims of the spirit were otherworldly. So it was not until the industrial revolution had altered the traditional mode of life that the vista was opened at the end of which men could see the possibility of the Good Society on this earth. At long last the ancient schism between the world and the spirit, between self interest and disinterestedness, was potentially closed."[18]

The New Age critics' preoccupation with other people's wealth is deadly to an understanding of capitalism. What really matters is the capitalist's act of creation. It is the source of growth and riches. The capitalist, Gilder tells us, begins with a blank canvas and creates. Most who work in this world do so with the expectation of contractual remuneration, but the capitalist's expectation is based solely on faith. The capitalist is a bold, adventuresome, self-reliant citizen who looks ahead trying to ascertain what his fellow citizens' needs will be in the future. Economists, in the main, believe in *Homo economicus,* man as a slug moved to action solely by financial inducement. It is as gross a generalization as the belief that all redheads are hot-tempered or all fat people are jolly. Some men will roost under their favorite shade tree no matter what the economic inducement. Others will work until they have attained a certain level of material comfort and no more. Yet there are those whose restless gropings never end. This, Gilder tells us, is the true capitalist. Taking on Adam Smith's theory of the invisible hand, Gilder argues that the psychology of the eternal groper or tinkerer is more fundamental to economic growth than the existence of markets; only capitalism allows this fellow his opportunity to bring us material progress. Gilder's argument is audacious and perplexing, especially for the grim socialist.

Parting company even with most champions of capitalism, Gilder believes that capitalism is an eminently moral system. "Capitalism begins with giving," says Gilder in a buoyant humor. "Not from greed, avarice, or even 'self-love' can one expect the rewards of commerce, but from a spirit closely akin to altruism, a regard for the needs of others, a benevolent, outgoing, and courageous temper of mind. Such a universal trait as self-interest—altogether as prevalent in any socialist backwater or deadening bureaucracy as in the realms of great enterprise—will reveal virtually nothing of the rare sources of riches in human society. Not taking and consuming, but giving, risking, and creating are the characteristic roles of the capitalist, the key producer of the wealth of nations. . . ." Gilder asserts that capitalists are chiefly stimulated not by the desire to consume or to make pigs of themselves, "but by the freedom and power to consummate their entrepreneurial ideas." Even more important than hedonism or economic inducement, Gilder believes, is the capitalist's drive to tinker with the world and try to understand it. Here, he says, is the source of wealth, which is to say "value defined by others."[19]

Is Gilder right? I have no doubt that he is right to take on the notion of *Homo economicus*. As for the capitalist's altruism, I reserve judgment. It certainly is a lovely thought. For centuries those who have been most proficient at creating wealth have endured some of mankind's bloodiest atrocities. Wealth maddens the mob. It maddened the Nazis against Jews and the Soviets against Kulaks and Jews. It accounted for the slaughter of the Ibo in Nigeria, and the deaths of more than a million overseas Chinese in Indonesia. The record is long and horrible. Yet always the slaughter is undertaken for high ideals. If there is any truth in Gilder's claim about the capitalist's altruism, the greed and envy of others stands revealed as even stupider and uglier than it appears.

11

The Egalitarian Placebo

"I Want My Mommy"

TIME goes by. All life is transitory. Perhaps these victims of other people's envy and greed have little ground for complaint. After all, nothing shaped by man can long endure the ravages of time: the fire of other men's passions, the mutilations wrought by nature's elements.

No matter our station in life, we distinguish ourselves from the herd by grasping one melancholy fact. It is the source of all great art and honor and every redeeming snicker; it is that every man lives out a tragedy: the promise of his youth fades into the certainty of his decomposition and death. Then he is gone. Soon all that has stood around him vanishes too; the landscape changes completely. For many Liberals, trapped in modernity's habit of mind, the news is as unbearable as its truth is inescapable: no matter how many plastic surgeons, physical therapists, or other such magicians are in one's service it is always a very brief trip from swaddling clothes to that last public appearance in charnel garb. The mortician applies his art to our cold, silent carcasses, and with us into the grave go all our laughs and groans and moments of ecstasy, never to echo again, not even in a friend's memory—at least not for long. The suntans and the elegance are reduced to dust, and in time the dust is being swept around on a kitchen floor belonging to someone we never dreamed would be here. Over thousands of years men have sought solace from these unhappy facts through the consolations of art, philosophy, heroics, the bottle, or speculations on that gaseous domain for which the Temple and Chartres were raised and in whose service the prophets and saints have hectored us.

By the 1970s Liberalism had shed many of the traditional considerations of politics. Now it took on the bizarreries of a religious cult.* This Liberalism, however, had denied itself all the ancient consolations, and so without such refuges the faithful were left to fill their aching voids with little lies, fashionable quirks and foibles, plus the enthusiasms whose most fantastical versions have absorbed the better part of our inquiry.

The ritualizing of thought that accompanied Liberalism's evolution through the years had left the faithful in desperate straits. They were chained to the present moment, the past having been anathematized and left contemptible, the future having been rendered so remote as to seem academic—a kind of dream world, any provision for which might be deemed an unconscionable flight from the dire present with its multifarious injustices and crises. Here in the dire present the Liberals shivered, forlorn and unsolaced even by a reassuring place in a Burkean chain of generations or under the eye of a loving God. The Liberal was in a hell of a mess, and neither recourse to freedom nor recourse to reason could assuage his anxieties and fill the aching void. In fact, freedom and reason made him very testy. He needed a new lie, a stupendous lie, one that would keep him occupied and comforted.

The lie was egalitarianism. Freedom and reason were a problem no more. Egalitarianism is a bracer for those who have been unnerved by the specter of freedom. It is the placebo for the spiritually and philosophically queasy, and it

---

* Not surprisingly, even a cult as weird as the People's Temple attracted amiable, if perhaps unwitting, endorsements from eminentoes like Congresswoman Bella Abzug, Congressman Phillip Burton, former Vice President Hubert Humphrey, Mrs. Jimmy Carter, and Vice President Walter Mondale.[1] Would Harry Truman or Lyndon Johnson have endorsed such a wild group?

works—at least for a while, for it holds out hope of splendid New Dawns, and it keeps the yokels busy and *ipso facto* free from dwelling on their problems. Then things get worse.

Egalitarianism never could solve the New Age Liberal's problem. Delusory as it is, it only compounds problems, making them more intense and leaving the Liberal rootless, timorous, fatalistic, and confirmed in the opinion that all life is aleatory, so what the hell. The sanguine Liberal of yesteryear gave way to a sad new Malvolio, pessimistic and surprisingly superstitious.

Of course, at first egalitarianism had dazzling uses. It was so ennobling, conferring upon the egalitarian an exalted mission that would enjoin him to intrude into every aspect of American life. Pursuant to the egalitarian ideal, nothing would be left unpoliticized. Here egalitarianism filled the Liberal's most pressing political need. By the late 1970s so many of the Liberal goals had been achieved, so many of the Liberal reforms had been tried. In America there was freedom and prosperity. The poor were better off than they could hope to be anywhere else on the globe. There was even equality, or as much equality as one could reasonably expect.

Now the Liberals had little left to do. As pontificators and public servants they were facing unemployment. Egalitarianism would allow them to pursue the only goal they had left: cultural and political domination of the Great Republic. But to what purpose? Alas, the Liberals had no purpose. Their only goal was to stay on top and to avoid facing up to that feeling of meaninglessness that gnawed within.

As ideas go egalitarianism is all cheap cologne and rhinestones. It was a futile undertaking for America. Tocqueville had observed that "When inequality is the general rule in society, the greatest inequalities attract no attention. When everything is more or less level, the slightest variation is noticed. Hence the more equal men are, the more insatiable will be their longing for equality."[2] Having now lived through the 1970s and endured all the pious pishposh about equality I must tender a qualification to the great Frenchman's wisdom. Sometimes the more a society is leveled the more its individual members will strain to stand out from the mob. In Mao's

China did the cheeky Chinese guy leave a shoelace untied? Did the fashionable Chinese gal roll up her left pant leg? In America, as the egalitarian reforms of the Liberals set in, a huge outburst of pretension grew: exceptional lifestyles being adopted, designer goods being proudly displayed, gold chains around the neck, weird pets in the living room, Perrier water where seltzer and a twist would suffice, and adults of every configuration affecting the fashion and even the behavior of youth. Suddenly one saw the guy sporting a Cartier tank watch or the gal bearing a $500 Louis Vuitton handbag while wearing jeans and a T-shirt, the message being: I can afford grandeur, though I choose to be pure lovable prole. Here is the kind of chaotic crassitude that egalitarian measures evoke.

Egalitarianism is always a futile thing; for it is a denial of nature, of the biological order that gives us different talents, strengths, and tastes. To pursue it one has to be at once foolish and ruthless, or at least hypocritical and ruthless. Irving Kristol tells us of his repeated attempts in the 1970s to induce an egalitarian economist or sociologist to submit an essay to his journal *The Public Interest* wherein we might be apprised of the specifics: an egalitarian society's proper income distribution, the prescribed degree of social mobility—that sort of thing. No one ever took Kristol up on his offer. Instead there was only the huge moral justification that rumbled forth from the philosopher John Rawls, and he left the specifics for the time when all the hellish institutions and markings of inequality had been swept away, as Mao swept them away in China—egalitarianism's record is not peaceful.

"A more equal society is a better society even if its citizens prefer inequality," one of the New Age's most luminous egalitarians, Professor Ronald Dworkin, has written.[3] Here is how far the journey from freedom and reason had taken the faithful. I may be a bad man, but I for one would rather not have the likes of Dr. Dworkin defining the boundaries of my freedom or my equality. Our only safeguard from incipient bullies like Prof Dworkin and from all the baseness that issues from egalitarianism is reverence for personal liberty as the ultimate political value. If a society properly esteems freedom its members will not be brought to a broil by tales of someone's debut at the Met or arrival into the *Fortune* 500. Nor will it be stampeded into the hopeless and barbaric business of forcing one mold down on a myriad of peoples who have been created different by nature. The intelligent quest is for the free society with equality of opportunity. The quest for equality of result is the path to the widest inequality of all: despotism.

In the New Age, apace with all the idiotic enthusiasms and lies, a huge fatalism arose and seeped into the ritualized thought of the faithful. Having depreciated all social hierarchy, tradition, kinship, and every other sort of distinction, the New Age Liberals were left believing only in an egalitarian tomorrow while today was made uncomfortable with alienation, anomie, identity crises, and other such modern horrors. The New Age Liberals themselves now constituted an undifferentiated mob of feckless souls, tremulous and impotent before the vast, uncontrollable forces they spied: capitalism, science, world revolution, fate. In a world that they had stripped bare of distinctions and significance, where family and community—Burke's "inns and resting places" of the human spirit—had been sorely diminished, the Liberals were left with no idea where they stood or who they were or what effect they might have on the shape of things. As a consequence of their own fatalism, life lost its meaning. All effort seemed futile, which in part must account for the frivolousness with which they confronted serious matters. They no longer believed that ideas or even actions had consequences, certainly not malign consequences.

Fatalism has overtaken other peoples in other times. It was dominant in post-Alexandrian Greece, for example, and in the Rome of the Caesars. In such times belief in one's capacity to influence events diminishes. All is foreordained by fate. There is pessimism and nihilism. All resides with chance, and every striving depends on luck. As Robert Nisbet, who has written so thoughtfully on all this, points out, there is renewed interest in the occult. Certainly this was the condition of the New Age Liberal watching with ambivalence as his friends and children entered into the cults. When his leaders began to act like cult leaders themselves he was too far gone to object. He admired their "charisma," their oratorical wizardry, their style.*

This was the wretched state of the New Age Liberal when along came a pert hill-jack from Plains, Georgia, whose desire to be president was as preposterous as Mozart's table manners. Yet the Liberals said, Why not? They took a gamble. How could it go wrong? Had they ever been wrong before? If so they had convinced themselves that their errors bore no consequences. All that really mattered was that they stay on top. And so they opted for Jimmy Carter's residency at 1600 Pennsylvania Avenue. Four years later they denied any responsibility for this last botch. Experience and reality were confected for them by their ideological gurus. Nothing else was real.

---

* The rise of the cults in the 1970s never created much of a stir with the Liberals. A generation earlier their appearance would have been viewed with alarm as a threat to reason and freedom. Alas, the Liberals' appetite for both had now turned into an allergy.

12

New Age Liberalism's Noble Goal

A Misdemeanor

In conclusion, what do the Liberals of the New Age think in their heart of hearts? Since the late 1960s these ardent pontificators have infiltrated the Republic with sundry brands of cheap thought, all promising the esoteric insight, the higher understanding, good vibes, or some other infantile desiderata. They have politicized heretofore virgin areas of American life. They have pelted us with misnomers, presumptuous cant, and suffering situations that leave the world appearing lugubrious and pathetic. By the early 1980s the *gringo* citizenry had been dragged through hundreds of unlovely episodes of which Vietnam, Watergate, Jonestown, the racial hullabaloo over the Atlanta murders, and the Iranian "hostage crisis" were only the most clamorous.

Still what the Liberals of the New Age really favor remains mysterious. As the era aged, the incoherence of their credenda worsened, suggesting that a kind of uninhibited senility was settling upon the movement. Their whole agenda was in flux. Smoking in public places, once a chic right defended by the forward-lookers, is of a sudden a deadly affront, subject to a new prohibition. Exuberant carnality, previously boomed as salubrious and liberating, is devalued, reassessed as "sexual harassment," and considered a prelude to rape. Throughout the era the number of good causes the Liberals abandoned was exceeded only by the number they betrayed. What, then, is it that they are really after?

Studious analysis of all relevant materials and much prayerful meditation have led me to conclude that Liberals in the New Age have, indeed, had one sublime goal that unites all the diverse enthusiasts: all felt enjoined by high principle to disturb their neighbors, most of whom they dismissed as idiots. This mighty goal is the great constant of their public lives: their ad hoc committees, letters to the editor, protest demonstrations, and every "issue" from "peace" to animal rights.

At times, I admit, it appears that Liberalism's goal is really to abridge the Bill of Rights and to limit personal liberty, for their reforms are frequently being frustrated by the common man's liberty-loving ways, and they often leap to restrain him. But then, just as we are ready to categorize the New Age Liberal as *au fond* an opponent of freedom, he begins thrusting upon us exotic freedoms whose *bona fides* even the late Jean-Jacques Rousseau might have doubted—for instance: our absolute dirty-book rights, the right to deaden our brains with drugs, the right to pull down our pants in public. Does this make the Liberal an absolutist for freedom? As likely as not he is equally vehement for mandatory and inescapable automobile seat belts. To what is he really devoted? The only constant in all his multifarious good causes and pious tantrums is the noble goal of disturbing his neighbors; and, if peace and justice be our goals, it is worth noting that this noble goal is legally termed "disturbing the peace," a misdemeanor in all civilized criminal codes.

Sometimes the noble goal is merely adumbrated, as when the New Age consumerist forced upon the Republic medicine bottles that were nearly unopenable, particularly by the sick; or when the career do-gooders, acting with their customary furtiveness, suddenly plowed up our sidewalks, leaving mischievous channels through which a solitary wheelchair might pass. In the meantime thousands of us stumble into the infernal depressions, presenting the Liberals with the happy prospect that still more of us may become handicapped, at least temporarily, thus qualifying as fit subjects for their odious compassion.

Yet at other times the New Age Liberal has been very forth-coming about his noble goal, which, as I have suggested, is probably criminal. "Challenge the orthodox," the pol of the New Age is wont to say. "Confront the iniquitous" is another of his lines, along with "Afflict the comfortable." Once re-moved from the coy realms of politics the New Age Liberal is even more blatant. The art critic bases almost all his aesthetic judgments on the oft-repeated belief that art's transcendent purpose is to disturb us: to scrape the bones, crack the skull, gouge eyes, and tear off an ear. Modern art, if it is truly aglow with Minerva's light, is supposed to make us feel like morons. The New Age cleric is just as avid for disturbance. Today he hounds the faithful into holding hands in church and embrac-ing perfect strangers; tomorrow he will have them placing their thumbs perpendicular to their noses while wagging their fingers at their next-door neighbors. Then there is the New Age prof who abominates all Christendom on the premise that his students must experience his violence if ever they are to shake the bourgeois coil and enter the palmy provinces of Dr. Karl Marx and Dr. Leo Buscaglia. Yet no New Age eminento that I have ever known has believed that he is similarly im-proved by having his life disturbed. That is going too far, and those who would disturb him are the agents of reaction or the late Senator Joseph McCarthy or some other horror from the dank of American history.

In strict political terms, then, the New Age Liberal has been neither libertarian nor authoritarian. He has been a pest, a public nuisance, and somewhat deranged at that.* To probe the cause of his derangement is to discover the causes for the

---

* Notwithstanding all the Liberal's poesy about compassion, tolerance, and decency, his capacity for intolerance, violence, and hatred is often quite breathtaking. Time and again he and his colleagues fall upon some poor fish who is out of harmony with them politically or intellectually, and when they have finished abominating him in all their forums of in-fluence he is a ruin, his name having been transformed into another of America's metaphors for evil. One thinks of the assault on James Watt, Ronald Reagan's first Secretary of the Interior. He may have been im-prudent; he may have been a fool; but when the Liberal brethren were done with him he had been transformed into the embodiment of evil; and even after bouncing him from government they kept up the abuse, reviling him at every opportunity. These are colossal haters.

New Age itself. It was created willy-nilly by those who could not bear the burden of personal freedom, rationalism, relativism, and affluence, all of which proved to be too much for vast herds of our progressive brethren and sistren. Thus they attempted to soothe themselves with a new system of values and ideas. The values and ideas are, as we have seen, very wretched; but that did not restrain progressives from attempting to inflict them on their fellow Americans. Happily, some areas of American life have remained tolerably invulnerable; but other areas—for instance, academe—have almost wholly capitulated and so gone to seed.

A fundamental cause of the New Age was the Liberal's inability to tolerate freedom. It is a matter of record that throughout the 1970s, despite all their sententious testimonials to liberation, many a vaunted absolutist for liberty called in the cops at the first sign of discomfort. Very few New Age Liberals could abide a society in which others too were free. Some could not even endure their own freedom. They had worn bikinis. Now they yearned for straitjackets.

A second cause of the New Age was the Liberals' reaction to rationalism. It is an old story: after rationalism has done its work irrationality enters. After Socrates came the mystery religions. After our own protracted examination of all that ordinary Americans had customarily taken on faith, many were left fearful; even many so-called rationalists were shivering. On came the 1970s cults, their members for the most part coming from the ranks of the reputedly well educated. A generation before, the Liberals would have subjected the cults to the utmost scrutiny and even derision. Now, however, many stalwart Liberals were themselves cowering in rationalism's wake.

Our whole belief system, every aspect of human existence had for a century been exposed to rationalistic analysis. All those timeless arrangements, traditions, prejudices, and nods to the supernatural that comfort ordinary men and women had been rendered dubious. The certitudes of a certain morality fell into doubt. Furthermore, prodded by rationalism and relativism, the Liberals abandoned practically all standards of judgment. The ensuing chill and pitiless reality were too much for the weak-witted children of rationalism and the free society. They mutinied against both and opted for unreason and statism. Some even accepted gods as long as they were suitably Oriental, inscrutable, and idiotic.

Yet if freedom, rationalism, and relativism were fundamental to the New Age's rise, affluence gave it its childish imbecility and unique staying power. At no other time in Western history had the flotsam and jetsam floated and jetted so comfortably. All the sages of the hour agreed that the inner life had grown painful, but material life was becoming wonderfully painless. The consequences of one's most egregious botches could be relieved or hidden away with a new purchase: the failed husband diverts himself with a new Corvette; the failed government diverts the voters with a new political giveaway. In the New Age affluence turned large numbers of supposedly well-educated citizens into arrested adolescents, lost in idiot bliss, bereft of any sense of tragedy or even danger. They ignored history. They grew oblivious to reality. On those rare occasions when some glint of it peeped through their clouds of fantasy they became very angry. The Liberalism of the New Age had become a long, angry war with life.

The major casualties of their war have been reviewed in past chapters, though the subtlest has only been alluded to. I have in mind trust. By ascribing ignoble values so widely throughout our society, they gravely damaged all faith in institutions, in individuals, even in the future; and without faith societies begin to fall apart. The Liberals' problem was that they had come into the world as idealists, and every idealist exits a cynic. Better it is to be a realist facing up to the world as it is than to fall into the stupidity of the cynic, the fool who praised gods that never were only to end up admonishing against bugaboos equally quixotic. After the New Age Liberal had had his say women did not trust the marriage bed, blacks did not trust whites, no one trusted a producer of any kind. Many doubted the arrival of tomorrow. Doctors, lawyers, businessmen, scientists—in fact, experts in almost every walk of life—saw their authority evaporate. As in decadent societies of old, morale sagged. The reward for doing right was abuse or disbelief. The smart fellow was encouraged to cut corners. That is the legacy that the moral hams of the New Age brought into American life, and whether America could ever recover what the founding fathers called its Republican virtue would be in doubt for years to come.*

Notwithstanding all the historic reforms, no one ever said Thank you. For well over a decade the American people conferred benefits on a growing mob of suffering situations, but gratitude and increased affection for the Grand Old Republic were not to be included in the transaction. Throughout the 1970s "rage" among the beneficiaries of government programs seemed to grow apace with the programs until their contempt for the Republic surpassed that of the late Confederacy's wildest firebrand. Certainly I cannot recall any Confederate denunciation of the Union to equal the criminal allegations lodged in the editorials of that composite of New Age beefs, *The Nation*, or heard at an assemblage of the National Organization for Women or the Congressional Black Caucus. My guess is that A. Lincoln would have taken one glance at the rants against the Republic issuing from these sources, and he would have sent Grant's constabulary into action.

With the exception of redressing the legitimate grievances of Southern blacks, none of the benefits showered upon the suffering situations in the 1970s would have been ordered by the founding fathers, most of whom would laugh deliriously to hear of the Santa Clauses and Utopias that New Age Liberal bureaucrats and judges claimed to find in the Constitution. Yet sometime in the 1960s the extravagant potlatch began, bestowing fanciful rights and hundreds of billions of dollars upon millions of Americans. Sometimes the government had to send out beaters to locate the newly authorized recipients of these so-called entitlements. Other times, stern groups led by professional rabble-rousers demanded aid under penalty of some horrible response—say, the immolation of their own neighborhood. At any rate, by the early 1980s largess beyond the wildest dreams of Franklin Delano Roosevelt had been

---

* Republican virtue is different from the democratic virtue of the Liberal. It calls for self-restraint, self-government, self-reliance. Democratic virtue, on the other hand, encourages aggressiveness against one's fellow citizens and reliance on government to establish "social justice" in the society.

spent on the poor and the angry, yet no one seemed to be grateful. Nor were the poor better off. In fact now they were often totally dependent on federal programs and practically everyone was indignant. America was becoming one of the most emotional nations on earth. There was more public sobbing than at an Iranian funeral; and the fist-pounding could be deafening.

No Americans were more angered by the Republic than the New Age Liberals; yet, as I have argued, it is a mistake to believe that their contempt issued from "Liberal guilt." It issued from a colossal egotism. One that swelled into grandiosity. One that left them seeing themselves as giants standing athwart the nation and admonishing 225 million idiots and miscreants. These braggarts made life in the Republic very uncomfortable for civilized Americans. In the most unlikely settings one of them, inflated by the grandiosity of the age, might begin boasting of his compassion, sensitivity, and worse. Self-dramatics replaced civics; at times it even replaced personal morality.

I found that dinner parties could become particularly gruesome affairs. There you would sit while the guest next to you launched into a sugary monologue whose sole point was to display his or her personal goodness: how he or she had wept over the morning news, or been overcome while trying to empathize with some victim of misfortune, how he or she could no longer bear the suffering of a cut flower. When the bilge began to flow I would feel a premonitory queasiness. I would try diligently to get drunk in hopes of seeing the world from my dinner companion's point of view. This helped, particularly if the wine was good.

What is odd is that as the world became decidedly more unstable and parlous these self-regarding snots never smartened up. They acted as though America could continue to be diabolized and debilitated with no attendant danger to themselves. They abominated Washington, D.C., and all lesser outposts of its authority much the same as V. S. Naipaul tells us the Third Worlder rejects the West—that is to say, "within the assumption that there will always exist out there a living, creative civilization, oddly neutral, open to all to appeal to."[1] At his first tremor of distress the New Age Liberal reflexively turns to Washington. All his schemes to save mankind have been predicated on using the power of the very country he is execrating and deauthorizing. Yet he has gone on shouting, as though that source of power would always be there "open to all to appeal to."

The derangement of the New Age Liberal grew eerily similar to the universal mental derangement of the Third World *enragés*. At American universities or wherever the Liberal brethren and sistren dwelt in large numbers one could perceive inchoate stirrings of what appeared to be The Resentment and The Confusion. As with some Oxford-educated jurist in Uganda, the seemingly well-educated New Age Liberals were slowly but perceptibly slipping back into primitivism. One saw it in their suspicion of science, the profit motive, and that agglomeration of manners and values we call civilization. One saw it in their mode of debate wherein syllogisms had been replaced by jeers: "trickle down, trickle down," "domino theory, domino theory"; speakers out of favor with the regnant bunkum were barred from the podium amidst terms of high opprobrium: "Cold Warrior! Cold Warrior!" "fascist! fascist!" Finally, one saw it in the New Age Liberals' policy alternatives, which amounted to empty incantations: "Neo-Liberalism," "high tech," "New Industrial Policy."

There the descendants of the proud New Deal stood, five decades after the original great doings, like members of some ever-hopeful cargo cult on a far-off atoll. At the appointed hour all would break into gibbers, weird and incomprehensible. There was nothing new about "Neo-Liberalism" whatsoever; all that had changed was that these Neo-Liberals had moved closer to socialism and appeasement. New Industrial Policy merely meant still more social and economic planning of the kind that had failed so thunderously during the heady days of the Great Society when such programs as Model Cities were established to "revitalize" our older cities. A decade later Model Cities had achieved just the opposite: our major cities had been transformed into decaying shells. The most vacuous incantation of all was "high tech." What could high tech possibly mean to people who had no idea of how wealth is created, no understanding of its value, no sense of personal responsibility, no reasonable expectation for life whatsoever? Aside from disturbing others, New Age Liberalism had become a pointless affair; and pointless civilizations cannot endure. By comparison even the civilization of the Marxist-Leninists on the far side of the Iron Curtain had more point to it. The Soviets were for coercion; the American Liberal was for petty mischief. Of the two, the former's prospects are more promising.

This has been a criticism of ideas and to some degree a piece of cultural criticism. It has also been a book of quotations. I suppose that for quoting so many voices of the New Age I shall be accused of hitting a new low in American intellectual debate. "Tyrrellism," the pedagogues will have it: "the technique of blackening an opponent's reputation by quoting him. Viewed as vulgar." Well, what is done is done, and so let me proceed with one more stimulant. On September 23, 1976, that veteran New Age cackelocutionist, Anthony Lewis, wrote: "It is indecent for those who care about sensitivity and humanity in politics to talk of the decency of Gerald Ford."[2] Gerald Ford? Yes, Mr. Lewis is speaking of the very same firebreather. Mr. Lewis is also speaking about a man who had survived two assassination attempts. Had a third been successful would this winner of two Pulitzer Prizes recall that line from his nationally syndicated column as he tapped out his requisite dirge on violence, intolerance, and unreason in America? The New Age Liberal had come to approximate much of what he had set out years before to mitigate and remove from public life. Liberalism had become virtuousness to the point of viciousness.

At some point in the 1970s Liberals like Mr. Lewis came to assume that all the New Age prejudices and policies that their bureaucrats and judges had so furtively implanted upon American polity were never to be revised. Anyone, even an elected official, who tried to put the Republic on a new path was fallen upon with the utmost cruelty and violence. Impeachment became a frequent threat. Political opponents were haled before congressional committees and browbeaten. Private lives were scrutinized so that public lives could be destroyed. The New Age Liberal had become a genuine reactionary. Like the Southern racist of yore, he held out desperately against progress. The Southern racist battled to preserve a world that looked increasingly unjust and unfeasible; the New Age Liberal battled to preserve a world that Jimmy Carter had shown to be futile and dangerous. Yet the Southern racist never claimed to champion tolerance, freedom, and reason. He merely wanted to keep the black man out and nostalgia in. Of these two bigots which is more hypocritical?

Would the New Age Liberal win the cultural struggle in America? We have seen how he dominated and distorted so many of the issues of the day. More encouragingly, we have seen how each New Age fanaticism was thumpingly dispatched. The refutations come from scholars and scientists of a very high order, men like P. T. Bauer, Petr Beckmann, Walter Berns, Martin Diamond, Richard Herrnstein, Samuel McCracken, Julian Simon, Thomas Sowell, and James Q. Wilson. Then there were the writers like Midge Decter, George Gilder, Irving Kristol, and Norman Podhoretz. As editor of *The American Spectator*, I noticed a growing group of intelligent writers emerging from the besotted gaggle of 1960s *enfants terribles* and urged them to appear in our pages. They were part of a remarkable intellectual transformation that was taking place in the Republic, though New Age pundits strenuously avoided mentioning it. Traditional Liberals from the Democratic Party of Roosevelt were joining with traditional conservatives from the Republican Party to battle against the enthusiasts and for the Constitution. It was part of an intellectual movement that was spreading all over the Western world propounding the ideas of freedom, intellectual and artistic excellence, and a more reasonable conception of man's condition than the idiotic whoop-whoop of the New Age.

So which side would triumph in the 1980s? Alas, I am not a seer, and anyway America has already had too many such solemn and dubious fellows. I do know that the enthusiasts of the New Age cannot win. Their view of the good life is too pointless and idiotic. Yet if their dominance of the cultural and intellectual life of the Republic is not broken the sad fact is no one else will win either. All will lose as the Greeks lost, and the Romans too.

Notes

CHAPTER ONE END NOTES

1. Norman Mailer, "The Search for Carter," *The New York Times Magazine*, 26 September 1976, p. 20.

2. *Facts on File*, 1977, p. 35.

3. *Facts on File*, 1979, p. 661.

4. *Ibid.*, p. 639.

5. *Ibid.*, p. 622.

6. Joseph A. Califano, Jr., *Governing America* (New York: Simon and Schuster, 1981), p. 415.

7. Edward Walsh, "Carter's Monastic Meal Surprises Other Leaders," *The Washington Post*, 24 June 1980, p. A12.

8. Betty Glad, *Jimmy Carter* (New York: W. W. Norton & Co., 1980), chapter 7, passim.

9. James David Barber, *The Presidential Character*, 2nd., (Englewood Cliffs: Prentice-Hall, Inc., 1977), p. 534.

10. Mailer, p. 70 & p. 92.

11. Barber, p. 535.

12. Jack Newfield, "Why Democrats Can't Stand Pat," *The Village Voice*, 19–25 November 1980, p. 7.

13. Associated Press, "Carter Hired Outside Agitators, Made Inside Agitators of Them," *The Indianapolis Star*, 4 January 1980, p. 26.

14. *Ibid.*, p. 12.

15. Arthur Schlesinger, Jr., "The End of an Era?", *The Wall Street Journal*, 20 November 1980, p. 26.

Notes

CHAPTER TWO END NOTES

1. Francesco Guicciardini, *Selected Writings*, trans. Margaret Grayson, ed. Cecil Grayson (London: Oxford University Press, 1965), p. 22.

2. Kenneth Minogue, *The Liberal Mind* (New York: Random, 1963), p. 7.

3. Frederic Lewis Allen, *Only Yesterday* (New York: Harper & Brothers, 1957), p. 246.

4. Jean-François Revel, *L'Express*, 24 November 1979.

5. Friedrich Nietzsche, "Twilight of the Idols," *The Portable Nietzsche*, trans. Walter Kaufman (New York: The Viking Press, Inc., 1954), p. 553.

6. "Playboy Interview: Andrew Young," *Playboy*, July 1977, p. 70.

7. Carl Gershman, "The Andy Young Affair," *Commentary*, November 1979, p. 32.

8. George Gilder, *Wealth and Poverty* (New York: Basic Books, Inc., 1981), p. 129.

9. Thomas Sowell, *Pink and Brown People* (Stanford: Hoover Institution Press, 1981), p. 15.

10. Edward D. Sargent, "Graduate Charles Diggs Looks to Future," *The Washington Post*, 14 May 1983, p. B5.

11. Nick Kotz & Mary Lynn Kotz, *A Passion for Equality: George A. Wiley and the Movement* (New York: W. W. Norton & Co., 1977), p. 302.

12. "U.S. Seeks Developer, Sets Claims Settlement for 'Soul City' Project," *The Wall Street Journal*, 27 June 1980, p. 4.

13. Susan Harrigan, "An Old 'New Town' Hangs On," *The Wall Street Journal*, 19 April 1979, pp. 1 & 32.

14. "Current Wisdom," *The Alternative: An American Spectator*, April 1973, p. 30.

15. Joseph Shattan, "Andy's Martyrdom," *The American Spectator*, December 1979, p. 7.

16. Nathaniel Sheppard, Jr., "Arab Businessmen Give $10,000 to Jackson's Rights Organization," *The New York Times*, 17 October 1979, p. D22.

17. Harold Cruse, *The Crisis of the Negro Intellectual* (New York: William Morrow and Co., Inc., 1967), p. 481.

18. Murray Friedman, "Black Anti-Semitism on the Rise," *Commentary*, October 1979, p. 31.

19. Bernard Gwertzman, "Vance Chides Young For Holding Talks with P.L.O. Official," *The New York Times*, 15 August 1979, p. A1.

20. Ellie McGrath, "Exploiting Atlanta's Grief," *Time*, 6 April 1981, p. 18.

21. Charles Euchner, "Questions the Press Didn't Ask About the Atlanta Murders," *The Washington Monthly*, October 1981, p. 45.

22. *Ibid.*

23. Keith B. Richburg, "Mayor's Remarks on Jews: Careless or Calculated?" *The Washington Post*, 26 March 1981, p. DC-1.

24. Jesse Jackson, "Letters," *Time*, 4 April 1981, p. E5.

25. Euchner, p. 46.

26. Gilder, p. 111.

27. Daniel Patrick Moynihan, *The Politics of a Guaranteed Income* (New York: Random House, 1973), p. 54.

28. Gilder, p. 111.

29. *Ibid.*, p. 120.

30. *Ibid.*, p. 118.

31. Guicciardini, p. 62.

32. John Lewis Gaddis, *Strategies of Containment* (New York: Oxford University Press, 1982), p. 235.

33. Richard Holbrooke, "A Sense of Drift, A Time for Calm," *Foreign Policy*, No. 23, Summer 1976, p. 112.

34. "Clark's Hanoi Comments," *The New York Times*, 25 October 1974, p. 22.

35. "His Mood at Mid-Term," *Newsweek*, 28 August 1978, p. 21.

36. "Jane Fonda Grants Some P.O.W. Torture," *The New York Times*, 7 April 1973, p.11.

37. Noam Chomsky, "The Meaning of Vietnam," *The New York Review of Books*, 12 June 1975, p. 31.

38. "A Fond Farewell to the Finest, Funniest Show on Television," *Esquire*, February 1977, p. 77.

39. Christopher Lehmann-Haupt, "Books of The Times," *The New York Times*, 11 June 1981, p. C21.

40. Anthony Lewis, "Avoiding a Bloodbath," *The New York Times*, 17 March 1975, p. 29.

41. Anthony Lewis, "Cultural Arrogance," *The New York Times*, 12 May 1975, p. 27.

42. Richard Dudman, "Cambodia: A Land of Turmoil," *St. Louis Post-Dispatch*, 15 January 1979, p. 3B.

43. Peter W. Rodman, "Sideswipe: Kissinger, Shawcross and the

Responsibility for Cambodia," *The American Spectator*, March 1981, pp. 7–15.

44. "Caring for 'Bag Ladies,' " *The Wall Street Journal*, 2 June 1982, p. 24.

CHAPTER THREE END NOTES

1. Edmund Morris, *The Rise of Theodore Roosevelt* (New York: Coward, McCann & Geoghegan, Inc., 1979), pp. 285–286.

2. William O. Douglas, *The Court Years: 1939–1975* (New York: Random House, 1980), p. 392.

3. Peter Steinhart, *Audubon*, March 1982.

4. Frederick Kempe, "Violent Tactics," *The Wall Street Journal*, 19 April 1983, p. 20.

5. Robert Moses, "Bomb Shelters, Arks and Ecology," *National Review*, 8 September 1970, p. 939.

6. John R. Silber, "Of True and False Apocalypses," *Bostonia*, February 1982, p. 21.

7. Julian L. Simon, "Global Confusion, 1980: A Hard Look at the Global 2000 Report," *The Public Interest*, Winter 1981, pp. 8–9.

8. "Asides," *The Wall Street Journal*, 18 August 1983, p. 22.

9. Edgar Berman, "We Must Limit Families by Law," *The New York Times*, 15 December 1970, p. 5.

10. Charles Krauthammer, "The End of the World," *The New Republic*, 28 March 1983, p. 15.

11. Mary Louise Weber, "Add Water and Stir," *The New Republic*, 14 April 1979, p. 12.

12. Julian L. Simon, "Environmental Disruption or Environmental Improvement?" and Paul R. Ehrlich, "An Economist in Wonderland," *Social Science Quarterly*, March 1981, pp. 31–49.

13. Paul Ehrlich, *How to Be a Survivor* (New York: Ballantine Books, 1971), p. 6.

14. *Bureaucracy vs. Environment*, ed. John Baden and Richard L. Stroup (Ann Arbor: The University of Michigan Press, 1981), pp. 1–8.

15. Simon, *The Public Interest*, pp. 3–4.

16. *Ibid.*, p. 4.

17. *Ibid.*, p. 6.

18. Petr Beckmann, *Eco-Hysterics and the Technophobes* (Boulder: The Golem Press, 1973), p. 80.

19. Simon, *The Public Interest*, pp. 9–10.

20. Simon, *The Ultimate Resource* (Princeton: Princeton University Press, 1981), p. 3.

21. Roger Starr, "Exporting Environmental Havoc," *The American Spectator*, April 1978, p. 5.

CHAPTER FOUR END NOTES

1. Anna Mayo, "Geiger Counter." *The Village Voice*, 5 February 1979, p. 31.

2. House Republican Research Committee: Task Force on Energy and Natural Resources, "The Future for Nuclear Energy: Will America Support It?", 30 September 1983, p. 14.

3. Anna Mayo, "Allen Ginsberg and the Mother of Us All," *The Village Voice*, 29 January 1979, pp. 29 & 31.

4. Samuel McCracken, "The War Against the Atom," *Commentary*, September 1977, p. 39.

5. Anna Mayo, "Geiger Counter," *The Village Voice*, 17 September 1979, p. 8.

6. Anna Mayo, "Geiger Counter," *The Village Voice*, 5 February 1979, p. 31.

7. Petr Beckmann, "Antinuclear Malpractice," *The American Spectator*, October 1981, p. 22.

8. *The Village Voice*, 5 February 1979, pp. 30–31.

9. Joseph Shattan, "The No-Nuke Wind Ensemble," *The American Spectator*, March 1980, p. 7.

10. *Ibid.*

11. *Ibid.*

12. *Ibid.*

13. Mark Hertsgaard, "Nuclear Comeback: There's Life After T.M.I.," *The Nation*, 8 March 1980, p. 271.

14. Shattan, p. 7.

15. *Ibid.*

16. *Ibid.*, p. 8.

17. *Ibid.*

18. Robert Richter, "Nurturing Vietnam," *The New York Times*, 3 August 1979, p. A23.

19. "The No-Nuke Movement," *Newsweek*, 23 May 1977, p. 25.

20. *Ibid.*

21. *Ibid.*

22. "Scientists Say Nation Badly Needs Atom Plants," *The New York Times*, 17 January 1975, p. 12.

23. Daniel Machalaba, "Nuclear Fallout," *The Wall Street Journal*, 24 August 1983, p. 1.

24. Stanley Rothman and S. Robert Lichter, "The Nuclear Energy Debate: Scientists, the Media and the Public," *Public Opinion*, August/September 1982, p. 47.

25. Shattan, pp. 7–8.

26. James M. Perry, "Cosmic Candidate: Jerry Brown Runs to Protect the Earth," *The Wall Street Journal*, 8 November 1979, pp. 1 & 41.

27. Robert Pack, *Jerry Brown: The Philosopher-Prince* (New York: Stein and Day, 1978), p. 222.

28. R. Emmett Tyrrell, Jr., "But to a Conservative Polemicist, He Is Simply the 'Mullah Brown,'" *Los Angeles Times*, 11 March 1979, sec. VI, p. 1.

29. Alexander Cockburn and James Ridgeway, "Jerry Brown: Loser Tells All, Part 2," *The Village Voice*, 9–15 July 1980, p. 15.

30. George Skelton, "Brown Gets High Marks on Handling of Prop. 13," *Los Angeles Times*, 10 July 1978, pp. 1 & 22.

31. Tyrrell, sec. VI, p. 1.

32. Perry, pp. 1 & 41.

33. Wayne King, "Brown Image: Chief Problem," *The New York Times*, 8 January 1980, p. A16.

34. Wayne King, "Gov. Brown, His Dream Ended, Returns to California," *The New York Times*, 3 April 1980, p. B10.

35. King, p. A16.

36. Donald Lambro, "Synfuels Boondoggle Produces Waste, Not Oil," *The Herald-Telephone* (Bloomington, Indiana), 10 October 1983, p. 11.

37. Fred and Geoffrey Hoyle, *Commonsense in Nuclear Energy* (San Francisco: W. H. Freeman & Co., 1980), p. 29.

38. McCracken, p. 36.

39. *Ibid.*, pp. 35–36.

40. Hoyle, p. 24.

41. *Ibid.*, p. 21.

42. McCracken, p. 43.

43. *Ibid.*

44. Hoyle, pp. 13, 34 & 36.

CHAPTER FIVE END NOTES

1. Maurice Cranston, "What Ever Happened to Liberalism?", *The American Spectator*, December 1982, p. 11.

CHAPTER SIX END NOTES

1. Anne Barton, "Shakespeare a Chauvinist?", *The New York Review of Books*, 11 June 1981, p. 20.

2. "Current Wisdom," *The American Spectator*, May 1982, p. 42.

3. *Ibid.*

4. Alexis de Tocqueville, *Democracy in America*, trans. George Lawrence (New York: Harper & Row, 1966), p. 565.

5. "Current Wisdom," *The Alternative: An American Spectator*, April 1977, p. 38.

6. Karen Stabiner, "The Storm Over Women Firefighters," *The New York Times Magazine*, 26 September 1982, pp. 102–103.

7. Adrienne Rich, *Of Woman Born* (New York: W. W. Norton & Co., 1976), p. 34.

8. "Current Wisdom," *The Alternative: An American Spectator*, February 1977, p. 38.

9. H. L. Mencken, *In Defense of Women* (New York: Time, Inc., 1963), p. 113.

10. A. James Rudin and Marcia R. Rudin, *Prison or Paradise?* (Philadelphia: Fortress Press, 1980), p. 62.

11. John Leo, "The Warm Success of Dr. Hug," *Time*, 15 November 1982, p. 84.

12. "Best Sellers," *The New York Times Book Review*, 8 May 1983, p. 32.

13. William L. Riordon, *Plunkitt of Tammany Hall* (New York: E. P. Dutton & Co., 1963), p. ix.

14. Deborah Rankin, "Women's Bank: Dour Audit View," *The New York Times*, 21 December 1978, p. D1.

15. Anne Crutcher, "The Second Stage," *The American Spectator*, February 1982, p. 30.

16. Gloria Steinem, "What Is a New *Ms.*," *Ms.*, November 1979, p. 4.

17. Harriet Lyons and Rebecca Rosenblatt, "Body Hair: The Last Frontier," *Ms.*, July 1972, p. 65.

18. Carole Rosenthal, "Rejecting Equality," *Ms.*, February 1977, p. 46.

19. Andrea Dworkin, "Phallic Imperialism: Why Economic Recovery Will Not Work for Us," *Ms.*, December 1976, p. 101.

20. "Letters," *Ms.*, August 1976, p. 12.

21. "Current Wisdom," *The Alternative: An American Spectator*, February 1977, p. 38.

22. Martha Shelly, *Sisterhood Is Powerful*, ed. Robin Morgan (New York: Random House, 1970), p. 308.

23. "Letters," *Ms.*, August 1977, p. 7.

24. "Letters," *Ms.*, December 1982, p. 7.

25. Werner J. Dannhauser, "Back to Nature," *The American Spectator*, December 1982, p. 30.

26. "Current Wisdom," *The American Spectator*, May 1982, p. 42.

27. Betty Friedan, *The Second Stage* (New York: Summit Books, 1981), Passim.

28. George Will, "The ERA Fixation," *The Washington Post*, 9 January 1983, p. C7.

29. Joanna Omang, "NOW Concedes Defeat in ERA Battle, But Vows to Make Strong Comeback," *The Washington Post*, 25 June 1982, p. A2.

CHAPTER SEVEN END NOTES

1. Kasum Nair, *Blossoms in the Dust* (New York: Frederick A. Praeger, 1961), p. xvii.

2. *Ibid.*, p. xiii.

3. Bernard D. Nossiter, "U.N. News Supplement Down to Its Last $53,000," *The New York Times*, 27 August 1981, p. 2.

4. Henry Kissinger, *Years of Upheaval* (Boston: Little, Brown & Co., 1982), p. 231.

5. V. S. Naipaul, *Among the Believers* (New York: Alfred A. Knopf, 1981), p. 168.

6. *Ibid.*

7. *Ibid.*, pp. 173–176.

8. Shiva Naipaul, *Journey to Nowhere* (New York: Simon & Schuster, 1980), p. 31.

9. Theodore White, *America in Search of Itself: The Making of the President, 1956–1980* (New York: Harper & Row, 1982), p. 225.

10. Clark R. Mollenhoff, *The President Who Failed: Carter out of Control* (New York: Macmillan Pub. Co., 1980), p. 224.

11. *Ibid.*, p. 226.

12. White, p. 223.

13. Mollenhoff, p. 223.

14. "Current Wisdom," *The Alternative: An American Spectator*, May 1977, p. 38.

15. George McGovern, "A Talk with Castro," *The New York Times Magazine*, 13 March 1977, p. 20.

16. "Current Wisdom," *The Alternative: An American Spectator,* May 1977, p. 38.

17. Doug Hostetter, "Correspondence," *Worldview,* January/February 1977, p. 2.

18. Clare Crawford-Mason, "Sen. Lowell Weicker Angles for Lunch with Fidel Castro—And Pulls Off a Feat of Shutter Diplomacy," *People,* 10 November 1980, p. 48.

19. Richard Falk, "Khomeini's Promise," *Foreign Policy,* Spring 1979, p. 32.

20. Jesse Jackson, "Jesse Jackson's Manifesto: A Call to Black America," *Chicago Tribune,* 18 April 1976, Sec. 2, p. 1.

21. "2nd Plenary Meeting," *U.N. General Assembly Official Records, 11th Special Session 1980* (New York: United Nations, 1982), p. 27.

22. Kwame Nkrumah, *Africa Must Unite* (London: Heinemann Educational Books, Ltd., 1963), p. xiii.

23. June Kronholz, "Dark Continent: Ghana's Economic Skid Illustrates Bleak Spiral of Poverty in Africa," *The Wall Street Journal,* 4 January 1982, p. 1.

24. P. T. Bauer, *Equality, the Third World and Economic Delusion* (Cambridge: Harvard University Press, 1981), p. 70.

25. *Ibid.,* p. 72.

26. *Ibid.,* pp. 67 & 72.

27. Pranay B. Gupte, "Mobutu's Rule Seen as Growing Shaky," *The New York Times,* 25 May 1980, p. 4.

28. Gregory Jaynes, "Famine Marches with a Nomadic Tribe in Uganda," *The New York Times,* 27 August 1980, p. A10.

CHAPTER EIGHT END NOTES

1. Kenneth Reich, "Carter Returns Home, Vows to Maintain Strong Ties with the People of Plains," *The Los Angeles Times,* 17 July 1976, p. 3.

2. Tom Wolfe, *The Purple Decades* (New York: Farrar Straus & Giroux, 1982), p. 288.

3. Daniel Seligman, "Keeping Up," *Fortune,* 20 April 1981, pp. 97–98.

4. "Alan Alda's Prescription for Doctors," *Good Housekeeping,* October 1979, pp. 78–79.

5. David Margolick, "A Reporter's Notebook: A.B.A. Blends Inspiration and Adoration at Its Parley," *The New York Times,* 14 August 1982, p. 9.

6. "People & Things," *The Indianapolis Star*, 23 February 1983, p. 64.

7. Harry F. Waters, "A Man Who Cares," *Newsweek*, 9 March 1981, p. 57.

8. "Current Wisdom," *The American Spectator*, May 1982, p. 42.

9. George Jean Nathan, *The Intimate Notebooks* (New York: Alfred A. Knopf, 1932), p. 221.

CHAPTER NINE END NOTES

1. Robert H. Ferrell, *Peace in Their Time* (New Haven: Yale University Press, 1952), pp. 13–14.

2. Winston S. Churchill, *The Gathering Storm* (Boston: Houghton Mifflin Co., 1948), pp. iv–v.

3. John Lewis Gaddis, *Strategies of Containment* (New York: Oxford University Press, 1982), p. 23.

4. "Human Rights in Iran," *The Nation*, 24 March 1979, p. 292.

5. Richard Falk, "Khomeini's Promise," *Foreign Policy*, Spring 1979, p. 32.

6. Albert Camus, *The Myth of Sisyphus & Other Essays*, "The Myth of Sisyphus" (New York: Alfred A. Knopf, 1955), p. 4.

7. Bruce Buursma, "Catholic Bishops Taking Aim at Nuclear Weapons," *The Chicago Tribune*, 18 October 1981, Sec. 2, p. 2.

8. "Current Wisdom," *The American Spectator*, June 1980, p. 41.

9. "Current Wisdom," *The American Spectator*, March 1982, p. 42.

10. Leonard Bernstein, "Just Suppose We Disarmed," *The New York Times*, 10 June 1980, p. A19.

11. Richard Grenier, "The Greatest Peace Movement of Them All," *The American Spectator*, March 1983, p. 12.

12. "What Next?", *The Nation*, 26 June 1982, p. 771.

13. "Soviet Defense Spending $710 Billion Above U.S. for Past 10 Yrs.," *Defense Daily*, 22 February 1982, p. 265.

14. "Military Implications of the Treaty on the Limitation of Strategic Offensive Arms and Protocol Thereto (SALT II Treaty)," *Hearings before the Committee on Armed Services: United States Senate (Ninety-sixth Congress, First Session)* (Washington: US Government Printing Office, 1979), 23–26 July 1979, pp. 116–117.

15. John Barron, *KGB Today: The Hidden Hand* (New York: Reader's Digest Press, 1983), p. 280.

16. Judith Miller, "Arms Control Drive to Open," *The New York Times*, 18 April 1982, p. 34.

17. Shana Alexander, "A Sentimental Binge," *Newsweek*, 28 April 1975, p. 88.

18. "We Lied to You," *The Economist*, 26 February 1983, p. 56.

19. Robert D. McFadden, "A Spectrum of Humanity Represented at the Rally," *The New York Times*, 13 June 1982, p. 42.

20. "Text of President's Commencement Address at Notre Dame on Foreign Policy," *The New York Times*, 23 May 1977, p. 12.

21. Jimmy Carter, *Keeping Faith* (New York: Bantam Books, 1982), p. 143.

22. Richard Holbrooke, "A Sense of Drift, A Time for Calm," *Foreign Policy*, Summer 1976, p. 112.

23. Bernard Ledwidge, *De Gaulle* (New York: St. Martin's Press, 1982), p. 37.

CHAPTER TEN END NOTES

1. *Survey of Current Business*, July 1961, p. 16, and *Survey of Current Business*, July 1981, p. 15.

2. "Embattled America: The Experts Polled," *Saturday Review*, 7 July 1979, p. 34.

3. George Gilder, "The Numbers Tell a Supply-Side Story," *The Wall Street Journal*, 13 June 1983, p. 22.

4. See George G. Graham in "Oversight on Nutritional Status of Low Income Americans in the 1980s," testimony delivered at a hearing before the Subcommittee on Nutrition of the Committee of Agriculture, Nutrition, and Forestry, United States Senate, 6 April 1983, p. 102.

5. Hugh Drummond, "Dr. Drummond Loses His Patience," *Mother Jones*, August 1977.

6. The Media Institute, *Crooks, Conmen and Clowns: Businessmen in TV Entertainment*, ed. Leonard J. Theberge (Washington: The Media Institute, 1981), p. vi.

7. Michael Novak, *Confessions of a Catholic* (San Francisco: Harper & Row, 1983), p. 101.

8. George Gilder, "A Supply-Side Economics of the Left," *The Public Interest*, Summer 1983, pp. 36 & 38.

9. George Gilder, *Wealth and Poverty* (New York: Basic Books, Inc., 1981), p. 12.

10. Gilder, "A Supply-Side Economics of the Left," p. 37.

11. Sidney Lens, "On the Contradiction of Socialism," *The Progressive*, March 1979, p. 24.

Notes

12. Baron de Montesquieu, *The Spirit of the Laws*, trans. Thomas Nugent (New York: Hafner Publishing Company, 1966), p. 316.

13. Thomas Paine, *The Complete Writings of Thomas Paine*, ed. Philip S. Foner (New York: Citadel Press, 1945), p. 36.

14. Adam Smith, *The Wealth of Nations* (New York: P. F. Collier & Son, 1905), II, p. 107.

15. Michael Novak, *The Spirit of Democratic Capitalism* (New York: Simon and Schuster, 1982), p. 118.

16. Garry Wills, "Carter and the End of Liberalism," *The New York Review of Books*, 12 May 1977, p. 18.

17. Novak, *The Spirit of Democratic Capitalism*, p. 121.

18. Gilder, *Wealth and Poverty*, p. 8.

19. George Gilder, "Capitalism Is for Givers," *The American Spectator*, February 1982, pp. 7 & 9.

CHAPTER ELEVEN END NOTES

1. Robert D. McFadden, "Leading Americans Backed Jones Sect," *The New York Times*, 21 November 1978, p. 16.

2. Alexis de Tocqueville, *Democracy in America*, trans. George Lawrence, ed. J. P. Mayer & Max Lerner (New York: Harper & Row, 1966), p. 510.

3. Irving Kristol, *Two Cheers for Capitalism* (New York: Basic Books, 1978), p. 192.

CHAPTER TWELVE END NOTES

1. V. S. Naipaul, *Among the Believers* (New York: Alfred A. Knopf, 1981), p. 168.

2. Anthony Lewis, "Decent Is as Decent Does," *The New York Times*, 23 September 1976, p. 41.

Index

Index

Index